You[r Career]
in Animation

How to Survive
and Thrive

David B. Levy

**ALLWORTH
PRESS**
NEW YORK

School of
VISUAL ARTS

11 10 09 08 07   7 6 5 4 3

Published by Allworth Press
An imprint of Allworth Communications, Inc.
10 East 23rd Street, New York, NY 10010

Cover illustration: SAMURAI JACK and all related characters and elements are trademarks
  of and © Cartoon Network. (s06)
Cartoonnetwork.com and logo are trademarks of and © Cartoon Network. (s06)
Cover design by Derek Bacchus
Interior design by Mary Belibasakis
Page composition/typography by SR Desktop Services, Ridge, NY

ISBN: 1-58115-445-3

Library of Congress Cataloging-in-Publication Data
Levy, David B.
    Your career in animation: how to survive and thrive / David B. Levy.
        p.   cm.
    Includes index.
    ISBN 1-58115-445-3 (pbk.)
    1. Animation (Cinematography)—Vocational guidance—United States. I. Title.

NC1765.L48   2006
791.43'34023—dc22

                                                          2006007274

Dedication

I dedicate this book to the birthplace of the animation industry, and my home, New York City. For more than one hundred years, from *Felix the Cat* to *Blue's Clues* and beyond, this city has housed some of the most innovative and commercially successful animation. Outside of its status as an industry Mecca, New York City contains the world's most prominent community of independent filmmakers, from the Hubleys to Bill Plympton. This book is dedicated to New York City, its thousands of animation artists, and the animation artists to be.

Table of Contents

Acknowledgments

This book project has enabled me to take stock of my career to date. It's humbling to look back and see all the help I received along the way. With much gratitude, I present the following acknowledgments:

Allan Neuwirth and Birte Pampel, for providing the connection to the wonderful folks at Allworth Press, without whom this book would not have been possible. Machi Tantillo, for recommending that I take over her career strategy course at the School of Visual Arts (SVA), inadvertently starting me on the way to writing this book.

Mark Heller, for giving me my first professional work experience while still a student. Michael Klein, for pushing me out onto the pavement to search for my first job. Michael Sporn, for giving me my first job in the industry, providing me with an opportunity to learn from a modern master of animation. Robert Marianetti, for teaching me so much in those first couple of years.

Howard Beckerman, for relentlessly encouraging me to join The International Animated Film Society Northeast/New York Chapter (ASIFA-East), which opened more doors than I could have ever imagined. Linda Simensky, for being my first mentor in the business. She will always be my model for a successful career in animation.

Nancy Keegan, for providing an introduction to the production of *Blue's Clues*, which did so much to set the direction of my career in motion. To the senior staff of *Blue's Clues* and especially David J. Palmer, who gave me my first opportunity to direct and taught me to always raise the bar and push for the highest standards possible.

To the fabulous crew of Cartoon Pizza's *Pinky Dinky Doo*, which proved that it is possible to create a great product on schedule in a happy work place.

To John B. Sebastian, for taking a chance on little ol' me and writing some terrific music for my cartoon proposal. To my pitch partners Dale Clowdis and Rich Gorey, for their unflagging creative energy.

Debbie Staab, for not only being my better half, but for being patient with me this last year as my time was sucked away by a full-time job, writing this book, and a constant stream of pitch projects.

Many thanks to all the animation artists and experts who so readily gave interviews, loaning their time and expertise to this project. Also to Mira Scharf, Tina Moglia, Ollie Green, Liz Artinian, and Barbara Jean Kearney for helping to make some important introductions, leading to numerous interview opportunities.

To my mom and sister for all the support and encouragement over the years. Finally, thanks to my dad for being my lifelong career hero and for passing along his incredible work ethic to me.

Introduction

Although I never set out to be an author, it almost seems I was destined to write this book. Unlike many of my peers in the animation industry, I grew up knowing that one could make a living in commercial art. My father, Bob Levy, achieved remarkable success in advertising. In the span of four decades his career ran the gamut from creative vice president of Benton and Bowles, to creative director at Grey Advertising, Bozell, Jacobs, Kenyon & Eckhardt, and J. Walter Thompson. The demands of a high profile career in advertising would be enough to zap anyone's strength, but for my father, that was just his day job. At night, his second identity as a freelancer would begin. From his home office, he often worked until 2:00 A.M., creating logos, designs, and illustrations for high profile clients including Pfizer and Procter & Gamble.

Growing up in suburban Long Island, New York, most of my friends bonded with their dads over a shared interest in sports. With both of us hopelessly non-athletic, my dad and I bonded over the world of commercial art. Our nightly ritual went like this: Dad came home around 8:00 P.M. I would follow him upstairs, where he would take his shoes off to relax a moment before supper. This was when I would get a vivid debriefing of the day's events at the workplace. The stories unfolded like mini radio plays, with my dad providing all the voices, the most interesting being his own.

I'm not sure why he did this. Perhaps he was looking for closure or clarity that can sometimes only come by talking about problems. For a while I was probably too young to offer much back. Yet these talks taught me at a tender age the meaning of words like client, rep, art director, copyeditor, traffic person, account person, and portfolio. I first suspected my dad was giving me a unique education when the distinguished animator/illustrator Lee J. Ames came to lecture at my school. I was only eight or nine years old at the time. More than a few eyebrows were raised when I asked if Lee sent out samples of his art in a portfolio to try to get new clients. Lee laughed and said I must be a "budding artist" to have such a question.

Every night, for nearly twenty years, my dad was giving me valuable lessons on how to survive and thrive in the business. In return, I don't think my dad could have asked for a more enthusiastic pupil. I got caught up in the drama of each office story and I would eagerly await the next installment the way some people anticipate the daytime soaps. As successful and brilliant as my dad was, he never told stories to try to present himself in the best possible light. These were warts and all stories.

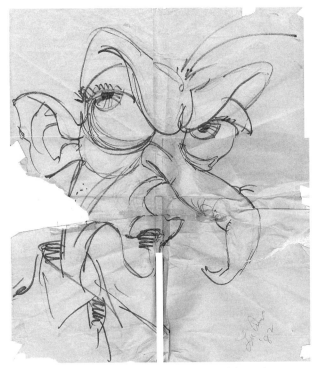

The sketch is by Lee J. Ames, presented to me at age eight or nine, at Willow Road School in Valley Stream, NY. The wear and tear is all mine.

My father, Bob Levy, Master Art Director at work, February 1980.

There were great mistakes, cataclysmic defeats, and long torturous times of stress and misery. On the other end of the spectrum were avalanches of creative inspiration, promotions, and other great victories in the workplace.

To my delight, the stories didn't stop when I grew up and moved out on my own. Like some wonderful jukebox, my dad still recounts favorite stories. Now these memories are often jogged after I share some of my own stories. This book is written in the same spirit of shared experiences. My hope is, with this book at your side, you will see that you need not go through your stories alone.

YOUR CAREER IN ANIMATION

This book is as much for those with hopes of entering the field of commercial animation, as it is an industry survival guide for those already working.

The worldwide animation industry rakes in billions of dollars of business each year. It's hard to imagine a day going by without being confronted by an image of SpongeBob SquarePants, Mickey Mouse, Bugs Bunny, or *The Simpsons.* Although animation dates back to the birth of film, it continues to evolve, as evidenced by the recent groundbreaking computer generated successes of Pixar's *The Incredibles* and DreamWorks' *Shrek.* Scads of books abound on how those films and your favorite animated TV shows are made. DVD commentary tracks regularly give us the voice of directors as they break down their creations. The curtain has been lifted and would-be animation artists now have more access to technical information than ever before.

Despite this flood of information, there are crucial aspects of the animation business that remain unexplored:

+ How do you begin a career in animation?

+ What kind of portfolio, reel, or experience do you need?

+ How do you meet the local community of animators?

Likewise, those already working may be asking:

+ How do you ensure that your skills stay marketable for years to come?

+ What can you do to network more effectively?

+ How do you make the leap from working for others to pitching and selling a show of your own or going into business for yourself?

No single book has ever sought to focus on these important topics until now. Utilizing interviews with those at the top of the industry, this book will offer up answers, advice, and personal anecdotes on all those questions and more.

What is the life of an animation artist? Ask one hundred artists, as I did for this book, and you're likely to get just as many different answers. The average animation artist is a nomad, ready to offer his or her talents on a work-for-hire basis. Occasionally, the down time between jobs may out-number the weeks that end in a paycheck. Health insurance, 401K plans, and pensions are scarce to non-existent. For every Mike Judge, Matt Groening, and Steve Hillenburg, there are one thousand animation artists staffing the ranks in complete anonymity to the general public. Yet, within the close-knit animation community, the best animation artists are known and sought out for job after job.

WHO IS THIS BOOK FOR?

On the surface, it may seem that this book is best suited for students and beginners in the field of animation. I might have made that assumption too, if experiences didn't constantly show me otherwise. Just before I proposed the idea for this book, I met a recently laid off lead animator fresh from fifteen years of animating on features at Disney Animation in Florida. In his time at the house-of-mouse, he'd animated on nearly every feature from *Beauty and the Beast* to *Brother Bear*. One would think that sort of experience as a lead animator would prepare a person for working anywhere in the industry. Surprisingly, the animator hadn't the slightest idea of how to find work. He didn't know what types of animation jobs were out there in the non-Disney world and he didn't even know what those jobs were called.

How can this happen? Well, it's easier than you'd think. Someone can excel at a job and rise to the top of a studio and still work with blinders on. In the case of this Disney animator, his isolation from the larger industry was several fold.

First, Florida is not an animation hub. The isolated geography ensured that it would be difficult for him to meet his peers outside the Disney walls. Animators working in Los Angeles, New York, San Francisco, Toronto, and Vancouver tend to work on diverse projects that involve hopping from studio to studio. Such frequent cross-pollination creates a more savvy workforce than could come from working within the vacuum of a large studio in com-parative isolation.

Second, at large studios like Disney Florida, there is a uniformity of style, technique, and work method. Jobs are narrowly defined and compartmental-ized. Workers in such a system develop the tunnel vision that lets them excel at their posts at the expense of learning or understanding the myriad of other creative and technical jobs going on around them. Is it any wonder that this Disney animator could work in a top job for more than a decade and still not know how work is divided at a typical animation studio?

Lastly, the comfort of working on such a long-term job doesn't allow for the advantages that freelancers enjoy by going from job to job. Chances are the freelancer knows where the work is, how to get it, and how to be asked back again. The freelancer needs to be a successful networker. For this reason, the freelancer has probably made his home close to or within a major animation producing city.

Don't get me wrong. Long-term employment is not akin to getting the plague. Many freelancers would trade all their diverse experiences for a crack at a stable job complete with benefits and a health plan. Successful freelance careers do not happen overnight. Honing your creative skills and building a large client base takes years. There's also the problem of isolation that comes from working from home or from not having enough time in any one studio to truly fit in to a team environment.

Ironically, freelancers and staffers face many of the same challenges. Recently I had a discussion with another animation industry veteran. He's a successful New York–based animation artist with ample experience in 2D (traditional or "hand drawn") and 3D (computer generated or "three-dimensional") animation. He wondered whether he should pursue freelance work or look for a full-time staff position. While it's an interesting question to ponder, it's important to note that such choices are often made for us, not by us. Often the strength of the economy dictates how many long-term staff positions are available. In leaner times, there is a greater number of freelancers bouncing between short-term projects.

In many ways, a career in animation is not like any other imaginable. If you're a doctor working at a hospital, you will not likely be expected to take a job as a nurse or an intern as your next job. Yet, in the animation business, such an equation is surprisingly common. Directors on one project may be animators or storyboard artists on the next. Not surprisingly, salaries swing up and down with these variations in titles and responsibility. On the subject of salary, it would be hard to find a career where salaries vary more. A small independent studio may pay one-fifth of the salary that a large studio such as Pixar can afford to pay. We'll come back to this subject later.

As a guest speaker in my animation career course at SVA, animation artist and independent studio cofounder Candy Kugel explained what she looks for in potential employees. "I look for someone who not only has the talent for the job, but is also someone that I can be around for eight hours a day." Now, following that same train of thought, picture yourself working in animation for eight hours a day, five days or more a week, for your entire career. You have to live with yourself and look after your own happiness and livelihood. Is a career in animation the right fit for you?

This book is for the hopeful, those who are hoping to break into the industry and those already working that would like to "toon up" to an even better career in animation. For some, this book might be the proof they need that animation is not a viable career choice. That's not a tragedy. It's considerably faster and cheaper to read this book than it would be to attend four years at film school, only to find that out. Nor is the purpose of this book to convince someone to enter this very specialized field. This book will not glamorize the industry. Instead, this book paints a realistic portrait of many different careers in animation.

ANIMATION ARTISTS, NOT ANIMATORS

We'll use the term "animation artists" and won't presume to call everyone animators. Animator is but one job in the collaborative atmosphere of a studio environment. This book focuses on all "animation artists." It need not matter whether you work in 2D or 3D animation. The distinction between the two is a mere matter of technology. The industry is the same for both. While it's true that computers are now a part of even the 2D animation process, it is unlikely that there will ever come a time when drawing skills will not be important in this business, or at the very least, a marketable asset to possess.

You won't find specifics here about voiceover acting, editing, musical composition/scoring, sound design, or marketing. While all of those jobs are integral to the animation industry, there is nothing about them that is exclusive to animation. Those who perform those jobs in our industry also work just as often outside of it.

HOW TO USE THIS BOOK

Although only one chapter serves as this book's official industry resource, this whole book is one big resource. As a reader, you have the flexibility to read chapters in any order. You may be first drawn to a chapter that deals with your immediate needs or interests. I welcome that approach to reading this book and I also recommend that you utilize the index in the back to further help you pinpoint what information you'd like to read at any particular time. However, like most things about this industry itself, topics presented in this book are highly interconnected. No chapter or idea presented here is an island to itself. The most useful information to you may live in a section you're least interested in. Sneaky, huh? My fantasy is that most readers of this book will find *all* of the information gathered here of interest and even more important, of vital and practical use.

So You Want to Be in Pictures?

"I'd recommend any art school that will give you a good understanding of the basic principles of animation and access to good film equipment is a good start. However, some of the most successful people I know went to a state college and made animated films in their garage in their spare time. The thing that will teach you the most is experience."
—Eileen Kohlhepp, stop motion animator

Today, it is possible for animation artists to pick up the skills of their trade without going to a special school to study animation. There are numerous great books that teach animation techniques, such as Richard Williams's *The Animator's Survival Kit* and Howard Beckerman's *Animation: The Whole Story*. By following the exercises and instructions in these books, you can conceivably teach yourself the nuts and bolts of animated filmmaking. Taking the home instruction idea even one step further, some books are now equipped with CDs or DVDs, providing living examples to the reader. Throughout this book there will be listings of recommended reading that I hope will become a part of your personal library. Richard Williams

The author interviewing famed Yellow Submarine *producer Al Brodax at an ASIFA-East event held at SVA. James Lipton, eat your heart out!*

is famous for saying, "You don't know what you don't know." Believe me, he's not speaking exclusively to the beginners out there. He's talking to everyone, including, amazingly enough, himself. The best talents in animation know that there is always more to learn. In a healthy career, we don't reach a point where we throw our books or our tools away. We need them too much. Our journeys are over when we stop, not when we think we've learned all there is to know.

So, if books play such an important part in our learning and development, why the need to enroll in an animation school? Why should one put in the time and expense required to get a degree in animation from one of the fine schools listed in the appendix of this book? It would be hard to imagine a field where a college degree or a good grade point average means less than it does in the animation industry. When it comes to finding a job, talent, enthusiasm, and relationships all take precedence over where you got your degree.

WHY GO TO SCHOOL?

Yet, before all the school recruiters faint in shock, I'd like to make the case for going to school. While it's true that there are many great books teaching the art of animation, a book cannot critique your work. It is the trained eye that can help advance your skill by leaps and bounds. With the structure provided by teachers, assignments, and grades, the availability of equipment, and the inspiration supplied by peers, one has the best shot at learning the animation arts. A great book sits on the shelf until you read it. The exercises living in its pages do not do themselves. With a book, you can easily fall into the habit of picking and choosing what you'd like to learn and in what order. Even a valiant start, when learning from a book, can lose steam because there's no one there to cheer you on. Nobody cares if you stop midway through or never even get started. Learning the animation arts is a discipline. It's not always fun. In school (or on the job, for that matter) we're not always drawing what we're comfortable drawing. We are pushed to go beyond what we could or would be doing if left to our own devices.

Perhaps most importantly, animation schools employ teachers that are working in their field. While this does not automatically make them great teachers, it does help students have the opportunity to make those first vital connections they'll need if they're to break into the industry. Animator Justin Simonich advises students to, "Pick a school in the city you want to live and work in. The contacts you make through your teachers will be the ones that get you into a studio and start you on your career. They will most likely have worked in that city and have formed contacts with studios, directors, and animators throughout their careers."

Schools also provide the animation student opportunities to meet some of the legends of the business. In my dual role as president of ASIFA-East and a faculty member of SVA, I have presented events featuring Ray Harryhausen, Richard Williams, Paul Fierlinger, Jimmy Picker, Yuri Norstein, Chris Wedge, Al Brodax, and Bill Plympton. Guest speakers at NYU Tisch Animation have included Chuck Jones, Frank Thomas, Ollie Johnston, Nick Park, Marc Davis, Jule Engel, Tissa David, Michael Sporn, J.J. Sedelmaier, Andreas Deja, Giannalberto Bendazzi, Pete Docter, Joe Ranft, Jonathan Annand, Michael Dougherty, Dan Sheffelman, David Zung, Faith Hubley, Emily Hubley, George Griffin, and Kathy Rose, among others. Even Dartmouth University, a school only offering a few animation classes, has hosted Karen Aqua, Nelson Shin, Piotr Dumala, Jerzy Kucia, David Anderson, Ishu Patel, Frederic Back, Rao Heidmets, Barry Purves, Michel Ocelot, Bordo Dobnikovic, Lejf Marcussen, Priit Parn, Nikolai Todorov, and Noori Zarrinkelk, etc. In addition to guest speaker engagements, schools also often host festivals and special events. For instance, Parsons School of Design in New York hosts the ASIFA-East annual Animation Festival as well as annual events with SIGGRAPH (The International Conference on Computer Graphics and Interactive Techniques).

Whew! That's a lot of opportunities; it's no wonder the Beach Boys sang, "Be True to Your School."

Job Placement

"We have an outstanding career services office that works with graduates indefinitely as a career placement resource. They provide services online as well as in person."
—*Judith Aaron, vice president for enrollment, Pratt University*

Animation schools, particularly those in or near animation hubs, offer students valuable job placement assistance. Schools recieve frequent job postings from neighboring studios and often host annual recruitment events with the big studios such as Pixar and DreamWorks. These services are open to both students and alumni. Perhaps even more useful to the student are school/studio internship programs. With internships, students have the opportunity to venture into the industry while still accumulating credits toward their graduation requirements. According to Parsons School of Design's Anezka Sebek, students in her school's animation sequence are encouraged to spend one or more semesters in internships with animation studios. As internships are largely prolonged job interviews, many students have snagged their first job fresh off a successful internship.

Peer to Peer Connections

One advantage of going to school to study animation is that you're automatically in the position to make connections with your student peer group, as well as with your instructors. The school becomes your first animation community. Here, the seeds you plant or the bridges you burn set the direction your career will take post-school. Some schools promote a sense of "healthy" competition among the students. A better idea would be for students to learn that each member of their class is a potential collaborator, partner, ally, and friend.

Everything a student does affects the reputation he has among his peers. As a guest speaker and an instructor I always encounter a moment when everyone in the whole class rolls their eyes or grumbles when a certain student talks or asks a question demonstrating tactlessness or an oversized ego. Such students are usually oblivious as to how they're really perceived. Students also keep watch as to who regularly botches homework assignments, delivers lazy work, or is sloppy and careless in his or her craft. Students and instructors make mental records of such behavior and work. These evaluations stick to people long after the school grades have faded. These are the marks you can't erase. So, why start accumulating them in a negative column?

Positive behavior is also noted by our peers. Humility, interest in what others are doing, and hard work are qualities that win the respect of others. After graduation, when the students scatter like billiard balls, who are they going to recommend for a job when in a position to do so? Our reputations matter as much, if not more, than the portfolio or reel we carry around. Learn to value relationships and you've already taken a major step towards a successful career.

My First Key Moment in School

One day in my second year at SVA, instructor Mark Heller, who ran a successful animation studio with John R. Dilworth called Streamline Film Manufacturing, popped into the small pencil test room I was occupying. Closing the door behind him, Heller asked me if I would be interested in doing some paid work on a commericial. If I'd been wearing a beanie with a propeller on it, it would have started spinning up into the air. Instead, I had to get by with smiling widely and nodding my head "yes." For six bucks an hour I would be doing mat-inking for a thirty-second commercial for Land O'Lakes butter. In the days of traditional animation, this was one of the techniques used to add depth to flat animated characters by adding controlled shadows. Mat-inking is a process by which shadows on characters are drawn on separate levels of paper. The shadow areas are filled in with a black marker. These blackened-in drawings would then be shot under the camera on a separate pass from the backgrounds and character animation. The blackened-in areas could then be set to any desired opacity or softness by means of a digital process.

This was my big break into show business and I don't think I'd ever been happier to pick up a marker in my life (and no, the marker fumes had nothing to do with my euphoria). As I knocked out the work, balancing speed and accuracy, I was able to finish and deliver the job on schedule. I wondered why I had been selected by Heller out of the twenty other students in the class. I knew I wasn't the best draftsman, but I certainly projected a lot of enthusiasm for animation and the class itself. That attitude and enthusiasm had a lot to do with success was an epiphany. Employers want to work with people who are enjoyable to be around. The opportunity to work while I was still in school made me realize that being a student was my first chance to make the right impressions on potential employers (my instructors) and future collaborators (my classmates).

Instructors were looking at us as a pool of potential hires. They searched us for signs of enthusiasm and talent. This was both exciting and nerve-wracking. Wasn't school supposed to be a sanctuary of learning, free from commercial and industry tampering? Most students want school to be a safe haven before they are forced to strike out into the big bad world. Art schools, like SVA, deliberately blur the lines by using instructors who are working in the industry. Unsurprisingly, this brings a great deal of "the industry" into the school and into the teaching process itself. In this environment, students enjoy access to and information about the industry while also being nurtured as independent, thinking, artistic filmmakers within the safe confines of the school.

My Second Key Moment in School

Mark Heller continued to throw good opportunities my way during my years at SVA. One day he announced to our class that his company was bidding on some spots to promote *The Flintstones* return to prime time as reruns on cable TV. He offered the sum of five hundred dollars to any student who proposed an idea that landed the job. As a student with a full load of homework, my available time was fairly limited, but I still wanted to come up with at least one idea for Mr. Heller's project. I used my only window of free time: my daily commute. Living on Long Island, New York, provided me with a two-hour ride in each direction. As kids, my sister and I would sometimes go to work with my dad and we would watch him use the commute to fill every bit of paper he had with ideas and designs. He might be working out a new campaign as an art director, or maybe figuring out a design or a logo as part of a freelance job. From my dad I learned that I could use anytime and any place to be creative. What better a time or place to be creative than when you're stuck on a bus or train? Now I was using this beast of a commute to conjure up some creativity.

On the subway I came up with a fun idea for *The Flintstones* bid: a live-action family of four is wearily driving home in their station wagon. Suddenly someone in the car remembers that they've got to race home to catch *The Flintstones* in prime time! Bare cartoon feet grow underneath the car and the family drives "Flintstones feet-style" all the way home.

"Hi, I'm Bill. I need approval."
"Hi, I'm Larry. I withhold approval."

Each year I draw hundreds of fish gags on my commute, six or seven of which have been subsequently published in newspapers and magazines.

Mark Heller liked the idea, had one of his artists draw it up, and showed it in his bid meeting. The promoters didn't end up using Mark Heller's company for the spots, but it was still exciting to participate in a real bid for an account.

I worked for Mark Heller two more times as a student. On one occasion, he needed help shooting a John R. Dilworth animated commercial for Sesame Place Amusement Park. This time there was no money available, just experience. Still, I leaped at the opportunity to spend a Saturday afternoon working on the project. After that came a three-week job assisting Heller's other business, a stock footage supply company. I'm forever grateful that Heller took a chance on me and encouraged my talents during my formative school years. I learned that working hard, being enthusiastic, and doing good work bring rewards that go beyond a paycheck. The first reward is getting asked back to work on another job.

My Third Key Moment in School

The final and most important lesson I learned while at school was that fear can be a great motivator. At the end of my junior year, an animator named Michael Klein called me at the recommendation of my favorite instructor, Howard Beckerman. Klein had graduated from SVA a few years prior. He had worked at several New York studios including Jumbo Pictures (now called

Cartoon Pizza) and Michael Sporn Animation, Inc. Klein's side gig was teaching animation to children in an after-school program at the prestigious York Preparatory School.

Klein tried to talk me into teaching the program, telling me that it would be a valuable experience. I have to admit that teaching had never been part of my plan, and certainly not teaching while I was still a student myself. Not quite convinced, I agreed to meet up with Klein in person. He turned out to be an even better salesman face to face than he was on the phone. Klein's easygoing personality calmed me and, despite my fear of this new experience, I soon found myself making a commitment to take over his class.

Twice a week for the next year and a half, I headed uptown to teach a group of children ages nine through twelve something about animation. We watched and analyzed classic cartoons and spent the second half of class working out exercises in movement. At the end of each class I'd scoop up the drawings and then shoot them on a video pencil test system at SVA. The following class the students rushed to the monitor to see their scribbles come to life. Before long, many of the children showed up to class with a stack of drawings ready for the camera. Holding a bunch of restless kids' attention for two hours twice a week was an invaluable experience. Best of all, in taking on the class, I'd made a connection with Michael Klein. A short time later, his good advice launched me into my first real job in the industry. Fear can be healthy and normal. I've trained myself to use fear as a gauge. If I have fear it is a sign that I'm out of my comfort zone. With this realization the fear yields to the excitement of a good challenge. The main thing we fear is failure. I like to give myself permission to fail, knowing that it can be the best teacher of all.

IT'S NOT ABOUT STYLE; IT'S ABOUT EXPERIMENTATION

I'm always amazed to see college students defending poor work, calling it their "style." Style is their get-out-of-jail-free card. Most of us draw what we have always drawn, the way we've always drawn it. This isn't style. Style is something you arrive upon after going through a journey of experimentation. Pablo Picasso didn't wake up one day and declare, "I'm a cubist painter now. This is my style." Picasso developed by studying and exploring classical drawing, painting, and sculpture first.

Every drawing you make is a record of where you are as an artist based on the sum of your experiences. How well you draw reflects your natural talent and the amount of effort you've put forth. While in school, instead of focusing on style, free yourself to borrow, steal, or experiment. Being a slave to your style can hold you back from taking in other ideas and growing as an artist. It's important to not use style as your crutch or device to hide behind. For example, many students these days have got the Anime bug. While there is nothing wrong with Anime as a genre or drawing style, students often cling to its drawing formula as law. How open can you be if you're busy processing all you see through such a limited point of view? As you begin your school career, check your style at the door along with your ego. Now it's time to stretch, stumble, and grow.

ANIMATION IS NOT FOR EVERYONE

My first year of animation class at SVA was filled with twenty-five students ready to have "fun." By our senior year, eight students remained. So much for fun. Of the eight, one student, who had done as little work as possible in four years, remarked on our last day of class, "I don't like animation. I think I'll do something else." Some students gravitate towards studies in animation because of the implicit fun of animated cartoons. They're fun to watch, so they must be fun to make. Many students grow quickly frustrated that their first animation tests don't immediately look like the TV shows and movies they admire. There's no quick way to get to the fun stuff, the finished work, without the labor-intensive and comparatively mundane (storyboard, layout, and design) stages.

Still from my thesis film, Get Off My Back, *revealing limitations, not style.*

School is a very expensive and time-consuming place to discover that you can't get past the "fun" of animation. The irony is that those of us who seriously respect the process of animation and the variety of skills and talent required to do it well, are the ones who have fun doing it.

Anezka Sebek, director of Parson's School of Design's animation program, feels that students often expect computers and technology to take care of the tedium of animation. "If students have paid attention to build their sense of timing and applied animation principles, they do well. Students should know that animation is essentially creating life, and creating life is not easy."

REEL STUDENT ADVICE

Twenty days prior to the release of his film *The Incredibles*, writer/director Brad Bird presented the film to an appreciative audience at SVA. Following the (forgive me) incredible film, Bird was interviewed on stage by SVA's chairperson of the film, video, and animation department, Reeves Leehman. Leehman asked Bird how important 2D skills are in this 3D digital age. Bird replied that 2D is still the fastest and most direct route for students to learn timing, acting, and design for animation. "From one character sketch, you can immediately throw a character into action. CGI is far more time-consuming to get started. You need to design a character, build a skeleton, cover it with textures, create all the points of movement, light it, and so on. Nowadays most people in the biz assume that a good 2D animator can learn 'the box' (computer animation)."

ASIFA, THE NOT-SO-SECRET WEAPON AGAINST SENIOR-ITIS

ASIFA (Association Internationale du Film d'Animation) was formed in 1960 by an international group of animators to coordinate and increase worldwide visibility of animated film. ASIFA's membership includes animation professionals and fans from more than fifty countries. The group sponsors international animation festivals in Annecy, Ottawa, and Hiroshima. I first heard about ASIFA-East (the Eastern United States chapter of ASIFA, based in New York) from fellow SVA student Silvie Nueman. Nueman was an energetic and fearless Belgian transplant, already making a name for herself in New York animation. She had interned for Jumbo and MTV Animation; she knew Beavis and Butthead creator Mike Judge. Nueman was only one year ahead of me in school, but she might as well have been light years away. She had already figured out that success in the animation industry is largely about plugging into the local scene to make relationships. Every chance she could she talked to me about ASIFA-East and how she attended all their monthly events, helped out on the board of directors, and worked with then ASIFA-East president Linda Simensky.

I remember the day Nueman told me about an ASIFA-East event in which a group of pros, including John R. Dilworth and Michael Sporn, blew off the dust from their student works and screened them before an audience. Nueman was giddy with excitement when describing the films and was energized to see that even local

A sample of the ASIFA-East newsletter, which goes out monthly to over four hundred members. Note: John R. Dilworth's Life in Transition *on the cover. Newsletter image courtesy of editor Mark Bailey.*

animation heroes came from a place to which students could relate. The idea of plugging into ASIFA as a means of joining the community of animators intrigued me. Still, I stayed away despite instructors Don Duga and Howard Beckerman constantly nagging my class to join ASIFA-East or check out an event. What was I afraid of? In my fantasy I imagined all eyes would turn to me as I walked in the door. They'd ask me to do the secret handshake or name all the Nine Old Men of Disney.

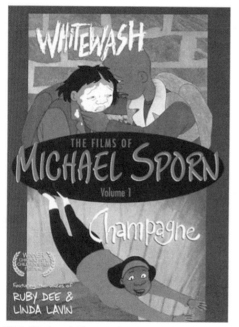

WhiteWash *and* Champagne, *available on* The Films of Michael Sporn Volume 1, *DVD. Courtesy of Michael Sporn Animation, Inc. and First Run Features.*

It wasn't until my senior year that I finally got involved with ASIFA-East. My impetus was the thought of graduating and not having enough connections in the animation community. The ASIFA-East Animation Festival, an annual event that's been around for decades, was the three-hour event that changed my life and career forever. As a newcomer to the scene, I remember thinking at once how big and how small the local animation industry was. The three-hundred plus in attendance were representatives from every large studio and independent shop in town.

Winning two prizes that night was *Whitewash* by Michael Sporn Animation, Inc. This was my first introduction to Sporn's work. I was at once struck by the subject matter in *Whitewash* and the imaginative way it was translated into animation. A few months after the festival, I went to work at Sporn's studio, setting my career in motion.

ASIFA-East helped smooth my transition from school to employment by introducing me to an entire community in one night. All the animation hubs in North America have ASIFA chapters of their own. Why not plug into the one near you? Tell them I sent you.

YOU GET BACK WHAT YOU PUT IN

Schools are like living, breathing organic things. As technology takes animation into new territories, schools struggle to keep up so their students retain a competitive edge in the marketplace. As a result, schools always seem to be restructuring the way they teach the animation arts. Your experience at a

school could be very different from someone else's experience a few years earlier or later.

One constant is that there will always be good and bad teachers. It remains up to the student to exploit every resource the school has to offer (regardless of the school's limitations). The best animation curriculum in the world will not make you a success. The onus, as it will be for the rest of our careers, is on us. We decide if the debt incurred by four years of school is worth it or not. Showing up at school, paying tuition, and breathing the school's oxygen for four years only entitles us to what we've earned.

If you have a lackluster instuctor, not only should you give him a poor performance review, but you should also spring into action to salvage your education. Instead of complaining to kindred spirits, sit in on a class taught by a better instructor, or better yet, work with your teacher to help him become the teacher you need. Teachers need students who communicate their educational needs clearly and consistently. Bring a list of questions to each class and ask them. Demand critiques on your work. Challenge yourself to do your best under any circumstance.

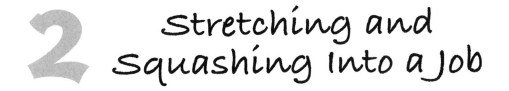

2 Stretching and Squashing Into a Job

"The first few years out of school, work was scarce. I lived at home with my parents and made my own cartoons and experimented with Flash, After Effects, and some 3D programs. I felt like Boo Radley with a computer. I got a little Web notoriety, and taught myself things that give me a big technical edge over many other directors."

—Mike Overbeck, animator/director

In a typical animation career you wear many hats. You may have a specific expertise, but chances are that just as often, you'll juggle many skills and titles from job to job. Animation artists find most of their work via word of mouth. No offense to agents, reps, and recruiters, but to succeed in finding work in the business of animation is to develop and maintain relationships. We are, as Barbra Streisand sang it, "people who need people."

A postcard mailing from Frederator sent out to filmmakers and friends makes a great device to sustain relationships. Call this our field's version of "going postal." Image courtesy of Frederator.

THE SIMPLE TRUTH

The key to finding work in animation is to accept that this is a people-driven industry. People who know people who recommend people who hire people. Those who take a negative view of the importance of relationships to the job hunt boil it down to, "It's all based on who you know." This makes "who you know" sound like some random act of luck. In reality, you are responsible for "who you know," for the relationships you create and sustain. Relationships require energy and effort.

The business of animation in North America is small enough that even within a few short years, you could know someone connected to every studio on the continent. We're all six degrees from our animation Kevin Bacons. Simple enough, right? But these truths are not self-evident and if they are, we certainly don't behave all the time as if we hold this to be true. This simple truth will show up over and over again in this book.

While there's no guaranteed way to find work in the animation industry, there are a lot of things we can do to create the best possible odds for success. Happily, finding work in the animation industry is something that gets easier over time, as you expand your network of contacts and your reputation opens doors for you. If you're already working in the field you might be tempted to skip over this chapter. Hold it right there, buster! There's a lot that can be learned from the experiences of others.

SUSTAINING RELATIONSHIPS CAN LEAD TO WORK

"The most effective opportunities that have
come my way have been from relationships I have
developed over my lifetime. Some of those
relationships go back to childhood, some of them
are ones started last week (seriously)."
—*Fred Seibert, producer, president, Frederator*

In the animation industry, sometimes the most effective job-hunting happens in the most indirect way. Often, even when we make a good connection at a studio, the timing is not right for an immediate job. So, what can we do to "hang around" until something opens up without risking a restraining order? My favorite solution is to stay in touch with people via the occasional e-mail.

Recently I was in a producer's office when he received an e-mail from a mutual friend of ours. "I guess he's out of work again," said the producer. I asked how he knew that without reading the e-mail. The producer replied, "This guy only e-mails me when he needs work."

Since I've been writing this book a few people have approached me for some career advice. One thing that keeps coming up when I ask them how they look for work is that people are not keeping in touch with their contacts enough while they are working. I hear about the great interview a person has had at a certain studio and then that person gets a job somewhere else and lets that contact die away. We need to nurture our contacts.

Periodically send out updates to your contacts. Let them know where you're working and why it's a great experience. Keep an eye and ear out for news about your contact in the trades, online, or via the grapevine, then send an e-mail offering congratulations. When I come across a media item on a contact I'll photocopy it and mail it to him. Who knows, he may have even missed it in the trades himself. Either way, your contacts will be tickled that you thought of them. It's a great way to spread good vibes. Our careers are all linked so let's acknowledge that and support one another's endeavors.

Over the years, I have received a few job offers as a result of mailing out some congratulatory messages. While I wouldn't say sending out e-mail messages and updates should be anyone's main focus for job-hunting, they are a part of what builds up a career over time.

TACT IN CONVERSATION

"Know-it-all students with chips on their shoulders go nowhere fast."
—*Mark Simon, A & S Animation*

Savvy animation artists with healthy careers make the time to network with others on a regular basis. Networking most often takes the shape of an in-person, casual conversation. In this way we sniff out possible jobs or share a tip on work with someone else. Sometimes just bumping into someone you haven't seen in a while could lead to an unexpected offer for work. Didn't someone famous once say that showing up is half the battle? We are each other's secret weapons when it comes to looking for work.

In my years in the business I've been in many networking conversations, sometimes giving tips and sometimes receiving them. These encounters are like a delicate dance. Each time is different, depending on the players, their moods, the weather, the shape of the economy, or what they had for lunch. The only important thing to remember is that you should never make someone feel on the spot or uncomfortable. If the conversation turns to work opportunities make it crystal clear that you will go through the officially recommended channels and procedures to apply for the job. You can't assume that the person giving the tip will also be your conduit into a job. However, it's okay to ask if you may use his name as a referral. Above all else, use restraint and look out for people's comfort zones. Step over the line and you'll risk cutting off hearing about future opportunities. For more on networking and its important role in your career, see chapter 10—"Networking: People Who Need People."

HOOFING IT: HOW I GOT MY FIRST JOB

I graduated from SVA in 1995 when gross, ugly, and edgy humor in animation was king. These were the heydays of *Beavis and Butthead*, *Ren and Stimpy*, *The Simpsons*, and *Spike and Mike's Sick and Twisted Festival of Animation*. My SVA thesis film, *Get Off My Back*, was a gentle story of two characters trying to single-handedly solve the overpopulation problem by encouraging everyone to walk "piggyback" to save vital space. The softness of my colored pencil technique coupled with the "family-safe" humor made the film seem like a throwback to the seventies more than an audition piece to land a job at the time.

Still from my thesis film, Get Off My Back, *in which the main characters are moments away from a horrible death. Well, maybe in a different film.*

New York in the mid-nineties was not at its peak for industry production. Jobs were scarce. Most people gravitated to two large studios, MTV Animation (which was banging out *Beavis and Butthead*) and Jumbo Pictures (then recently bought by Disney and working on numerous series projects). Outside of this were a smattering of small shops and fragile partnerships spread across town. Where would I fit in to all this?

On the plus side, I'd just finished *Get Off My Back* two weeks before its due date. This meant I had two weeks to do with whatever I pleased. I wanted to work. I turned to one of my few contacts in the field, Michael Klein, whose class I'd taken over, teaching animation to children at York Prep School. He pushed me to make a bold move. Klein gave me the contact info for three studios all in the downtown area of Manhattan and told me, "You have a finished film! What are you waiting for? Go to the city tomorrow and start knocking on doors. Don't call ahead of time. Just show up!" The next day I packed a messenger bag with five VHS copies of my film and just as many resumes.

First, I hoofed over to Jumbo Pictures. I had been to this studio once before on an SVA class outing. Two fine folks from Jumbo, Jack Spillum and Rick Allen, had spoken to our class. These were the names I asked for when I showed up at the reception area, unannounced and uninvited. The reception people were nice to me just the same. They tried to ring up my two contacts. When they proved to be out that day, someone else tried (unsuccessfully) to arrange an impromptu meeting with an animation director. I was grateful for the hospitality and encouragement to come back another time.

Next I hoofed down to Michael Sporn Animation, Inc. Sporn was well known for animating long-form (half-hour TV specials) completely in-house. It was rare for New York studios to tackle half-hour specials. Most of the smaller studios scraped by animating thirty-second commercials. The larger studios working on TV series farmed all their animation work to South Korea where there is a larger and cheaper workforce. In the industry this practice is known as outsourcing. Sporn's studio was a place where one could learn the nuts and bolts of filmmaking from a man who had been trained by some of the industry's most stellar talents, including John Gentilella, John Hubley, Tissa David, and Richard Williams.

As I rode up the elevator to Sporn's fourth floor studio, I suddenly felt very calm and confident. Something told me the sensitive films coming out of his studio might mesh with my own sensibility, and perhaps he would appreciate my gentle thesis film. Michael Sporn, himself, came to the door to let me in. At the time I thought I'd interrupted a staff meeting, but later he told me, "It was only lunch." Sporn was gracious and kind to me. His studio was long and narrow, which reminded me of pictures I'd seen of Pat Sullivan's *Felix The Cat* studio. Sporn and I chatted for a few minutes. We talked animation history. I asked him questions about his recent film *Whitewash*. Emboldened, I asked if I could come back later that day for feedback on my film. Amazingly, Sporn agreed!

The next and last studio on my list was Stretch Films, John R. Dilworth's then one-room operation. Out of such a humble space poured some of the best animation in New York, including the Oscar-nominated short *The Chicken from Outer Space*, which was later spun into the Cartoon Network series *Courage the Cowardly Dog*. Stretch Films was my most poorly timed visit of the day. I never made it past the doorjamb. Dilworth's nice office manager invited me to come back when he would have the time to review my work. In

Michael Sporn's animation studio circa 1995. Can you spot a young bearded Dave Levy? Photo from the author's collection.

I challenge anyone to find two better mentors than Michael Sporn (standing) and Robert Marianetti (seated), seen here in a rare moment away from drawing. Photo from the author's collection.

the background I could see Dilworth animating with one hand and holding a phone receiver with the other.

When I returned to Sporn's studio, his office manager, Christine O'Neill, asked me, "You were in here earlier, right? Michael would like to offer you a job." My eyes went as wide as two animation discs. The offer was for a studio runner job. I was to fetch art supplies, drop off packages, and use the rest of the time to help out wherever I could in the studio. I accepted the job, which I began three weeks later. Oddly enough, my first day of work was the day after graduation. It all seemed so tidy.

None of this is to say that dropping by unexpectedly is the best way to find work. In fact, I haven't repeated this method since that fateful day. Now I use "hoofing it" as a metaphor for putting the necessary energy into the job hunt. It's important to get out there and start making relationships. Our mission is to meet real people, face to face. The rest can surely follow.

THE THREE NEVERS

A very talented Russian animator recently asked me to help her find work in New York animation. The first thing I did was give her ten studios to contact. A week later she called me sounding very disappointed. "Nobody will hire me," she sighed. "I called everyone on the list and asked if they had work and nobody needed any help." This is one of the most common mistakes people make when looking for work in the animation industry. Never ask an employer *if they need help, have work, or will be hiring soon.* I call these questions The Three Nevers. Nine times out of ten, whether the industry is up or down, if you ask these three questions, you will be told "No." Like the craft of animation itself, timing is very important. However, unlike the craft, this timing is out of your control. Often you'll hear about a project too late or too early to be considered for a position.

When cold calling, contacting a potential employer who is unfamiliar with your work, put yourself in the position of the person on the other end of the phone call. The average-sized studio may not have a designated person handling inquiries. Whoever answers is likely juggling duties in production or may be the head of the studio themselves. If you immediately ask the three nevers, the person who answers is likely to ask you to call back in a few weeks or send in your reel and resume. If this sounds like success, remember that your reel will probably sit in box for a year and may never be viewed at all. This isn't because the animation business is full of jerks. Reels sit in boxes because studios find it nearly impossible to make the time to sit still and watch unsolicited material. If you follow up with a call back in a few weeks, you'll just be putting yourself in a position to go through the same thing all over again. After you've asked the three nevers and been dismissed, you're already forgotten. Looking for work this way could take up to a year to snag a job, and that's if you're lucky and the industry is healthy.

GET THE MEETING

Now you know to avoid the three nevers, but what's a person to do—especially someone looking for a first break into the industry? Fortunately the answer is easy: Get the meeting. Your single goal, whether cold calling or calling on a recommendation, is to get the meeting. It doesn't matter if the company you call has an opening because the best way to look for work is to set up informational interviews. When you cold call a company you're a perfect stranger to them. Change that as soon as possible and create a relationship with them. Informational interviews are low-pressure affairs. You're much more likely to be your relaxed self if you're not worried about wearing the right shirt, saying the all the right things, or showing up with perfect timing.

Getting the meeting is already a measure of success since it gives you the chance to make a real impression. Your work will be seen because you're the one showing it. Plus you have the opportunity to pick the brains of great animation artists and tour their animation studios! *Blue's Clues* co-creator Traci Paige Johnson adds, "I always left informational interviews with one or two more people to meet. Contacts would grow and grow. Afterwards I always sent thank you notes, and sent updates of new work to people I really clicked with."

The most surefire way to get the meeting is to snare a referral before you make your call. That way you can say that so-and-so recommended you call. This is always better than calling cold. However, it's common courtesy to ask permission before using someone else's name to land your interview. This is a small business and word will travel quickly if you lie about a referral. Your reputation is too valuable to soil it with such an error in judgment.

What if you don't know anybody yet to secure a referral? If that's the case, at least find out a name to contact at the studio. In addition, do your research before approaching any studio or employer. Be familiar with their work and achievements so you can talk about specific projects the studio or employer has tackled.

Making the Call

Early in my animation career, I'd prep a cheat sheet of some important things to say before calling a studio or employer. As I got more comfortable, I relied on this less and less and finally no longer needed it. Don't get carried away, though. There is no point to trying to script out a two-way conversation. The main points to hit are:

+ Briefly introduce yourself and your area of expertise.

+ Name your referral and/or why you are attracted to the studio's work.

+ Ask if you can come in to show your work and get a quick tour of their operation.

This approach is successful because it gets you in the door. Period. The rest is up to you and your work. No amount of superior schmoozing will land you a job if you aren't qualified to do the work. When you get an in-person meeting, the employer has a chance to look over you and your work and draw conclusions about where you might fit in to the studio.

Dressing for the Meeting: No Suits, No Ties

Just one look at the busy Hawaiian shirts worn by Pixar's top dog, John Lasseter, and his cohort *Monsters, Inc.* director Pete Docter, and you'll see that the dress code of the animation industry is loose and sometimes even loud. This is cause for celebration. For a time, I worked on an animation job at Merrill Lynch, smack in the heart of the World Financial Center. I was decked out in flannel shirts and jeans surrounded by a sea of accountants and corporate types dressed to the hilt in their finest suits, skirts, and ties. I never felt so happy to be working in a creative field in my life. Casual and comfortable dress is the uniform of creativity. This is as true when dressing for a job interview as it is when working on the job itself. Of course, good hygiene and proper grooming is not to be forgotten, but please, no suits and ties at interviews. It's just not that type of business. Be grateful for that.

EFFECTIVE COVER LETTERS AND RESUMES

I know what you're thinking: What about portfolios, resumes, and reels? Portfolios and reels will be discussed in chapter 3, "Designing a Career", but here we'll address cover letters and resumes.

We know that the animation industry is not like most other businesses. If I were an accountant looking for work I would research a hundred accounting firms and then do a mass mailing of cover letters and resumes. Accountants find work this way. Animation artists usually do not. We are a people business, a small industry. Although word of mouth is how most animation artists find work, it is important that we understand the value of effective cover letters and resumes as a key component of the job hunt. Often in this field, cover letters and resumes work as handy follow-ups to an interview. Ila Abramson, who runs her own successful creative recruitment company, I Spy Recruiting, was kind enough to describe the ingredients of successful cover letters and resumes:

Tips to Create Effective Cover Letters and Resumes

+ Cover letters should be addressed to a specific person in the company. Make sure that the name and title are accurate and spelled correctly.

+ If there is any way you can establish some kind of personal connection, do so. For example: you were referred by someone this person knows, you heard the person speak, or you read something about him.

+ Cover letters should be concise, but not form letters! Know the company that you are applying to. Try to think of something unique or show your knowledge about the company.

+ Make sure to do your research and that your facts are accurate.

+ If you are applying for a specific job you saw posted, note it. If you are not responding to a job posting, still make sure to state the type of position for which you are applying, and the relevant skills or experience you can bring to that job.

- If you are applying for a job in a different state or far away, mention specific dates you will be in the area in case they are interested in meeting.

An effective resume should list the following information:

- Contact Info: Make sure it is all current. List name, address, phone number, e-mail, and Web site address. If you are a student or plan to move, make sure to include a permanent and temporary address. When you have moved, send a postcard or e-mail with your updated information.

- Goal/Objective: Be as specific as possible and make sure your resume supports your goal. If not sure of your objective, include a brief summary of your professional qualifications instead.

- Skills/Software Knowledge: List them, and be specific. Make sure to note your level of proficiency with each program. Be honest and accurate about your skill level.

- Experience: List the company and your job title, and provide a brief description of your duties. You may want to include internships or other work-related experience. List your experience in reverse chronological order with the most recent job at the top.

- Education: List where you went to school, your area of study, and degrees you obtained.

- Awards, organizations, and other interests that relate to the industry or job for which you are applying: Do not include extracurricular activities that do not apply to the industry or information that is too personal.

Always make sure to:

- Check your spelling—do not rely on your computer's spell-check feature alone.

- Make sure your layout is consistent and that there is overall continuity in your resume.

- Often resumes need to be photocopied many times—graphics and images will not read well.

- Have different versions of your resume depending on the job and company to which you are applying. For example, have one version that is more job-specific for applying to a larger company, and another more general resume that emphasizes your versatility for a smaller production house.

- Make sure you know the proper submission requirements. Does the company accept e-mailed resumes? Web sites? Do they only accept hard copies of your resume and reel on VHS or DVD?

+ If you are sending your submission via e-mail, make sure the digital copy of your work is easy to open and read. Use Microsoft Word, pdf, or text pasted into the body of the e-mail. Do not use Photoshop or Illustrator files. Test any attachments by opening them on both a Mac and a PC.

+ Never send out a mass e-mail with your resume/cover letter. Continually review and revise your resume to keep it current. That goes for your reel and portfolio as well. Your resume, reel, and portfolio are always works in progress.

GETTING TESTY: FOUR RULES TO KNOW

It's a fairly common practice for studios to give out tests to potential employees to try them out in a no-risk manner. Some tests are to take home; in other cases a studio prefers to test people at their facility. Under their supervision, employers have the ability to test you for speed more accurately than if you took the work home. If the test is for 2D or 3D computer animation, employers also get a chance, via testing, to find out just how well you know the software. In this business, tests are given out most often for storyboard, storyboard revisions, character/backgrounds/props design, layout, and animation. Rare, but not unheard of, are tests required for directing or sheet timing.

There are a few things to keep in mind with regard to testing. The first law of testing is that you should *never take a test for a job that you are completely unqualified to do*. If there is no way you can turn in a decent test in the given area, don't take it. You don't want to risk turning in a poor test that wastes everybody's time. Ask the studio to show you samples of finished work so you can gauge how well suited you are to take that test. You are allowed to say, "No thanks." Not every job offer is the right fit, even for the most in-demand animation artists. Only take tests that demonstrate your areas of strength. Traditional animator Travis Blaise can relate. "I took a couple of tests. Unfortunately they proved unsuccessful. This was, however, due to my lack of experience with Maya."

The next law of testing is that *time is always a factor*, no matter what you're told to the contrary. Animation is a business with tight deadlines. Talent, time, and resources are what get work done and done right. Slow turnaround times can cause projects to go over budget and fall behind schedule. Meeting the deadlines on a test displays efficient time management skills, which makes you a less risky proposition. Early in my career, I took a traditional inbetweening test at a studio that did commercials. To complete the test, I needed to create two drawings falling inbetween two extreme positions. The director gave me the test on the premises and advised me to take as much time as I needed. I painstakingly sketched out the two inbetweens and then spent even more time doing clean-ups on the roughs. Three hours later I re-emerged with the two completed drawings. "You took too long," said the director as he pegged them and began a flip-check. I didn't get the job, but I did get the lesson.

The next law is that *you've got to stay on script*. Know the particular rules of the project in terms of style, budget, and its intended audience. It's easier if you're testing for an existing show because you can research the material easily. When I took the storyboard test for *Blue's Clues*, the show had only been on TV for six months. In anticipation of the test, I ordered cable and starting taping episodes of the series as a reference. This research proved invaluable and gave me the confidence I needed to wrap my head around the show's idiosyncrasies. Upon reviewing my test, the producers were impressed by how well I knew the show. I got the job.

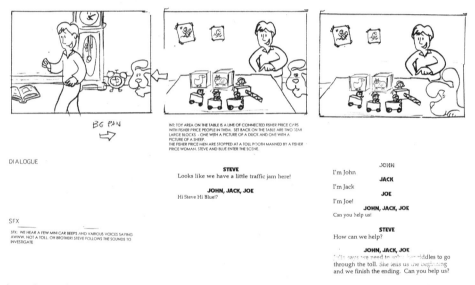

A sample page from my storyboard test for Blue's Clues. *This particular test took me four days to board out fifteen pages of script (which was nearly a full half-hour episode!) In case you're wondering, that is one of the longest tests you could ever be asked to take.*

When testing for a project that's not already available for reference, ask lots of questions and get them answered before you begin. It's not enough to simply learn the rules of a project when testing; you've got to follow those rules. One animator I know learned the hard way that testing is not the time to show how a project could break new ground or be flipped on its ear. This animator, a skilled and gifted writer, took a writing test for the TV series he was working on. He decided to use the test to write a sample episode that broke every rule particular to the series, even forsaking its intended audience, young children. Unsurprisingly, the test was met with bafflement, and the opportunity to write for the series was wasted. We should always assume that there won't be a second chance.

Last, but not least, *tests are really tests of employability.* David J. Palmer, the supervising director at *Blue's Clues,* had an ingenious system for getting the most out of the testing process. He would give out a ten-second scene, in which the tester would animate a frog interacting with the live action host, Steve Burns. The short test demonstrated an animator's level of familiarity with After Effects and her grasp of the principles of animation. Yet much of the assessment happened after the test was turned in. Palmer would sit down to critique the work in a meeting with the animator. He would poke through the After Effects project structure to see how expertly the animator had set up the work. After asking the animator to defend and explain his creative choices, Palmer gave notes on the work. Animators that really wanted the job were excited by the notes and by the chance to take their work to another level. This interaction simulated the collaborative process by which the director and the animator would work together on the job.

PATIENCE IS KEY. DESPERATION IS A TURN-OFF

"Don't be discouraged if work doesn't come right away.
My film's exposure in ResFest 2000 got me my first
commercial directing gig three years later in 2003."
—*Mike Overbeck, animator/director*

OK, let's say you're chomping at the bit to land a dream job or your first gig in the industry. You're bursting with enthusiasm. You've been building up to this moment and now you're ready, by golly. Use this energy to help yourself stay motivated during the search. Create new samples for your reel and portfolio. Attend every animation event in town. Don't obsess on any one job lead or studio contact. I've seen otherwise sane people go down this path. One student in my career class mentioned a storyboard test he'd taken just after the conclusion of an internship months earlier. All semester he obsessed over this one opportunity. He tortured himself by wondering what had happened and if he should contact the employer one more time to get the final word. He rationalized the panic because the employer had told him the job needed to be filled quickly. "Surely, the company needs someone now. They said so," he said. I replied, "They know when and if they need to fill a position. I'm sure they haven't dropped the ball. Consider the time on the test well spent and move on to the next thing." My words fell on deaf ears.

On another occasion, a more seasoned animation artist blew a job opportunity after leaving a string of increasingly desperate voice mail messages for a studio department head. This affair was particularly sad because someone at the studio had recommended this person as a potential hire. The contact was deeply embarrassed about the friend's behavior. Needless to say, this desperate person didn't even make it to an interview stage.

These examples probably sound extreme, but we all risk this behavior. It has to do with us being "ready." We feel that because we just graduated, ended a job, or decided to pick up a phone that somehow the universe should be attuned to our needs. It ain't so. The person you're calling may be busy, on vacation, or who knows what. Always leave people time to return your call. The less well you know them, the more time you should allow for them to get back to you.

THE HARD SELL

As a director on a TV series, I interviewed an animator who was more than qualified for a job that was open. For three years he had been doing similar work on a different production at the same network. He had experience with TV deadlines and knew many people on the crew. At the time of his interview we needed to hire four people. We gave this animator a take-home test and he turned it in a few days later. He nailed it. Sounds like he should have been a shoo-in. Yes and no. Although he was technically qualified, it wasn't that simple. For one, the animator was well known to bad-mouth our show and disrespect our team when he was working on another production. Now, out of a job, he came to us with his hand out. We were willing to give him the benefit of the doubt, but there was another cause for concern. In the interview and testing process he would often declare, "My work speaks for itself." Then he would go on to speak anyway, boasting and bragging. He was arrogant, cocky, and downright demanded the job. We let him know we'd be making our decision after two weeks.

He showed up several more times over these two weeks ambushing me and the other two directors in our offices. His tone grew more insistent and desperate. In our eyes, his star was fading with each encounter. My supervisor was the one who had to call him to let him know he didn't get the job. When he came in to retrieve his test CD, he walked into my supervisor's office, grabbed his stuff and marched out. That was a very ungraceful display and certainly not the actions or attitude of someone who was genuinely interested in working with us. We felt vindicated in our choice not to hire him.

CAST A BIG NET

If we all run the risk of desperate behavior when we're on the outside looking in, what can we do about it? We all have different personalities. Some of us may behave desperate because of insecurity. Some of us just lack experience. Heck, some folks are just wired that way, right? I propose a plan to help all types: Cast a big net! Don't focus on one job lead. Who is more likely to get a bite, the fisherman with one pole in the water or the one with ten? I like to cast a big net because every informational interview I set up is another chance to practice presenting my work and myself. I get to read how my work is coming across. I can use that knowledge to tweak my next presentation. Often, taking a meeting will lead to acquiring more contacts. With the big net method, we stay fresh, open, and increase our chances exponentially.

A GOOD PROBLEM TO HAVE

To repeat: Cast a big net. Don't put all your eggs all in one basket, put many lines in the water. While these are all familiar clichés, many animation artists don't follow this advice because they fear the problem of overlapping jobs or having different opportunities occurring at the same time. That would indeed be a good problem to have. That's the risk you take and it's well worth it. The alternative is to focus on one job opportunity and stare at the phone waiting for it to ring. I know many folks that have tried that method and it rarely leads to a job. However, there are times when overlapping opportunities may put you in a potentially awkward position.

Once, not so long ago, conflicting opportunities appeared at my door. I wish I could say that I handled it properly, but I did not. I went against my usually good judgment, hurt a friend and nearly damaged an important business relationship. It happened during my post-*Blue's Clues* run of freelance work. For six months straight I was never without a gig and I was usually juggling more than one at a time. One of my most reliable clients was a small studio run by two good friends of mine. They may be the nicest people in the business today. In recent years, their fledgling studio has grown by leaps and bounds, and I'm proud to say that I worked for them at their humble beginning more than five years earlier.

From time to time I took on freelance animation assignments from them while working full time at *Blue's Clues*. I sacrificed many evenings and weekends to work on their cool projects. Once or twice I had agreed to do a job for them only to see it canceled or delayed through no fault of their own. Now, I was on the freelance market again and they gave me two back-to-back jobs right away. It was nice to work with them again and even nicer to have the time to focus on their work as my only priority.

My mistake came a few months later when they called me on a Thursday offering yet another freelance job. I agreed to do the work, which would start sometime the next week. As I mentioned, their projects could sometimes be canceled on a whim. I used that knowledge to justify one of the worst lapses of judgment in my whole career. Shortly after I accepted their work for the following week, a different client called asking if I could work on a TV series. They needed help doing sheet checking. The pay was good and they needed help right away. It was a chance to work with new people, at a new studio, and on new TV series. Plus they dangled the opportunity of much more work to come. There was a good possibility that taking on their work would lead to a full-time job with benefits. Without thinking, I said, "Yes."

I kidded myself into believing that my previous commitment would get delayed or canceled so I didn't bother to call my friends and let them know that I'd accepted another job. Four days later when they called me asking if I could come in and pick up the assignment, I knew I had done wrong. It mattered little that I was able to recommend a replacement for myself, whom they hired. The issue wasn't that they wouldn't be able to replace me, but that I let them down.

Looking back, I could have done their job, which would have lasted a week or two tops, then taken the job on the series. As it turned out, the series job used a bunch of people to handle the demanding job of checking their exposure sheets. I could have jumped in and worked with them at any time. Regardless of what the job could have led to or whether I could have done both, my loyalty should have been to my friends who had offered me the first job. Even if they weren't friends of mine, this should have been so. It's just good business. We are our word. No opportunity is worth risking your reputation.

If you suddenly find yourself in a position where you have to make a tough choice, ask if you can give your answer later that day or the next day. Consider all the options and then decide. Yes, opportunities will come up and sometimes hard choices will have to be made. Yet, one should always give the proper notice and honor original commitments. I'm lucky and grateful that my relationship with my friends survived my mistake. To their credit, they gave me another chance and offered me more work a short time later. This is one mistake I don't need to make twice.

WHY YOU SHOULD SAY *NYET* TO THE NET

A former student of mine from SVA had been struggling to find work in animation for a year. Before I could help him, I asked him to describe the way he was looking for work. He replied: "Basically what I've been doing is looking for companies which have Web sites and e-mail addresses and I e-mail them. I've gotten some responses and I've sent out a few reels but aside from that I haven't heard much."

Recent graduates are not the only people who would have a hard time finding work via Internet postings. A very talented animator with five years of experience on a top TV series spent nearly an entire year out of work during a time when the animation industry was booming. What was the reason for his lack of success? He spent all of his energy putting together "the perfect reel" and then replying to every job posting he could find online. He didn't take a single meeting with a human being and only got a pittance of people to talk to him on the phone.

Most studios do not post their job opportunities online. The jobs that are posted are often woefully out of date and rarely include a direct phone number or contact name. Sending your resumes, reels, and portfolios to these phantom studios is tantamount to dropping your work down a bottomless pit and a colossal waste of your job-hunting time. The only time it remotely makes sense for you to send your work to an online listing is if you are out of state or are trying to apply to a dream factory such as Pixar. Large studios like Pixar have more in common with small cities than they do with the way the rest of the business works. Pixar has a recruiting department that handles job inquiries and a training department to wean new hires. Still, if you are really serious about applying for out-of-state work, there is nothing better than taking a trip there and spending a week or two doing in-person meetings.

Since we know that animation is a people business, the impersonal nature of the Web makes looking for work online a dubious bet at best.

Counterpoint

In writing this book, I was surprised to discover that some of my colleagues did in fact recommend looking for job leads on the Internet. However, all of them were in agreement that nothing beats having a face-to-face informational interview. It may be best to use the Internet to research the companies that are out there. After that, it would be advisable to pursue a human connection as soon as it is possible to do so.

Designer Dagan Moriarty found quite a few jobs, both full-time and freelance, on Web sites such as AWN.com and animationnation.com. Moriarty told me his use of the Internet goes beyond finding job postings. He said, "I have also met a ton of industry people from around the world online at various animation 'drawing boards' and 'message boards.' I would never have met some of these people pounding the pavement in New York."

Another good use of the Internet would be to set up Web sites and/or portfolio blogs to display your reel or work. One animation artist, only one year out of school, was just snatched up to storyboard a feature length stop motion film directed by Henry Selick. She was discovered after the director was introduced to her Web site.

Designing
a Career Part I:
The Animation Artists

"I feel like I'm at a point in my life where the decisions I make now are going to determine my future career. Ultimately, I hope to create a body of really memorable works of animation, something that will hopefully inspire others or future animated films."

—Chris Conforti, Animator

I would define a career as something you don't put off to think about tomorrow, but rather actively build up slowly each day. Careers are the progression of someone's working life or professional achievements. While careers imply careful planning and a disciplined focus of energy, there's some degree of chance involved as well.

Opportunities happen seemingly by chance, but only those who

Chris Conforti's SVA thesis film, Frog, *a silver medal winner at the Student Academy Awards.* Frog *can be seen on the DVD compilation,* Avoid Eye Contact Volume II.

have made themselves ready can take advantage of an opportunity wherever and whenever it may strike. Even the smallest of opportunities grow a career like a snowball rolling down a snowbank.

The function of this chapter is to flesh out (in the most realistic manner possible) the professional life of an animation artist. Find out what happens when art meets commerce. The experts are waiting for us below. Grab a snack. Hunker down and read on.

CAREER PATHS: STORYBOARD ARTIST

The storyboard is the visual shot-by-shot translation of a script and is the basis for the entire production process that follows, including design, background and layout, animation, and postproduction. Despite changing technology, storyboards are still mostly drawn by hand, although sometimes they're drawn directly into a computer program such as Flash, where the storyboard panels can be easily assimilated into an animatic.

Storyboards represent the finished product long before great time and expense goes into a project. The storyboard artist, working in the style of the production, maintains storytelling continuity, breaks down the script into scenes or shots, establishes the size relationships between characters and props, and indicates the acting by hitting strong poses on each story point. In addition, the storyboard artist is often the first to rough out new background locations, characters, and props. A storyboard artist balances strong drawing skills with a good knowledge of anatomy, acting, directing, staging, and the ability to think creatively and quickly. With such commanding skills, storyboard artists often develop into animation directors.

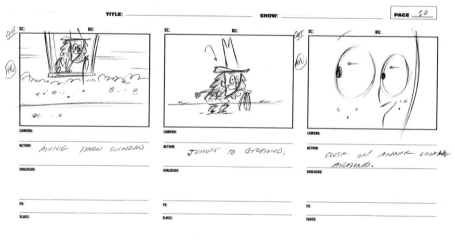

Storyboard sample by Otis Brayboy from a pitch, Teddy and Annie, *written and created by Debbie Staab and the author. Image courtesy of the author.*

Veteran storyboard artist and co-creator of Frederator/Nickelodeon's *Call Me Bessie!*, Diane Kredensor, describes the daily duties of a storyboard artist. "First, you go through the script and thumbnail out your shots. Then you pitch your thumbnails to the storyboard supervisor or animation director for notes and changes. From there, you flesh it out, adding the acting, into a full rough storyboard. Some productions already have the voices recorded, and the board artist will board to track. Otherwise, you create (draw) the acting and the voice actors match your board. Once your rough board is approved by the director, you make it pretty, putting everything on model, and then you're done (and ready for the next script!)."

Scott Cooper, who has storyboarded on such projects as *Blue's Clues, Maya and Miguel,* and *Clifford's Puppy Days,* says that a storyboard for a half-hour TV episode usually needs to be completed in three weeks. "After my thumbnail sketches get approved, I try to board about a script page a day." Storyboard artists Liz Rathke (*Smurfs, Brand Spankin' New Doug, Teenage Mutant Ninja Turtles,* and *Pinky Dinky Doo*) and Dev Ramsaran (*The Super Mario Brothers Super Show* and *Stanley*) agree on the importance of assigning yourself a daily page count. Ramsaran adds, "That way you're not wondering at 3:00 A.M. why you are on page three of the script instead of page nine."

What kind of training and skills does a storyboard artist need to develop to start out and to keep advancing in her career? According to Diane Kredensor, you want to be a good draftsman, able to draw the human figure in a variety of poses. "Other skills should include strong storytelling,

Illustration by Liz Rathke. Courtesy of the artist.

cinematography, staging, and composition. Storyboards should clearly communicate ideas to the entire production team, so strong communication skills are an important asset."

Kredensor never went to art school, but she knows a lot of excellent artists who have gone to Cal Arts and NYU. Her best advice: "Take any classes you can find on storyboarding, and look for a mentor, someone whose work you admire, and just start boarding as much as possible and use their feedback to keep learning and improving. If you can land a job doing storyboard revisions, it's a great way to immerse yourself in it and get paid at the same time."

Like Kredensor, Liz Rathke didn't go to art school, but she did watch a lot of Bugs Bunny cartoons growing up. "I would watch them frame-by-frame. I studied the comic timing, which is surprisingly important even in storyboards; but even more importantly, the composition, and what makes good action. You have to have a vivid imagination for images that move and be able to capture the essence on paper."

Rathke started out as a storyboard revisionist doing corrections on storyboards that were done by seasoned, talented artists. "I worked with producers; they would each explain why certain things had to be done certain ways. It made it easy for me to eventually go off on my own, knowing the rules of animation."

All the experts agree that the most intensive learning takes place on the job. Dev Ramsaran explains, "The more experience you have out there working with other people's good boards, the better your own boards become. In fact, you will even learn what not to do by working with bad boards."

Speaking of good boards, what should a storyboard artist include in her portfolio? For Diane Kredensor, the answer is variety. "I believe a wide variety of styles and shows make a strong portfolio; from action adventure, to comedy, to preschool. When I look at portfolios to hire potential board artists, I like to know that they can adapt to any style."

Scott Cooper advises showing only your best work. "You can always show additional work in an interview." Cooper adds, "Sequential art like comic books or newspaper strips are good to show as well. Also have some life drawings (both human and animal)."

For those just starting out, with no professional board samples available, Cooper recommends you write a script or find a script sample on the Web and simply board it out.

Political cartoon by Scott Cooper. Courtesy of the artist.

Career Advice

Diane Kredensor notes that while learning to board in Flash is now a great asset, you still need to know basic cinematography and storytelling, which will always be the same. For those starting out, Kredensor advises, "The best way to learn is by doing it, then ask your teacher/mentor/co-worker what's missing that would make your work stronger, and put it in. Animation is a team effort, and I believe the best shows come from a group of people who are willing to put their egos aside."

Scott Cooper adds, "Storyboarding requires you to work quickly, be able to take direction, and then make a lot of changes to your drawings. You can't get too precious about your work."

Dev Ramsaran stresses the importance of doing your *own* work, outside of studio assignments. "Sometimes your creativity can feel stifled even when working on some beautiful productions, because you've had no say in the initial designs or story. I have been working on a four-minute independent film for the past five years, whenever there is a spare moment. It is fantastic therapy for one's stifled creativity."

The Storyboard Artist's Bookshelf

Recommended reading list:

+ *Film Directing Shot by Shot* by Steven Katz, Butterworth-Heinemann (1991)

+ *The Five C's of Cinematography: Motion Picture Filming Techniques* by Joseph V. Mascelli, Silman-James Press (1998)

+ *Paper Dreams: The Art and Artists of Disney Storyboards* by John Canemaker, Hyperion Books (1999)

+ *Don Bluth's The Art of Storyboard,* DH Press (2004)

+ *Animation: The Whole Story* by Howard Beckerman, Allworth Press (2003)

+ *Inspired 3D Short Film Production* by Jeremy Cantor and Pepe Valencia, Premier Press (2004)

CAREER PATHS: ANIMATION DESIGNER

Animation history books pinpoint a time in the 1950s when designers began to dominate the industry. The results changed the look of animation on the screen, TV, and even on Madison Avenue. Animation was pulled away from its comic strip and storybook illustration roots and brought into the modern age, where the new influences might be cubism, abstraction, and surrealism. Animation designers not only create the final look of what you see on the screen, but also provide inspirational and conceptual art to sell shows.

What does an animation designer do? If we were to stalk one for a day, what would we learn? Animation designer Dagan Moriarty (*Leader Dog, Tortellini Western*) answers, "The main job is to design and draw within the visual parameters of the specific show or film and to have fun with it! A good designer will push to make the project as visually strong and appealing as possible. It's our job to stay inspired, and to some degree, to keep the whole crew inspired. It's our designs that everybody must work with day in and day out. An animation designer helps things stay visually coherent, too, usually working closely with the Art Director."

Design by Dagan Moriarty. Image courtesy of the artist.

Moriarty continues, "Design is usually a very collaborative step in the animation process. Most of the time there will be a design team, however small or large, working together on a show." Veteran designer Teddy Newton (*The Incredibles*) agrees: "I've often sat with other artists when creating a character. I love to bounce off of other artists such as Tony Facile and Ricky Neirva."

Most importantly, Moriarty reminds, "You are designing for 'animation.' How well will your designs work in motion? You train yourself to think that way."

What kind of training and skills does an animation designer need to develop starting out and also to keep advancing in his career? Animation designer Alex Kirwin (*My Life as a Teenage Robot*) believes versatility is important. "You have to know how to be just as expressive in a pre-existing drawing style as you are in your own, or you have to know how to invent a brand new set of stylistic sensibilities to best suit a new project. If a desire to take apart household objects to understand why they function designates a future engineer, then the same has to be true of almost any type of designer. You have to want to examine all sorts of art, graphics, and drawings, and break them down into their components to find out what makes them tick."

Animation designer Ian Chernichaw (*Blue's Clues*) answers that all animation designers have one thing in common: a thorough understanding of the animation process. "Animation designers need to know the current technologies, trends, computer software, and programs. You should also know how to animate because you will often have to supply animators with angles, positions, and turnarounds, and will be expected to be familiar with animation lingo."

Debra Solomon, who created the design of the animated *Lizzie McGuire*, thinks an animation designer should be able to create characters that feel real to the viewer and can emote. Solomon adds, "Drawing skills are important but some acting ability is good, too."

Now how do you best show off your animation design skills in a portfolio? Alex Kirwin talks about two criteria he looks for in a portfolio: appeal and imagination. Kirwin explains, "Appeal is a broad term which covers a lot of things, but I use it here to describe an artist's use of proportion, line, and shape in a balanced way to deliver the idea of a drawing most effectively. For some, this comes very naturally; others have to work at it a little harder, but this can be okay if it is compensated with imagination. Imagination could refer to the quality of the ideas presented in the drawings, the amount of personality or humor in a drawing, or the originality of the approach."

Animation designer and creator Elanna Allen (*Bing Can Sing!*) recommends including a variety of characters both in final form, and in sketch form, showing different poses and emotions, and character turnarounds to show the character from all sides. "It is good to see some strong figure drawing as well."

Animation designer Jason McDonald (*Sheep in the Big City*) believes people, objects, and places are the three main things you should have in your portfolio along with a strong emphasis on your ability to draw in different styles. "The person looking at your work should see that you have strong drawing skills and can handle just about anything that's thrown at you."

Ian Chernichaw stresses that a strong portfolio has continuity. "Organize your work carefully. A good presentation needs to be organized by style, content, and flow. You should also group vertical images separately from horizontal images; it makes for easier viewing. Consider your audience and create a special portfolio geared for that person. Last but not least, make your portfolio easy to handle. I've received portfolios with pages falling out and ones that are practically too big to fit on my desk. Although there are no standard

Illustration by Jason McDonald. Courtesy of the artist.

E

Design by Teddy Newton for The Incredibles.
© 2004 Disney/Pixar.

size criteria for portfolios, I suggest having a compact and organized presentation." Chernichaw concludes, "Your presentation should leave people saying, 'Wow!'"

Teddy Newton feels that a portfolio needs a distinctive "point of view." Newton explains, "Good drawing is sometimes not enough. H.R. Gigor and Charles Schulz may be very different in skill, but there is no denying the clear identity they both have created for themselves by having a distinctive point of view."

Finally, Dagan Moriarty shares his secret for keeping a portfolio fresh. "I have a funny little ritual that I like to do about once a month. I take out my portfolio and flip through it casually, front to back. If I put it back down feeling mostly content with what I just looked at, then the work is still working for me. If I come away telling myself that twelve of fifteen pieces need to be pulled, it's time for an overhaul."

Technology has changed the way many animation artists work. Is it any different for animation designers? Alex Kirwin answers, "Digital color has opened up many possibilities that weren't previously possible or practical. Not just the in the range of colors now available or the ability to use colored line work inexpensively, but also the luxury of experimentation itself. We can create dozens of different color options in the time it would take to create one test cel."

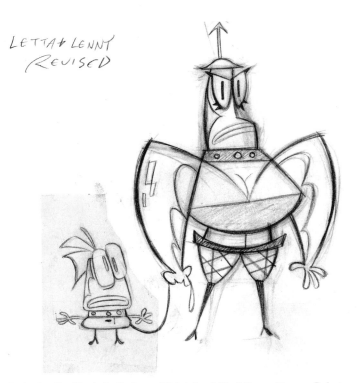

Design by Alex Kirwin for Frederator/Nickelodeon's My Life as a Teenage Robot. *Copyright 2005. Viacom International Inc. All rights reserved.*[†]

Elanna Allen utilizes a mixture of traditional and digital. She explains, "I always scan my drawings and color them in Photoshop. I just bought a Wacom Cintiq, which allows you to draw directly on screen. I use mostly Photoshop and Flash. For a Flash production, you want to be able to draw directly in Flash."

Dagan Moriarty has a way of staying current with technology. "Just look at the work out there that you admire and find out how it's executed. Also, if a good school is offering classes in certain software, you can bet that it is or is becoming an industry standard." However, Moriarty warns, "Never use the computer as a crutch. It will show one-hundred percent of the time if you do."

Career Advice

Alex Kirwin warns that it's important to balance being very confident about your work with being open to suggestions. Kirwin recommends that it's better to create a simple design that everyone involved can feel some ownership over than it is to "show off" with something complex that no one can recreate (including you).

Kirwin concludes, "I've learned to not present my least favorite option, and to never provide a drawing that I wouldn't want to see on screen."

Design by Ian Chernichaw. Image courtesy of the artist.

Teddy Newton believes designers should have more understanding of how to tell a story. He says, "The problem I find with most designers is that they don't think of how their designs fit into the film. Some people may be able to paint beautiful pictures, but they don't think about how it works in a sequence." Newton warns that sometimes too many outside views spoil the design. "Beware of overworking a design to the point of not recognizing what it is supposed to convey."

Jason McDonald shares, "If you're working for someone, don't fall in love with what you create. Once you've finished a design, it is taken from you and can change into something else. Be willing to let go. Only love your own work."

Collage Design by Teddy Newton for The Incredibles. © 2004 *Disney/Pixar.*

Still from Debra Solomon's award-winning independent film, Everybody's Pregnant, *showing off her design style. Image courtesy of the artist.*

The Animation Designer's Bookshelf

Recommended reading list:

- ✦ *Understanding Comics: The Invisible Art* by Scott McCloud, Harper Paperbacks (1994)

- ✦ *The Art of Robots* by Amid Amidi, Chronicle Books (2004)

- ✦ *The Art and Flair of Mary Blair: An Appreciation* by John Canemaker, Disney Editions (2003)

- ✦ *How to Draw Comics the Marvel Way* by Stan Lee, John Buscema, Simon & Schuster (1986)

- ✦ *Batman Animated* by Paul Dini, Chip Kidd, Harper Paperbacks (1999)

- ✦ *Anatomy and Drawing* by Victor Perards, Dover Publications (2004)

- ✦ "Vintage design books from the fifties and sixties and any fifties-era Hanna-Barbera book. My studio is filled with Picasso books and Bill Watterson's books. I really recommend having a wide variety of books, art books, comics, magazines, whatever you can go to in a pinch for reference or for inspiration. A huge and well-organized reference 'morgue' is essential to an animation designer."—Dagan Moriarty

CAREER PATHS: BACKGROUND ARTIST

Background art may be a supporting player to the main action occurring in the foreground, but that doesn't make it any less important to the finished production. As animation artist Kyle Neswald (*Wow! Wow! Wubbzy!*) puts it, background artists build a stage for the characters and tell the part of the story that the characters cannot.

Background art by Bob Levy for Scout Says, a film by Dale Clowdis and the author.

The development and refinement of background art in animation parallels animation history itself. Howard Beckerman, the author of *Animation: The Whole Story*, hosted a New York animation event showcasing background art through the decades. Beckerman's presentation showed that early on in animation history there was a bare minimum of background detail or design in cartoons. As animation developed, background art became sophisticated, innovative, and stylistically diverse. Today's background artists follow in that tradition, often juggling traditional painting tools with modern computer applications such as Adobe Photoshop to create background art.

Veteran background painter Kim Miskoe (*Doug*) describes the day-to-day duties of a background artist:

+ Attend preliminary meetings.

+ Transfer the layout to the surface to be painted. This can sometimes mean taking a rough layout and redrawing it into the style required. Next, transfer that to bristol or watercolor paper by hand or by copier.

+ Color the drawing with whatever medium is specified.

+ Return the background with the layout to the appropriate file, properly labeled as to scene and BG number.

Miskoe concludes, "A background artist communicates with the director or supervisor as to how the BG will work with the animation. You need to know when the animation is in front or behind objects on the BG or if the scene you are assigned must match to scenes being painted by other artists."

Mike Lapinski (*Teenage Mutant Ninja Turtles*) says that most individual designs are so time intensive that there is a heads-down, plow-through sense of completing a painting. "There are rarely sketches or drafts to start from. To really get something to work, you need to zone in on it, finding the shapes and harmonies. I often listen to music for a two-hour stretch while working on a painting."

BG design by Mike Lapinski for an episode of Blue's Clues.
*Courtesy of the artist. Copyright 2005. Viacom International Inc.
All rights reserved.*[†]

What would be the ideal background or skill set of a background painter? Beatriz Ramos, background artist and chairman/creative director at Dancing Diablo, answers, "Background artists should have a strong knowledge of composition, space, volumes, · and a sophisticated sense of color and understanding of light. They should be proficient in Photoshop and Illustrator and versatile in the styles it can handle." Ramos also values speed, organization, and the ability to work well with others. She concludes, "If you understand the complexities of animation production from beginning to end, you'll be able to do a better job. What you know or don't know is always reflected on those backgrounds."

Background painter and art director Paul Zdanowicz (*Pinky Dinky Doo*) answers that observation is the best practice for building your visual toolbox. "Every day on my walk home from work I pass a baseball field. I can tell you what color the grass is right before or after a storm. How shadows fall when it's bright or overcast. Looking and remembering is something you will be doing the rest of your life. Whether you are taking in a tree or a style you like from a show you saw on television, to retain and be able to call upon those visual memories is invaluable."

In recent years technology has changed the way most backgrounds are painted. Since starting in the industry in 1997, Paul Zdanowicz has seen the field take a complete turn from traditional to digital. "*PB&J Otter* at Jumbo Pictures was the first show that I saw change from hand-painted watercolor to digital. Now, it's nearly impossible to get a background painting job in television without knowing certain software. There are several reasons studios went digital. One key factor is efficiency. Software such as Adobe Photoshop or Painter can yield some pretty natural-istic results while cutting down on sup-plies, prep time, and revision time."

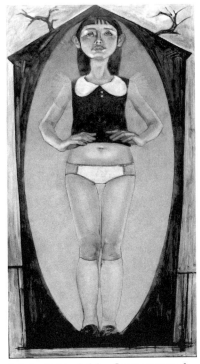

On the other side, Mike Lapinksi warns, "There is the danger of a produc-tion abusing a program like Photoshop. Because of its extreme flexibility and rela-tive speed I have both seen designs revised ad nauseam and excessive numbers of backgrounds heaped on a show with disre-gard to the manpower and time available."

Kim Miskoe suggests that if you want to work traditionally without the new dig-ital painting tools, you should look for work in California, where the big studios employ illustrators for inspirational and concept art.

Career Advice

Background artist Liz Artinian (*The Venture Brothers*) recommends avoiding getting locked into exclusively being a background artist. "The jobs are few and very competi-

Painting by Liz Artinian. Image courtesy of the artist.

tive. It's important to constantly remind people that you exist outside of the realm of animation background painter. You can draw, design, paint, and maybe animate too, and it's important to keep that information on the tip of your tongue."

Beatriz Ramos shares her personal mantra: "Once the background looks nice, what are you going to do to make it look amazing?"

Paul Zdanowicz reports, "My least favorite experience has to be anytime when you think you nailed a background and a director shoots it down. There is a reason they are the directors and nine and a half out of ten times they are right, so as much as I dislike when that happens, it is vital to the learning process. Taking any criticism personally is an easy mistake to make but a mistake nonetheless."

Kyle Neswald says his greatest mistakes usually come from overthinking what the director wanted. "Most of the time, intuition is a good guide for your design. Second guessing yourself can often lead to overworking your design. The greatest key, I have learned, is to keep design simple."

Background art by Bob Levy for Scout Says, *a film by Dale Clowdis and the author.*

The Background Painter's Bookshelf
Recommended reading list:

+ *The Fleischer Story* by Leslie Cabarga, Da Capo Press (1988)

+ *The Art of Robots* by Amid Amidi, Chronicle Books (2004)

+ *The Art and Flair of Mary Blair: An Appreciation* by John Canemaker, Disney Editions (2003)

✦ "Whatever art books would be in a painter's/illustrator's library: Caravaggio, Degas, Mondrian, Disney, Ryden, and everything in between, including great comic artists like Bisley and Miller."
—Liz Artinian

CAREER PATHS: CHARACTER ANIMATOR

Character animators work in 2D or 3D or in dimensions yet to be discovered, bringing life to talking rabbits, dancing hippos, anthropomorphic cars, near-sighted fish, and more dysfunctional families than you can shake a stick at. The principles of animation, including stretch and squash, weight, anticipation, and overlapping action, were fully developed (largely at the Walt Disney studio) by 1942. Since then, character animators have applied these principles to projects with an infinite amount of stylistic variation, from full (feature quality) animation to low budget (limited animation) for the Web or TV. The character animator is a journeyman, accumulating experience and expertise over the course of a career and a lifetime.

What kind of training and skills does a character animator need to start out and also to keep advancing in their career? Feature animator Travis Blaise (*Brother Bear*), advises starting with the grass roots. "Try to attend a school that teaches the fundamentals (figure drawing, painting, sculpting, art history) along with traditional animation." TV animator and director Jim Petropolis adds, "If you learn nothing else, learn how to draw a proper human figure."

Award-winning independent animator and TV commercial director Mike Overbeck answers, "It's also important to understand storytelling, continuity, and acting."

Student Academy silver medal–winning animator Chris Conforti feels it's less important to research technical "how-to-animate" books and more beneficial to find books on your favorite artists or illustrators. "It's better to develop your own voice and it's easy to get stuck animating the way everyone else does."

Setting the glamour of working in show business aside, what are the daily duties of a character animator? TV animator Justin Simonich answers, "As an animator you're responsible for any scene given to you by the director, animating any characters assigned to you, and handing it in by the deadline. The deadline is paramount; you have to

Still from Justin Simonich's independent film, Geriatric Hip. *Courtesy of the artist.*

be able to work in a quick, yet deliberate manner. I like to block out a scene first, get the basic poses down first; the keys. From there I will refine the animation to the minimum required to hand in the piece. After that, I decide where to spend the remaining time to enhance any key moments."

Jim Petropolis reports that an animator's job starts with at least a couple of meetings with the director (usually when handing in or picking up new scenes), followed by cranking out whatever scenes are on your desk, pencil test critiques (with the director, producer, and whoever else may be around), and probably the most dreaded duties of all, the inevitable scene revisions.

Petropolis says, "Even with tight deadlines, there is often too much 'hurry up and wait' time. This could be anything from waiting on new voice tracks to waiting for more paper. When that happens, one either checks up on the assistants, helps out someone who might be behind, or just waits for further instruction. One thing is certain; *no* two days are ever 100 percent alike!"

Chris Conforti says that even though character animators receive animatics and voice tracks upon which to base the movements, there are a lot of gestures and acting that are left up to the animator and that's what makes it fun. On the realities of production, Conforti answered, "Your scenes for the next episode are still coming in each week though you're still doing notes on the last show. It's not uncommon to be working on three different shows at once."

The daily duties of a character animator often go beyond their job descriptions. Jim Petropolis feels that once you are in the loop, expect to wear many hats simultaneously. "Over time you'll probably be asked (or told) to do something different than what you might have hitherto been accustomed to."

In Justin Simonich's experience, the more versatile you are, the longer a studio will be able to hold on to you. "If your department is winding down, another may need some help and the studio would much rather keep someone that they already know than bring in someone else from the outside. Being flexible with diverse skills will definitely increase your employment rate."

Character animators, whether they work in 2D or 3D, need to keep up with technology to stay employable. According to Jim Petropolis, "The recent technological changes in animation are as significant and radical as those during the industrial revolution of the nineteenth century. Cel painting is now extinct, and 2D traditional animation is an endangered species. It will be around for a while to come (on cable/TV and in commercials), but I do think we've seen the last of 2D feature animation. Flash, of course, is quite viable, and seems to be the tool of choice for a lot of 2D television work. I decided in 2002 to throw in the towel and learn 3D animation. I've been working with Maya for three years and I am just now becoming proficient enough to attempt to send out a reel."

To stay current with technology, Mike Overbeck likes to read articles about new software and new features. "If I see a cool look or effect on TV, I try to imitate with Flash and After Effects. It just helps me build an arsenal of styles and looks."

Still from Mike Overbeck's award-winning RISD thesis film, Tongues and Taxis. *Courtesy of the artist.*

TV animator and director J.P. Dillard (*Pinky Dinky Doo*) believes the two predominating factors affecting the field of commercial animation today are technology and shrinking economics. "Although animation revenues for the networks and distribution outlets appears to be robust, budgets continue to shrink in many cases as companies try to further increase their market share. As a result, 2D programs like Flash and After Effects have had a huge effect on how animation is being produced today. There are a lot of productions that probably wouldn't have happened here in the States if not for the availability of a program like Flash (with its ability to manage and reuse assets). I try to pay attention to what kind of skills are in demand and what kind of shows are being produced and how."

Illustration by animator and director, J.P. Dillard. Courtesy of the artist.

Chris Conforti notes the Internet's contribution to the changing technology in the industry. "I get so many e-mails about jobs and freelance work that if I don't check my mail every day, it's as if I went away on vacation."

As much as technology has changed the way character animators work, the ingredients of a good sample reel remain the same. Justin Simonich advises to open a reel with your best stuff first because it may be all a studio watches. Each reel you send out should be tailored to the job you're going after. Simonich continues, "Do a little research first. Go online and find out what projects the studio has worked on in the past and tailor your reel to what you think they may like to see. Show them that you will fit into their studio. If they specialize in pre-school series you don't want to send them a reel full of blood and guts, anime style work."

What should a character animator include on a sample reel? Simonich is always sure to include walk cycles and acting scenes with dialogue/lip synch. "Walk cycles are a good indicator of how you handle a figure in motion. Have fun with it and give the character some attitude. Pencil tests, or wire frame if working in 3D, examples are okay, but also include finished examples as well. The rest of my reel would be made up of scenes from a variety of projects I have worked on. I try to pick scenes that are funny. If you can get someone to laugh, they will remember that. I like to end my reel with some personal work in order to show what I like and what I can do as an animator on my own."

Career Advice

Travis Blaise feels that the most common mistake in this industry is miscommunication. "We work in an industry that calls on teamwork. When the lines of communication break down you can be rest assured mistakes will happen. Try to listen and take notes whenever possible."

Jim Petropolis agrees, adding, "Be observant and humble. Listen and learn. Fight the urge to rock the boat. Your turn *will* come, but not without first paying your dues. Take *all* constructive criticism and own up to your shortcomings. Improve upon them; never make excuses for them. Maintain the highest professional standards. Remember it takes many months and years to build a solid reputation, but mere minutes to destroy it. If you don't like a certain studio or job, find another one, but don't grouse about your job in the workplace. It's bad for team morale and *will* come back to bite you."

Illustration by animator Travis Blaise. Courtesy of the artist.

One of J.P. Dillard's first mistakes as an animator was to "not sweat the small stuff." He explains, "In a world where every thirtieth or twenty-fourth of a second counts, you must be very anal and detail oriented. Nothing about your work should be arbitrary and every line and/or dot should be there for a reason."

Chris Conforti learned not to be afraid to ask for help. "It can be a little intimidating, especially if you're new on the job, because you don't want to come across like you don't know anything or waste their time, but I've wasted a lot of time trying to figure stuff out on the computer. Then I would finally ask someone and they would solve my problem in a second and are usually happy to do so."

The Character Animator's Bookshelf

Recommended reading list:

+ *Technique of Film Animation* by John Halas, Pawprint Books (1963)

+ *Before the Animation Begins* by John Canemaker, Hyperion Books (1997)

+ *Artistic Anatomy* by Dr. Paul Richer and Robert Hale, Watson-Guptill Publications (1986)

+ *Atlas of Human Anatomy for the Artist* by Stephen Peck, Oxford University Press (1982)

+ *The Animator's Workbook* by Tony White, Watson-Guptill Publications (1988)

+ *Animation: From Script to Screen* by Shamus Culhane, St. Martin's Griffin (1990)

+ *Talking Animals and Other People* by Shamus Culhane, Perseus Books Group (1998)

+ *50 Greatest Cartoons* edited by Jerry Beck, Turner Publishing (1994)

+ *The Encyclopedia of Animation Techniques* by Richard Taylor, Running Press (1996)

+ *Producing Animation* by Catherine Winder & Zahra Dowlatabadi, Focal Press (2001)

+ *The Natural Way to Draw* by Kimon Nicolaides, Houghton Mifflin Company (1990)

+ *The Illusion of Life: Disney Animation* by Frank Thomas and Ollie Johnston, Hyperion Press (1995)

+ *Creating Unforgettable Characters* by Linda Seger, Owl Books (1990)

+ *The Animator's Survival Kit* by Richard Williams, Faber and Faber (2002)

+ *Cartoon Animation* by Preston Blair, Walter Foster Pub (1995)

CAREER PATHS: STOP MOTION ANIMATOR

Stop motion has never enjoyed the same attention in North America that it has received in other parts of the world. Europe and much of Asia, for instance, have a long tradition and appreciation of puppets and marionettes, which predate the birth of film. Understandably, there is a larger market for stop motion animation in these territories. North America's stop motion industry is like a stepchild to the 2D and 3D animation industry, the same way animation is a stepchild of the live-action film business. A niche within a niche, if you will.

Stop motion animator Eileen Kohlhepp (*Robot Chicken*) points out that at the present time, England seems to be the nation with the largest stop motion industry. "Unfortunately, the possibility for Americans to find work in England is rather difficult due to strict labor laws. Canadians, on the other hand, might find it easier since they are offered work exchange opportunities through their country. In any case, if you can get a company to sponsor your work visa, you're in."

Stop motion animators Mark Caballero and Seamus Walsh finished a short begun by Ray Harryhausen in 1952, called The Story of the Tortoise & the Hair. *Courtesy of Screen Novelties.*

In North America, stop motion animators tend to be a gypsy workforce, ready to move to any city currently engaging in even a short-term stop motion project. Currently, the cities with the most stop motion work are Toronto and Los Angeles. At times there has been long-term work at places such as Will Vinton Studios in Portland, Oregon, and (for a few years) at MTV Animation in New York with the series *Celebrity Death Match*. Eileen Kohlhepp says that most animators supplement their downtime between stop motion jobs with work in other animation/design areas. *Celebrity Death Match* animator and creator of Nick Jr.'s *Bing Can Sing!*, Elanna Allen, agrees. "I would really recommend not relying only on stop motion. So little of it is done these days, and studio/network executives are really resistant to doing it. You could have stop motion in your bag of tricks, and mix it in with drawn and After Effects animation and do fine."

There is some stop motion work out there, as well as a small community of stop motion animators working in North America. Eileen Kohlhepp describes a typical day animating on a stop motion project. "A normal production day might start around 9:00 A.M. Each animator is assigned a stage where she will spend a few days or sometimes a few weeks. You spend a few moments checking with the animation coordinator to clarify what shot you're doing that day. Then you head off to gather everything you need. First stop is the set department to get the set and props. Next is the puppet department. They supply you with all the characters you'll be working with on that shot. Then, you pick up the exposure sheets from the track reader.

"Once you have everything on your stage, you block out the shot according to the storyboard. You set the camera in a temp position and get the director of photography to come to your stage and take a look. The DP spends anywhere from five minutes to an hour lighting the set and adjusting the digital camera to the proper position and settings. Usually while the DP is working, you spend that time marking and numbering your X-sheets with directions. You listen to the voice track a few times; note the emphasized syllables and time out when certain actions should occur.

"The next person you speak with is the director. She gives the set a once over and suggests any changes. Then she usually gives direction, explaining the most important aspects of the shot. You add these to the notes on the X-sheets, fix any suggested changes on the set and get ready to start your shot. Depending on the length of the shot, you can spend a few hours to a few days animating. Most animators focus a great deal while working and don't like to have their concentration broken. This translates into many hours alone, just you and the puppets in a small room, experiencing little successes, little frustrations, and lots of problem solving.

"When you've finally finished the shot, you download the frames from the camera card onto the computer and assemble them in Final Cut Pro. You make a QuickTime movie of the shot and present it to the director. Once it has been approved, you start the process all over again with the next shot."

Elanna Allen adds, "If the production is a commercial, or a shorter shoot, you really can't leave a hot set. A hot set is when you are in the middle of a shot. If you leave, the lights might not be as bright in the morning, or the puppet could have sagged, just a tidbit, which would mess everything up. Therefore you stay until the shot is done, which can be all night." Allen describes further differences between traditional animation production and stop motion. "In stop motion you are standing up, and you may have to contort in some odd pose to reach the puppet. You don't get to key frame either, so you have to have a firm idea of what action you are doing."

What kind of training and skills does a stop motion animator need starting out and also to keep advancing in their career? Eileen Kohlhepp notes that although she studied animation/illustration at Rhode Island School of Design, most of her animation knowledge came from on the job experience, reading, and what she's learned from friends and co-workers. "As far as schools for stop motion, there is an experimental program at Cal Arts that has produced some great animators."

Seamus Walsh, co-founder of the stop motion studio Animation Novelties, believes you don't really need to go to a school to learn stop motion, adding, "If you have a feel for movement, you can just experiment on your own until you're proficient."

The stop motion animator straddles a line between working in animation and live action. How much does a stop motion animator have to know about lights, cameras, lenses, and the latest technology? Animation Novelties co-founder Mark Caballero believes like any industry, the more you know, the more invaluable you become. "The animator should know the whole process as well as appreciating and understanding all the hard work that goes into it."

Still from Jimmy Picker's famous stop motion sequence to the live action feature film Better Off Dead. *Courtesy of the artist.*

Oscar-winning stop motion animator Jimmy Picker (*Sundae in New York*) has worked primarily alone, creating a necessity for him to know how to do everything. Picker advises, "Outside of your skills as a stop motion animator, you have to be an engineer and know how to deal with lights, camera, etc." Kohlhepp agrees, "It's helpful to know as many aspects of production as you can, especially if you want to make your own films." However, she points out that on professional projects it really depends on the size of the production you are working on whether you will need to do tasks outside your special-ization. "Generally, if you are an animator, you just animate. The puppet department just works on the puppets. The director of photography deals with the cinematography and lighting. Everyone has their job to do and they are all very well trained in their area of expertise."

Kohlhepp described how technology has changed the way stop motion animators work. "While most stop motion movie productions are still shot entirely on film, the introduction of digital cameras to the field helped televi-sion and commercial productions to shoot cheaply without much loss of quality. The development of frame grabbers like the Animation Toolworks LunchBox and programs like FrameThief help animators see their animation in real time while they are working. Every production I work on has a different setup, so I learn new programs and work with new camera equipment every time I start a job."

Career Advice

Eileen Kohlhepp recommends interning or working as a production assistant at first. "It gets your foot in the door at a company and if you're a great intern then you're showing the company you could be an even better employee. Everyone pays their dues; in the beginning I did my share of taking out the trash and making coffee. Volunteer. Watch people work. Ask questions. You'll be surprised how many people love to talk about what they do and want to help you learn. Watch films. Watch people on the street and study their movements. Talk to other animators online and become part of the community. Lastly, people don't get into stop motion animation because they expect to make money; they get into it because they truly love it."

Elanna Allen, who learned stop motion animation abroad in Prague, recommends trying to intern or learn at British or Eastern European studios.

Seamus Walsh notes that stop motion jobs tend to come around in cycles, so have something you can do as a backup way to make money. "There can be periods of several years when there's almost nothing happening in stop motion . . . then a project comes along and they need twenty animators . . . quick." Walsh continues, "Always compare your work to the best stuff you've seen and don't limit that to stop motion only. Look at traditional animation and learn from the beautiful timing and acting found in some of the old UPA, Fleischer, and Disney stuff. Don't worry about 'smoothness.' Concentrate on good timing and dynamics. Learn as much as you can and be passionate about the history of the medium and learn how to build your own puppets."

The Stop Motion Animator's Bookshelf

Recommended reading list:

+ *Ray Harryhausen: An Animated Life* by Ray Harryhausen and Tony Dalton, Billboard Books (2004)

+ *Creating 3D animation: The Aardman book of filmmaking* by Peter Lord, Harry N. Abrams (1998)

+ *The Illusion of Life: Disney Animation* by Frank Thomas and Ollie Johnston, Hyperion Press (1995)

+ *The Animator's Survival Kit* by Richard Williams, Faber and Faber (2002)

+ *Cartoon Animation* by Preston Blair, Walter Foster Pub (1995)

CAREER PATHS: OFF-SITE FREELANCER

There are those among us that choose to work in the luxury of home, forsaking the hassles of the commuter crowd, the politics of the office, and the need for bathing (just kidding). Off-site freelancers have usually spent years in the on-site workforce learning their craft, establishing their reputation, and creating valuable contacts. Not every job in a studio can be outsourced, but storyboards, design, background painting, animation, and sheet timing may be assigned to an off-site freelancer.

Animator Dean Kalman Lennert (*Ice Age, Beavis and Butthead*) describes his average day as an off-site freelancer working from home:

+ 4:00 A.M.–8:00 A.M. animation.
+ 8:00–10:00 A.M. feed the family and get the kid off to preschool.
+ 10:00 A.M.–2:00 P.M. animation.
+ 2:00–3:30 P.M. lunch and housework.
+ 3:30–7:30 P.M. animation.
+ 7:30–8:00 P.M. run to FedEx.
+ 8:00–10:00 P.M. have dinner, get the kid ready for bed.
+ 10:00 P.M. Good Night!

As Lennert demonstrates, off-site freelancers need to organize their day very carefully for the work to get done. He adds, "You learn very quickly that being surrounded by the comforts of home equals being surrounded by the distractions of home. And what seems to be a minute here and a minute there away from the animation table quickly add up to an hour lost here and an hour lost there. One formula I like to use is that the amount of time wasted during the day will equal the amount of time that I am late for the last FedEx drop-off that night."

Technology, high-speed Internet connections, and ftp sites have made the lifestyle/career choice of an off-site freelancer possible. How do off-site freelancers make sure they are staying up to date with technology? Animation Stewdio co-founder John Serpentelli answers, "I keep up to date by being on e-mail lists of most software manufacturers and by reading newsletters such as those sent by awn.com."

Dean Kalman Lennert actually works on-site if the job calls for high-end computer graphics work. At home, Lennert uses a traditional animation desk, laptop computer, scanner, printer, and fax machine.

Animator Doug Compton (*Pinky and the Brain, Animamaniacs*) draws by hand on paper and pencil tests animation on a program called Toon Boom. He also relies on a Xerox copier so he can resize drawings.

Technology aside, working off-site usually requires contracts between client and freelancer. Lennert reports, "Contracts vary from client to client. For those folks that I have worked with for many years and trust completely,

I find that, while delivery dates are established, we don't necessarily discuss money until after the job is completed. On the other end of the spectrum I have signed contracts with companies that spell everything out down to the letter: my compensation for the work to be provided, delivery dates, and how missing the latter can and will affect the former. Most of the agreements, however, fall in the middle ground of discussing money and delivery date, and filling out a W-2."

Doug Compton also works on word-of-mouth agreements with clients he has long known and trusted. He adds, "Occasionally a studio will ask me to sign a NDA (Non-Disclosure Agreement)."

Stop motion animator and animation designer Elanna Allen learned the hard way to negotiate the number of revisions in a contract up front. She explains, "Since you are paid a project fee, the more requested revisions, the less you're paid. It's important to be very clear about what the client is getting, because acting on good faith doesn't always work."

Career Advice: Off-Site Survival Tips

John Serpentelli has found attending festivals and conferences to be invaluable to his career. "Independent animators spend a good amount of time by themselves staring into a lightbox or computer screen. Events allow you to not only meet other animators, but people in related professions such as producers, distributors, and agents. Festivals have been a great source of inspiration, not only for the aesthetics of animation but also for the practical reality of the business of animation."

Doug Compton warns, "One time FedEx lost a package I was sending and I had to do the work over again. "Now all my animation drawings that I pencil test are stored on my computer." Compton continues, "You need to be disciplined to make yourself spend the time necessary to get your jobs done in time. You need the skills to do whatever job you're given, and to know how much work you can handle, and when not to spread yourself too thin. Reputation is an important factor in a successful freelance career. Clients do like to have their projects completed on schedule, so you have to make sure you can do the job in the time allotted."

Dean Kalman Lennert recommends, when not working on freelance, to always, *always*, work on your drawing skills. "It doesn't matter what type of animation you do, having solid drawing skills will serve you well. Turn off the TV, radio, and any other personal entertainment device, get off the Internet, and avoid any other forms of potential distraction." Lennert concludes, "Make sure to pay quarterly income tax so that you're not hit with a big bill at the end of the year."

Designing a Career
Part II: Writers, Directors, and Producers

"My first boss in advertising production once told me that a good producer will always maintain a creative vision but guide the production in such a way that everyone else is credited with the good ideas and ultimately the project's success. I think this is as true about animation as it is about advertising. My most satisfying projects have been the truly collaborative ones where good ideas are welcome from the entire crew."
—Melanie Grisanti, animation producer

The top echelon of the animation studio is sometimes known as the senior staff, made up of writers, directors, producers, and department supervisors of all kinds. Most of these positions are filled by individuals who have come up through the ranks of production. Their time in the trenches working as animation

Still from Janie & Jerome, *created by Eric Weil with director/designer Jennifer Oxley. © Sesame Workshop.*

artists, production assistants, and coordinators serves them in their supervisory roles. This insider's perspective ensures that they know production: what it's like to do the work, how long each task takes, and what systems and conditions allow each employee to do their best.

The paradox is that, although these important positions are the result of years of dedication and hard work, the very nature of these jobs may take you away from why you got into this business in the first place; an animation director no longer animates, a storyboard supervisor no longer storyboards, and so on. It's not all loss, however. The senior staff member has the opportunity to help creatively shape the product in ways that the animation artists cannot. Supervisors creatively shape the entire production and the process by which the work is done. This is a far more sweeping influence than animating any one particular scene, for example, would be.

For many, a senior staff position is the natural progression of a career in animation. Certainly it was for the good people who share their stories below. This chapter demystifies what it's like to contribute to a production as a member of the senior staff. Not so long ago, an animator asked me what it was like to be an animation director. I answered that it gave me a chance to fail from a much higher place with far larger consequences. Yes, an animation director makes more money, but there are also increased expectations and responsibility. Despite the differences between worker and supervisor, I see much common ground. First, there is the shared goal of best serving the project. After that, whether you're an animation artist or a member of the senior staff it requires talent, hard work, and the building of healthy relationships to succeed in the workplace.

Without further ado let's meet the senior staff experts waiting for us below. Grab a refreshment to wash down that snack from chapter 3. Get comfortable and read on.

CAREER PATHS: ANIMATION WRITER

Animation writing has changed a bit in recent years. The current age of the creator-driven TV cartoon series has generated a different approach to writing for animation. On shows such as Nickelodeon's *SpongeBob SquarePants*, storyboard artists are the writers, developing their scripts visually. However, much of TV and feature film animation continues to be scripted by writers in a traditional sense. Using only words, these specialized writers write visually, staying true to the medium.

Animation writers write for audiences as diverse as preschool, tween, and adult.

Whatever the niche of animation, the animation writer is a storyteller. According to Adam Peltzman (*Blue's Clues, Backyardigans*), an animation writer must have a sense of story structure, character, pacing, tone, humor, etc. "Without those, you really can't write a good script, no matter what the medium. Writing visually is especially important in animation. You certainly never want to write a talking head scene and always have to ask, 'How can I make this scene as visually dynamic and active as possible?' Also, an ability to think big and exaggerate is important, especially in a comedic script."

Veteran animation writer Erika Strobel agrees, "Animation is visual by nature, so it requires more explanation to detail all the action and visual jokes. In live action, a writer can only minimally stage the scene where everything is taking place since the writer has no control over who will be cast as the actor, what the set will look like, what location will be used, what available props there are, etc. In animation you can be very detailed because anything can be 'drawn.' While 'less is more' almost always applies (to writing in general) I tend to overwrite my action sequences to give the director (and storyboard artist) more 'animation business' to work with." Strobel adds, "You must enter the world of your cartoon characters as if they exist (hear their voices, see their movements, feel their natural responses)."

Eric Weil, animation writer and co-creator of *Sesame Street's Janie and Jerome* (with designer/director Jennifer Oxley), feels that every project, whether animation or live action, has a story based in its own reality. "My job as a writer is to serve as a good caretaker of each project's world-within-the-show."

What kind of training and skills do animation writers need starting out and also to keep advancing in their careers? Allan Neuwirth, an award-winning writer, producer, director, and author (*Makin' Toons*, published by Allworth Press) feels that the best school to teach good animation writing is the "school of life." He adds, "There are a number of really fine universities that'll teach you the fundamentals about animation, generally speaking, and it really helps to *know* your medium . . . but writing is an art, like any other. You either have the talent for it or you don't. All a school can do is show you some of the rules and templates, and offer you a chance to practice and be critiqued by people who (hopefully) know good writing when they see it."

Eric Weil never went to school to learn animation writing. "I was an American Civilization major at the University of Pennsylvania, so it's fair to say that I wasn't consciously planning to be on the animation writing track. The key is to keep writing as much as you can. And whenever possible, *always* take advantage of opportunities to present samples of your work, including company-wide solicitations for ideas or contests. Do it for the exercise rather than to win. If you don't find ways to at least practice your craft, your work and career will tend to suffer and you'll likely want to rethink your career priorities."

Adam Peltzman didn't specifically set out to be an animation writer. He recalls, "Television writing, screenwriting, journalism, fiction, and comedy writing were all areas of interest. Not too long after graduation I was fortunate to get the opportunity to submit a sample script to a company that was developing a comedic/educational series for kids, and the producer there really took to my submission. She hired me to write the pitch materials for the show and a short pilot script. That show never happened, but I enjoyed the experience so much that I kept pursuing this kind of work. I was soon after hired as a writing coordinator for *Blue's Clues*, which was starting its second season of production, and shortly after began writing episodes for the show. This was a tremendous learning experience, and it eventually grew into a head writing job on the show."

There's a romantic notion of a writer as a lone person in a cramped office (maybe even in a remote cabin) with only a table, a lamp, and a laptop computer for companionship. In this age of instant long-distance communication, where do animation writers work? Allan Neuwirth answers, "It helps to be in LA. If you can't be in LA, be in New York, or Toronto, or London, or Paris, or Vancouver, or Sydney, or Bombay. Of course, there's animation work everywhere nowadays, but it is easier in a few big cities, where most of the work happens to get produced."

Erika Strobel adds that if you are starting out, it's a must to be in major entertainment industry city (since you need to be available for meetings). "Once you are established you can live anywhere; because producers don't care where you live, they care if the script comes in on time. The Internet makes it possible to live in Timbuktu."

Eric Weil likes to think that location would become increasingly less relevant as technology improves, but he believes, "New writers will always be best off being accessible to producers and busy production centers. At least for projects you don't originate, it's always to your advantage to be in the loop, whether you are on staff or an off-site freelancer. The more connected you are to a project, the better you can serve the production. Beyond that, I'd always advocate working where you can do your best work."

Adam Peltzman reports, "The writing itself is often done off-site, and sometimes productions will either be open to phone meetings or to giving notes via e-mail."

Whether animation writing is done off-site or on-site, it remains a specific, smaller niche within TV and screenwriting. With that in mind, how healthy is the market for animation writers? Is the industry strong enough to provide enough work for animation writers to stay employed year round? Erika Strobel was fortunate in 1988 to work for the cream of the crop, Nelvena, so she has never had to struggle, although she knows plenty of writers who do. "In the eighties when there were only three networks to develop/pitch for there were regular busy seasons and downtime cycles, but I don't think this is the case anymore with all the cable networks and Internet media outlets seeking content." Strobel believes, if anything, there are too many outlets, leaving room for a lot of low quality animation to be created.

In Allan Neuwirth's experience, when the economy is strong and business is booming, it's absolutely possible to earn a living exclusively writing for animation. When animation work slows down, it's helped Neuwirth to have other outlets. "I've always kept my hand in producing and directing, as well, and not just cartoons. I also write books and have had a syndicated comic strip [with Glen Hanson]. When work-for-hire slows down, there's only one thing to do: create, create, and create *new* projects."

Eric Weil explains, "Producing is a big part of the fun for me, and so I pursue opportunities to produce work that I've written or helped write, and may even consider some straight-up producing work should the right opportunity arise. I've also written for live-action projects and fielded other kinds of writing jobs."

Career Advice

Eric Weil advises that animation writers not overlook what they can learn about writing during other phases of production. "The voice-over recording process has been especially instructive to me because by watching a good actor perform (and come to think of it, even a not-so-good actor), I can learn how to serve the performer's range, instincts, style, quirks, etc., and write new dialogue and stories that make both the character and the actor sound great (or at least better than before). I've directed many voice-over sessions and observed many others, and the advantage it's given me almost seems unfair."

The realities of rejection are a common theme in this industry. Allan Neuwirth's remedy? "Write!!! Write tons of work! Keep writing and writing and keep submitting it, and don't ever get discouraged when people tell you 'no.' If it's what you love, no one can stop you when all's said and done."

Erika Strobel says, "Study the industry. Read as many books and scripts as you can. Watch cartoons. If you can, get a job (any job) in an animation studio. It's the easiest way to work your way up the ladder and see the process first hand. Be professional at all times to create an immaculate reputation. By the time a production company requires writers (when they are scrambling for time), they call 'who they know' and if those writers are busy, they ask if they can recommend anyone." Strobel continues, "The best advice I have for writers who want to work on a series that is in production is to write a spec script and send it to the story editor. If they are lucky the story editor will buy the premise. If they are really lucky they will get a script assignment. At the minimum (if the spec is good) the story editor will remember them for a future assignment."

Adam Peltzman feels animation writers should play to their strengths. "If you're a funny writer, showcase that; if you write good action stories, then show that off. Also, try out different forms of writing. A well-written play, screenplay, comedy sketch, or comic book could be a nice addition to a portfolio and show that you have range as a writer. Versatility is very important, because what producers and story editors care about is your ability to capture the voice of their particular show."

The Animation Writer's Bookshelf
Recommended reading list:

+ *Story* by Robert McKee, Regan Books (1997)

+ *The History of Animation* by Charles Solomon, Random House Value Publishing (1994)

+ *Makin' Toons* by Allan Neuwirth, Allworth Press (2003)

+ *Animation: The Whole Story* by Howard Beckerman, Allworth Press (2003)

+ *The Art of Creative Writing* by Lajos Egri, Citadel Press (1995)

+ *The Hero With a Thousand Faces* by Joseph Campbell, Bollingen (1972)

+ *The Writer's Journey: Mythic Structure for Writers* by Christopher Vogler, Michael Wiese Productions (1998)

+ *The Comic Toolbox* by John Vorhaus, Silman-James Press (1994)

+ *How to Write for Animation* by Jeffery Scott, Overlook Hardcover (2002)

+ *Toy Story: The Art and Making of the Animated Film* By John Lasseter & Steve Daly, Disney Editions (1995)

CAREER PATHS: SHEET TIMER
Sheet timing is one-way communication, often with someone thousands of miles away who may not speak the same language. Sheet timers, animating in their heads, mark a set of frame-by-frame instructions on exposure sheets, providing character poses, and timing out acting as well as technical things such as pans and camera moves. Even the smallest minutia such as blinks and settles are plotted out.

Sheet timers evolved out of the needs of "runaway" or outsourced productions, which are what we call projects where the majority of the tedious and expensive production work (animation and composite) is shipped to studios overseas, usually in South Korea. With the entire animation crew an ocean away, detailed exposure sheets are necessary to communicate the vision of the show and the instructions of the animation director. Sheet timers fill this role. Currently, North America has seen the return of in-house animation production due to the rise of cheap 2D production programs such as Flash and After Effects. In-house productions usually forsake sheet timers, requiring animation directors to work directly with the animation crew. However, more and more overseas "runaway" animation is being done in Flash, likely reducing the amount of in-house productions in North America. This may create an additional need for sheet timers.

Sheet timer Celeste Pustilnick (*The Simpsons*) describes the daily duties of a sheet timer. "Usually before starting timing on a section, it's wise to go over it with the director. He may have some specific ideas that he wants conveyed onto the sheets. Once you have your section of the show, the X-sheets, storyboard (or layouts), character and prop model sheets, background designs, script, audio recording, and animatic, you are set to go. It's the sheet timer's job to give instructions to the animators (anything that is written will be translated into another language, so be clear in what you are asking for). You listen carefully to the dialogue to hit all the acting accents and subtleties. For action sequences it is often helpful to use a stopwatch, especially one that includes feet and frames. All the elements should be properly exposed including characters, effects, props, overlays, backgrounds, etc."

What kind of training and skills does a sheet timer need starting out and also to keep advancing in their career? Sheet timer Karen Villarreal (*Codename: Kids Next Door*) answers, "I started as an animator, which I think was an invaluable help. I had to picture in my head how I would break down the action if I was drawing it." Industry veteran Dev Ramsaran had eight years of animation experience before he was given the responsibility to do sheet timing on a series. Ramsaran considers becoming an animator to be a prerequisite to becoming a sheet timer.

Celeste Pustilnick first had a background in visual art and theater. She recalls, "I got into the animation industry as a production person and early in my career met directors who helped me break into timing. I've been able to use my acquired skills to help me as a sheet timer." Pustilnick continues, "Skills should include basic drawing ability (you don't have to draw perfectly on model on the sheets), ability to convey what you want legibly and concisely, while including necessary details. Timing is a mixture of right- and left-brained thinking. It is creative problem solving and analytical brain work. It takes discipline and would help to not be easily distracted."

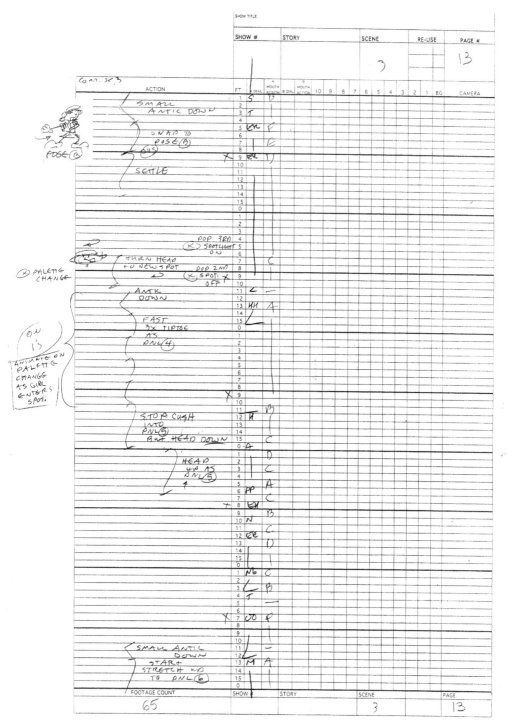

Sheet timing sample by Karen Villarreal. Note the pose sketches and notes for the animators. Courtesy of Curios Pictures.

Career Advice

Dev Ramsaran advises, "Always keep in mind that an animator here at home or overseas has to stick that sheet on their desk for possibly a whole day or two. You want them to care, understand, and follow your direction, so time that scene as though you yourself will have the joy and privilege of animating it."

Celeste Pustilnick offers, "Early in my career I would get insecure about my work if I saw that my timing was altered by the director. I have learned over the years (and have been reassured) that timing can be very personal and usually the director just sees the timing a different way."

Karen Villarreal cautions, "Be prepared to spend hour after hour alone at your desk, mired in minute detail, with just an audio track for company. Strap yourself to the desk, stare at the storyboard, and force yourself to write and write sheet after sheet until you've met your daily quota of pages. Resist the temptation to clean out the basement (or anything) instead of sitting there."

CAREER PATHS: ANIMATION DIRECTOR

Animation director Yvette Kaplan (*Beavis and Butthead, King of the Hill*) describes her job as being part of everything, hopefully in its proper and sufficient time. "Animation directors make script notes, put track together, oversee storyboards, approve, revise, look at designs, model sheets, create inspirational poses, look at layouts (if there are any), check mouth charts for lip sync, slug track or check slug, do animatics, or approve and revise them, check sheet timing, approve color, and start all over on the next episode. On features, it's more spread out. You can spend days, weeks, with the luxury of thinking."

Animation director David J. Palmer (*Blue's Clues, Backyardigans*) explains how animation directors sometimes handle all of the above responsibilities while leading a team or department of animators in a managerial capacity. "At my last directing job, I was also responsible for the hiring, firing, promoting, and everything else for a staff of over twenty. But that was a show with everyone in-house. The show I'm currently supervising directing is done with an outside studio, so none of that applies."

Palmer continues, "The most important quality for a leader is to be able to stay calm, cool, and collected while on the job. Every project is going to involve unexpected and unfortunate events, but if you've planned the project appropriately and are prepared to handle contingencies, you'll be able to weather anything. It's like you're the pilot of an aircraft; the passengers are depending on your skills, talent, and know-how to get them from points A to B. When unexpected events occur during the trip, the passengers will feel safe and secure as long as you keep your head and deal rationally with the problem, but the minute the pilot starts running around the craft screaming, 'we're all doomed!' Well . . . that would be alarming, to say the least."

a day at the office

Self-portrait by Dave Palmer showing the life of an animation director. Image courtesy of the artist.

Animation director J.P. Dillard (*Pinky Dinky Doo*) says there is also a creative responsibility of leadership. "Your primary responsibility is to develop, foster, and/or communicate the creative vision or the animation style for a show to the crew. It's your job to make sure the animation and show look good and meet or exceed the quality expectations of your employer. Although you like to strive for perfection you have to know when good or really good is enough and move on. Perfection costs time and money, which oftentimes you may not have, so use limitations as an advantage and opportunity to be more creative. Oftentimes less is more."

Self-portrait by animation director Sue Perrotto. Image courtesy of the artist.

I think we're beginning to get a sense of the many challenging duties and responsibilities of an animation director. What kind of training and skills does an animation director need starting out and also to keep advancing in their career? Animation director Sue Perrotto (*Billy and Mandy, Sheep in the Big City*) feels there is no typical journey to becoming anything. "I know some animation directors that started out as animators and worked their way up, others that started out in storyboards, and some that were producers or theater choreographers." Yvette Kaplan adds, "The ideal background for an animation director would be developing strong skills in both animation and story."

For David J. Palmer, you must have a goal to become an animation director and then take whatever opportunities lead to that goal. He adds, "A little luck helps, too. In my case, I did a couple of small freelance gigs for someone, which led to more work, which led to a pilot, and when the pilot got picked up, I started as an animator on it and moved my way up. Everything for me hinged on taking those first few jobs, doing my best at them, and learning everything I could along the way."

J.P. Dillard points out that it helps to have some innate leadership ability or at least be a good team player. "Even a director or lead animator role on your own personal project is a good start. You need something to show that you can communicate effectively with other artists."

Does changing technology have any impact on how an animation director works? For Yvette Kaplan, who has worked in both 2D and 3D, directing is always first and foremost about story and character, but she was surprised to learn how many differences there were between 2D and 3D. "In 2D, the shots I have been used to visualizing have been fairly simple, locked, other than pans and trucks. In 3D, in order to be most effective (to really use the medium) you have to understand the camera and all its possibilities. Of course, I still love that static flat shot for comedy."

Kaplan explains there are also unexpected limitations in 3D. "It takes a lot longer to build and model something, than to draw it. Adding another character walking in the background to keep a scene alive, for instance, is not so easy. A 2D character can just put his hands in his pockets. Interacting with fabric is more difficult with 3D. With budgetary and schedule constraints, some of the things you take for granted in 2D are now out of bounds. I am very proud when I find solutions that not only work within the constraints, but are also funny, effective choices. Ideally the audience should not be aware that you have compromised at all."

Career Advice

According to David J. Palmer, great directors are always learning and should never think they know everything there is to know. "Every project is unique in some way, in terms of style, mission, personalities involved, process, etc., so soak up as much as you can, because it all becomes part of the toolbox you'll bring to your next job, and the one after that, and so on."

Palmer explains that directing is to make a lot of decisions. He recommends that before making one:

✦ Listen to everyone involved.

✦ Gather all the information you can.

- Think about the information. And get more info, or check in with others, if you need to.

- Decide based on the above; make the best possible decision you can (Then decide!).

- Communicate your decision to the folks who need to know (and the reasoning behind it, if need be).

- Check in to make sure everyone really understands you.

- Repeat as needed, especially the check-ins. They're really important.

Yvette Kaplan advises that animation directors be true to themselves while being open to others' ideas. "Especially listen to experienced others if they have a suggestion." Kaplan continues, "Be true to the project and don't get attached to small pieces that don't make a greater whole. Also be true to your characters and really look and listen to what the script is saying. Number one: think about your audience. I can't stress that enough. Have fun in the process, and be sure those around you are having fun, too."

The Animation Director's Bookshelf
Recommended reading list:

- *The Elements of Style* by Strunk and White, Allyn & Bacon (2000)

- *Animals in Motion* by Eadweard Muybridge, Dover Publications (2002)

- *The Human Figure in Motion* by Eadweard Muybridge, Dover Publications (2000)

- *Animation: From Script to Screen* by Shamus Culhane, St. Martin's Griffin (1990)

- *Talking Animals and Other People* by Shamus Culhane, Perseus Books Group (1998)

- *Producing Animation* by Catherine Winder & Zahra Dowlatabadi, Focal Press (2001)

- *The Illusion of Life: Disney Animation* by Frank Thomas and Ollie Johnston, Hyperion Press (1995)

- *The Animator's Survival Kit* by Richard Williams, Faber and Faber (2002)

- *Cartoon Animation* by Preston Blair, Walter Foster Pub (1995)

CAREER PATHS: ANIMATION PRODUCER
Producers are involved in every aspect of an animated project from prepro-duction to post production. Working within a set budget, they hire a crew,

plan a schedule, run the day-to-day management of a production, and are responsible for delivering the end product to the client or network.

There is some longstanding nonsense in regards to producers that we should address before moving forward. The outdated notion is that there is an "us versus them" or "the artists versus the suits" mentality in an animation production. The reality is that producers need crews to make their projects and crews need producers to initiate or manage projects. To work in animation is to already be a part of this equation. In the end we are all part of the same (hopefully) winning team.

Animation producer Melanie Grisanti (*Doug, Pinky Dinky Doo*) described a day in the life of an animation producer. "There are lots of phone calls, e-mails, and meetings (especially the first season of a production). There will be meetings with the production partners and broadcasters, production process meetings, schedule and budget creation, staffing interviews, creative (script, design, or storyboard) meetings, negotiations with outside vendors, etc. Once things are up and running in a series production you will have many shows in the pipeline at various stages at the same time. It's a fast moving freight train, which requires daily maintenance and problem solving to keep it from derailing or stopping before it reaches its destination. Any good producer should be highly organized, flexible, adept at multitasking, and ready/willing to play a number of important roles including: fearless leader, creative problem solver, juggler, diplomat, negotiator, teacher, shrink, cheerleader, and even babysitter."

There are several different types of producers in the animation business. According to industry veteran Fred Seibert (*Fairly Odd Parents*), the show runner is a type of producer responsible for the day-to-day creative execution on a series. She supervises the entire art team and the writers, actors, and directors.

Seibert describes a line producer as the person responsible for making the production work smoothly. "The line producer manages the budgets, schedules, and will develop deadlines that allow the series to deliver (hopefully) superior episodes on time and on budget." Legendary animation producer Al Brodax (*Yellow Submarine*) adds, "The line producer does most of the worrying and most of the work."

At the top of the chain is the executive producer, who has the ultimate responsibility for a show. Seibert says that everyone looks to the executive producer for final adjudications of conflicts, how to deal with the network, and even for things like free t-shirts for the crew. Grisanti adds, "Executive producers may be creators or instrumental in selling the project. They may or may not be very creatively involved and they often step in to handle budget/political issues as needed."

What background and creative skills should an ideal animation producer have? Veteran animation producer David Steinberg (*Cats Don't Dance*) jokes that as a producer, he doesn't have to know anything. He reveals, "Don't ask me to come up with the technical specs for a 3D studio, or use Maya to animate a scene, or place a camera in virtual space and then light that scene. Forget it. The one thing that all animation producers must know is who to ask. That is the skill we all must have. To find the right experts, to solicit enough opinions to get enough understanding to hopefully make wise daily decisions on how to keep this ever more complex process on track."

Steinberg continues, "Animation is the hardest way of making movies. We start with nothing. I'd say that more than any other brand of producing, we in the animation corner need to have an attention and retention (anal retention?) to the details. As a general rule, I think animation producers have to be pretty good multitaskers, able to keep a lot of detail in their heads at one time and hopefully have the logical ability to connect all those details when weighing in on any given piece of this big million-piece puzzle we like to call a cartoon."

Fred Seibert has known animation producers who've been animators, writers, editors, commercial directors, students, producers of live action feature films, or former jazz record producers/network executives (like himself). Seibert says, "Story sense helps and a visual flair, too." Melanie Grisanti agrees, "You have to learn how to visualize a story from a storyboard and animatic. Unlike in live action, there's no shoot to go to, no multiple takes or multiple-camera coverage (at least not on a TV series schedule/budget), no dailies to screen, etc."

Al Brodax believes animation producers need a good eye and ear for what "works," adding, "If it's not in the genes, I'm not certain it can be taught. Trial and error were my mentors. Lots of trial."

Career Advice

David Steinberg feels that point of entry doesn't matter, saying, "What I find is that people who become producers are generally ambitious people, excited about the medium we work in and committed to looking at every job in the field as a learning experience and a stepping stone. Putting yourself in the right arena is half the battle. After a summer of varnishing desks at Don Bluth Productions, I took an "in-between test" and started drawing on production. I worked in nearly every department during those early summers in L.A., until the leadership at the studio recognized me as a guy who they could count on and who had developed a broad understanding of the production process. And I got along pretty well with people, too, which doesn't hurt. For An American Tail, Don Bluth asked me to be his assistant director, which led me into more and more opportunities to help helm productions."

Fred Seibert confesses, "Every producer, and I'm certainly no exception, makes mistakes every day. And on any given day, one would hope they've learned something, but one is never sure they've learned enough. The biggest mistake a producer can make is not trusting the talent of the creator(s) of a film or project." Additionally, Seibert stresses the importance of relationships and how they've impacted upon his career.

Al Brodax cautions that leaving some things to chance is a big mistake, warning, "Chance doesn't work." Brodax advises that a producer be in all departments all the time, to open and close the shop. He adds, "Have patience and always have a 'plan B' in hand."

Animation producer Lesley Taylor (*The Little Lulu Show, The Busy World of Richard Scarry*) has learned that every film is different and every director is different. Taylor reveals, "Ron Weinberg was the CEO of a company that I worked for and he showed me that whatever the problems with a show, you needed to find a solution where the film wins. John Gaug, a director, showed me that once a film is finished it stands alone on its own merit."

The Animation Producer's Bookshelf
Recommended reading list:

+ *Up Periscope Yellow, The Making of The Beatles' Yellow Submarine* by Al Brodax, Limelight Editions (2004)

+ *Animation: Script to Screen* by Shamus Culhane, St. Martin's Griffin (1990)

+ *The Encyclopedia of Animation Techniques* by Richard Taylor, Running Press (1996)

+ *Producing Animation* by Catherine Winder and Zahra Dowlatabadi, Focal Press (2001)

+ *The Animation Book* by Kit Laybourne, Three Rivers Press (1998)

+ *Makin' Toons* by Allan Neuwirth, Allworth Press (2003)

"THE BEST LAID PLANS . . ."

"Nothing ever goes according to plan. Ever. And as many films as I've worked on (I just counted fifteen on my fingers and toes), the stuff that goes wrong is never the same stuff that went wrong on the last project. Case in point, on *Pagemaster*, our Hollywood offices flooded and our overseas ink and paint studio burnt down; a third of our movie burnt with it. We're talking pencil drawings, gone. You know, none of that stuff was on the beautiful plan we had in the conference room."
—David Steinberg, *animation producer*

Animation producer, David Steinberg.
Courtesy of David Steinberg.

As David Steinberg's experience with *Pagemaster* shows, there are no guarantees on a project no matter how well one plans, just as there are no guarantees in life. The sad reality is that we don't all get to the finish line together, if at all. Yet, it's because of our sense of community, our need and support for each other, that we have the strength to keep going, through the good days, the bad, and the unimaginable.

It's easy for us to name the stars of the animation industry. In fact, many of the best and brightest are collected in this book. The longevity and accomplishments of our heroes put them forefront in our minds. Yet, hiding among the rest of us are some pretty astounding talents. One of the best and brightest was an animator named Paul E. Beard. Paul Beard died April 22, 2005, from injuries suffered the previous day in a two-vehicle crash southeast of Kansas City, Missouri. He was twenty-seven years old.

Gifted animator Paul Beard pictured in his home office in Queens, New York. Image courtesy of the Beard family.

I'm pleased to write that Paul was a friend of mine. We were neighbors in Astoria, Queens. This meant occasional brunches on Sunday and beers at the Bohemian Beer Garden. During the final season of *Blue's Clues*, from 2002 to 2003, I had the privilege of working with Paul as his director. Paul was a uniquely dedicated individual. Nobody worked harder or held higher standards for themselves than he. Post–*Blue's Clues*, Paul took a brief sabbatical from the industry, choosing to stay sequestered in his apartment to finish his first independent film, *Petalocity*. This film, miraculously finished the month of his death, should have been the beginning of a great second career for Paul as a top independent filmmaker. Paul was already in demand as a top freelancer and also as a staff animator on the *Wonder Pets!* (Little Airplane Productions, Nick Jr.).

Petalocity serves proudly as Paul's swan song. The film is a testament to his spirit, humanity, wit, and zest for life.

On May 1, 2005, it was my job, as host of ASIFA-East's 36th annual animation festival, to dedicate the event to Paul E. Beard. I looked out at the hundreds of animation industry people in attendance. With great difficulty holding back my grief, I managed these words: "In our animation community we're like a large family. Beyond our industry relationships, we're in each other's lives. Of course, the risk of connecting into such a large family is that the news about our members isn't always good."

Still from Paul Beard's independent film, Petalocity, *a film that demonstrates Beard's zest for life. Image courtesy of the Beard family.*

We screened *Petalocity* to open the festival. At the film's conclusion we gave Paul the standing ovation that he so richly deserved. Weeks later, hundreds of industry people gathered again to officially say goodbye to Paul at a memorial service held on May 26, 2005. As a family we laughed, cried, and remembered.

The more I grow and learn in this business the more I realize that it is all about relationships. In a career, we bounce from job to job, studio to studio, but it's the relationships made along the way that have the potential to last forever. It is my hope that this book helps to spread that point just a little bit further.

Illustration by Blue's Clues *director David J. Palmer, in memory of Paul Beard. Image courtesy of the artist.*

Illustration by Scott Cooper, in memory of Paul Beard. Image courtesy of the artist.

How to Get the Most Out of Long Periods of Employment

"When you're on a project it's easy to get overly focused and a little myopic. However, I would recommend keeping up with emerging animation talent and networking with others in the biz by attending festivals and events, joining industry organizations, and visiting art schools whenever possible. It's part of what makes this business fun!"

—Melanie Grisanti, animation producer

One of my sketches from a drawing class at New York's The Art Students League.

I n the 1934 Walt Disney Silly Symphony, *The Grasshopper and the Ants*, the ants are busily preparing for the winter ahead by gathering and storing food and other essentials. All the while they are chided by the happy-go-lucky grasshopper who merrily sings, "The world owes me a living." The inevitable winter comes and the grasshopper's philosophy of living in the moment suddenly leaves him cold.

In this business, it's easy to fall into the grasshopper's point of view when you're working on a long-term job. Animation work can be sporadic. Most animation artists work project to project and it's common for projects to last as short as a few days or a few weeks.

Long-term employment can mean working on a feature, a series, or for a bustling studio with a string of consecutive projects. In such a model, it is typical for jobs to last a year or longer. The first thing to do when long-term work stares you in the face is to get the celebrating out of the way quickly. Toast yourself with champagne, throw a big party, and set off some fireworks.

Now comes the hard part: avoid developing a sense of entitlement. This sort of thinking can have you coasting on the job and can ultimately cause you to slip into some bad habits in several areas. The two things you need to focus on are excelling at the work itself and making the most out of the opportunities that long-term work affords you. Showing up, learning the ropes, and doing your best daily is only part of what you need to succeed on the job and ensure success beyond it. Ironically, one of the best ways to excel on the job is by continuing to grow outside of it. What can you do at home to complement or supplement your experience at work? Don't answer yet. You'll spoil everything. The answer is the focus of this chapter.

MODEL STUDENTS

"It is always important to constantly improve drawing skills. I try to take a lot of additional classes and attend live model sessions."
—*Elanna Allen, character designer and stop motion animator*

As commercial animation artists on long-term jobs, we often work in compartmentalized ways. We are hired to do one task or use one type of skill for years at a time. The end result can be a loss of skill in other areas. For starters, are you working at a computer station all day? If so, your drawing skills are at risk of shrinking and dying. Drawing is not like riding a bike. You can't pick up a pencil after a ten-year absence and resume your best life drawing from college. Drawing needs to be maintained. Beat this problem by signing up for life drawing classes on evenings or weekends. The great thing about taking a class is that it imposes a structure on you. You can't blow it off as easily as if you were left to your own timetable.

Many colleges and community centers offer life drawing for free or at a very low cost. In New York City, our ASIFA chapter offers free life drawing once a week for members and students. For a few bucks a class, The Art Students League (also in New York City) offers life drawing sessions every Friday night. Find out what's cookin' in your town. If nothing turns up, pool your money together with other artists and hire a model once a week. In the early days of the Disney studio, animators began doing exactly that. Mr. Walt Disney saw the value in those sessions and decided to bring them officially under his studio roof. Years later, these life drawing classes, under the supervision of the legendary teacher Don Graham, led to the creation of the California Institute of the Arts (Cal Arts). Today's Hollywood animation studios are filled with former Cal Arts students. What a shadow those early Disney animators have cast!

COMPUTE THIS

"As animation artists, we should try to keep up with our industry. The more well-rounded, the more you'll have to offer. The goal for me is to maintain a place in the animation industry, so I have been learning different tools to continue my edge. Learning 3D animation is a must if you want to remain well rounded."
—*Travis Blaise, animator*

If you're a computer challenged, traditional 2D (two dimensional) "pencil" animation artist, don't let the industry leave you behind. Many of today's working animation artists juggle working between 2D and 3D (computer generated animation). In fact, even the traditional 2D animation process involving hand-painted cels shot on gigantic Oxberry camera

Drawing by Travis Blaise. Courtesy of the artist.

stands, has faded into memory as computers are regularly used for ink, paint, and compositing.

When it comes to learning new software, everyone gets there a different way. Some prefer to take classes, which provide structure, assignments, and a live teacher to help you get over any hurdles. Others prefer to sit with a friend who's an expert with certain software and ask questions and take notes. Others learn best at their own pace with a book and a CD in their home. Whatever your ideal method of learning is, you've got to keep using the software for the information to stick. If you can't use the software on the job, you should initiate a small project of your own to keep pushing forward. Why not take this opportunity to make a new sample for your reel? There isn't much time before your traditional studio workplace starts their first 3D project. Who are they going to lean on when that project arrives? Make yourself ready for the inevitable and the unexpected.

PROJECT YOURSELF

"My first self-published comic book led to a thirteen-year career in animation and TV because the right person saw it and liked it and gave me my next opportunity. And pretty much every leap I've made career-wise since then has been the direct or indirect result of some period of introspection, re-evaluation of priorities, and forcing myself to work on something of my own."
—*Jackson Publick, creator,* The Venture Brothers

Initiate your own creative project. It could be writing scripts, sculpture, photography, painting, preparing a pitch for an animated series, an independent film, or inventing a new use for cheese. The great thing about your own projects is that you don't have to be finished to start seeing the value of your effort. Show your work in progress to your peers on the job. Invite them to your script readings, gallery openings, film premieres, stand-up performances, or whatever creative endeavors you have going on.

Six-time Emmy Award winner and two-time Caldecott Honor recipient Mo Willems spent nine years as a scriptwriter and animator for *Sesame Street*. Willems was initially working for Children's Television Workshop (CTW) as a freelance illustrator in the research department. On the side, he was busy writing scripts and sketches for a biweekly stand-up comedy show performed at a small performance club on the Lower East Side of New York. Every other week, Willems would be sure to invite his colleagues at work to see his act. As Willems tells it, they never came to his performances, but the important thing was that the folks at the Workshop knew that Willems was actively writing and performing. Pulling off this biweekly act meant that Willems had lots of script samples on hand. The day came when CTW's *Sesame Street* needed to hire a new writer and they asked Willems to show them some writing samples. After eight months of audition scripts, Willems got the writing job and laid the foundation for a wildly successful career as the creator of the *Suzie Kabloozie* shorts for *Sesame Street*, Nickelodeon's *The Off-Beats*, and Cartoon Network's *Sheep in the Big City*. Willems was also head writer for Cartoon Network's number one rated series, *Codename: Kids Next Door*. In addition, he is making a splash as the author of several award-winning and best-selling children's books published by Hyperion Books for Children, including *Don't Let the Pigeon Drive the Bus!* and *Knuffle Bunny: A Cautionary Tale!*

Willem's spectacular career was set in motion by initiating and promoting his own creative projects. It's a great example of how our personal work can feed our careers. By initiating his own projects, Willems made himself ready for the unexpected (in his case, a writing job at Sesame Workshop). When opportunity comes your way, you need to be ready—otherwise it's someone else's opportunity.

MY ANIMATION SALVATION

"I've often found that it was my more personal work that made the greatest impression in interviewers' minds. Also, for an animator this may be your first opportunity to show that you can direct or that you have director potential."
—*J. P. Dillard, animator and director*

Early in my career, I did a variety of traditional 2D production work at Michael Sporn Animation, Inc., including inbetweening, animating, storyboards, layout, and checking art for camera. It was an education I wouldn't trade for the world. Shortly after a layoff period from Sporn's studio, I landed a job as a storyboard artist at Nick Jr's *Blue's Clues*. When I informed Sporn about the new job, he advised me to get all I could out of the experience. I took that advice to heart.

For a year and a half I worked as a *Blue's Clues* storyboard artist, where I made creative contributions at the earliest stage of each episode and worked closely with the producers, creators, writers, and research department. Despite this, I missed the variety of my work with Sporn and I missed animating. To remedy the problem I initiated and finished two independent films in a two-year period: *Snow Business* (1998) and *Hortonhow* (2000). On these films, I was writer, designer, animator, director, and producer. In this way, I was able to forge a separate identity from my *Blue's Clues* self, while at the same time, increasing my value to *Blue's Clues*. According to John Hays, co-founder of Wild Brain, "The most innovative directors are the ones who have always created new projects and films no matter what else is going on around them." Creating independent films enabled my employer to see me as more than just a storyboard artist, although I didn't realize I was planting these seeds. I just wanted to improve my skills outside of my specific job on the series.

Still from my film Snow Business *(1998). Besides the boost this film gave to my career, musician and composer Chris Jones used it as a sample to launch his own successful career.*

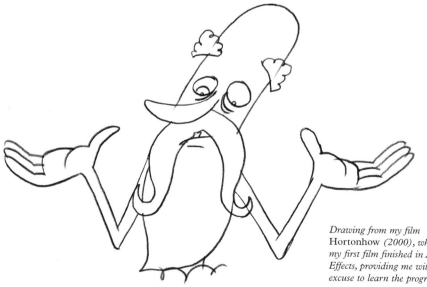

Drawing from my film Hortonhow *(2000), which was my first film finished in After Effects, providing me with a good excuse to learn the program.*

During this time, legendary animator/director Richard Williams (*Who Framed Roger Rabbit*) brought his three-day animation master class to New York City. I attended the costly class with three other *Blue's Clues* folks. Among them was David J. Palmer, the supervising director of animation. During one of the tea breaks in the course, Palmer asked me if I would consider animating for *Blue's Clues*, which was animated on Macs using Adobe After Effects. I didn't know the program at the time, but six months later I learned After Effects and, with the production's blessing, transitioned from storyboard artist to animator.

Less than one year later, directing my own independent films combined with my prior storyboard experience helped me earn a promotion to an animation director. Like Mo Willems, I was ready for an unexpected opportunity by pursuing and promoting my outside projects. Who knows to what heights your projects will take you? Elanna Allen, character designer and stop motion animator adds, "If you are looking to ultimately create, pitch, and sell your own stuff, then there is nothing more important than self-motivated projects."

STEREOTYPING AND TYPECASTING

"Would Nick Jr. call Ralph Bakshi to direct a new preschool show?
Probably not, which is not to say that he wouldn't do a great
job at it, or wouldn't love the job. Simply put, people often
only know you from the work you've done."
—*David J. Palmer, animation director*

Initiating your own projects can have many positive effects on your career. For one, your personal work can save you from being stereotyped or typecasted into one genre of animation.

Obviously, this becomes an important survival tool to ensure that you'll be as employable as possible after working for years on one project, in one style, and in a compartmentalized way. Ian Chernichaw, a designer who worked on *Blue's Clues* for many years, faced the danger of being stereotyped head on. He recalls, "I was actually told in more than one interview, 'You've mostly done preschool programming. What makes you think you can design for a big kid show?'"

Besides initiating our own projects, what else can we do to avoid being stereotyped, and therefore, limited in our career choices? Animation director and producer Ray Kosarin offers this answer: "Opportunities to expand your range usually happen because of other factors, such as already having a positive working relationship with a client." Chalk up another benefit for building and maintaining good relationships. Animation director Yvette Kaplan advises beating stereotyping by ". . . accepting a role on a smaller project to get a new sample. Usually a successful director who has proven him or herself over and over will be welcomed with open arms if enthusiasm is expressed for a particular project."

"YOU WOULDN'T LIKE ME WHEN I'M ANGRY"

The Hulk inside each of us can be set off by getting notes, revisions, or changes on the job. Were you asked to change the size of that cartoon mouse to smaller, to bigger, to smaller, and then to bigger again? Did you freak out? Well, chances are that you'd keep the commercial work you do in perspective if you worked on your own creative endeavors at home. On your projects, you have full control and the final say. The commercial work you do can never compete with the creative satisfaction and reward you'll get from doing your own stuff. In fact, commercial work has little to do with your personal creative vision. As a commercial artist, it is your job to use the time, resources, and skills you have to make the client happy. When you do this successfully, it is a source of great pride, but that should not be confused with the satisfaction of creating on your own terms. According to animation director Jeff Buckland, "The collaborative nature of commercial animation tends to dilute your contributions. Your personal work is really all you have to show people who you are." Storyboard artist Aaron Clark adds, "If nothing else, working on your own projects is a good way to keep yourself sane." You may not know there is a difference unless you go home and create.

THE PERILS OF A LACK OF PERSPECTIVE

"Being defensive about my work has rarely helped me. Feeling insecure about your work can cripple you too if you really start to believe it."
—*Alex Kirwin, Art Director and Character Designer*

I heard of a talented animation artist who blew many issues out of proportion, working at a long-term job. This artist complained about process, personnel, and procedures on a day-to-day basis. The artist's behavior, justified or not, clearly indicated a need for creative control and personal recognition. Not surprisingly, this artist was not engaging in creative projects outside of the job. As a result, his job became his main creative outlet, and every day at work his artistic ego was on the line. After a short while, it became quite a burden for producers and co-workers to hear his negative rants so often. For too long the artist offered complaints but no solutions. Needless to say, he was not asked back for future productions at that company. A bridge was burned.

If this sounds like you, take a moment and try to analyze why you complain and risk self-destructive behavior. For some, personal projects can keep a lot of these "artistic" demons at bay. When there is something to complain about, consider what you need out of the situation. Do you want personal acknowledgment or are you really trying to create an improved working environment for all? Some issues are worth complaining about, some aren't. For more on this subject see chapter 6, "Choosing Your Battles on the Job."

FREELANCE: THE ANIMATION ARTIST'S BEST FRIEND

In addition to initiating your own creative projects, freelancing on evenings and weekends offers many potential rewards to the full-time animation artist. So, why don't more full-timers do it? When we're working a long-term gig, the last thing many of us want to do is to do more work when we get home. For many, evenings and weekends are sacred. I'm not suggesting that you work yourself into an early grave, but the nature of our business can be boiled down into a simple sentence: When there's work, you should do it. Just be sure you don't take on more than you can handle. A great storyboard artist with a staff job once took a freelance storyboard job on the side. The freelance client asked him to create a board in too short a time period, but instead of walking away, he agreed to do the job. As a result, he was forced to turn in a storyboard far beneath his usual standards. The client was unhappy and the storyboard artist's reputation took a negative hit. Never accept a freelance job in which you cannot deliver your best, for any reason.

The wise sage Bugs Bunny said, "Another day, another carrot." The first benefit of doing freelance work will be felt in your wallet. Extra money (if there really is such a thing as extra money) is money you'll need to pay bills, rent, and for classes, supplies, and equipment, or even for that richly deserved vacation. In my career, taking on freelance work has provided enough financial security to help me weather any lean periods that may be ahead. Who knows what I'll need the money for? One day I might want to take a risk like moving to a new city or starting a business. Tomorrow is another day and chances are I will want another carrot.

The income freelance work provides can prevent you from being petty about accepting a small pay raise at work. Most pay raises on the job fall between a two and six percent increase on your yearly salary. These teeny percents will not change your life. They are designed to theoretically keep your income matching the cost of living. However, monies brought in from freelancing a month or two out of the year can nearly double your annual income. Now, that can change your quality of life. Tennis, anyone?

Taking on freelance work can also ensure that you're making enough connections to help land your next long-term gig. Jennifer Oxley is one of the most active and successful freelance animation artists in New York City today. Much of her success in the field is due to the fact that through all her periods of long-term employment at such places as Children's Television Workshop and productions such as Nickelodeon's *Blue's Clues* and *Little Bill*, Oxley has always made time for freelance work. She has even been known to take her laptop on vacation to animate for her many clients. I personally observed that many staffers on *Blue's Clues* and *Little Bill* had enormous difficulty making new job connections once their shows had wrapped.

The problem? Many of these talented artists did not seek out extra work in the "fat years" of employment. As a result, they didn't get to build a rich network of contacts. In contrast, Jennifer Oxley's prestigious career continues to grow. After years of freelance illustrating, animating, and directing for others, Oxley recently made the leap to creating original material for *Sesame Street*. Today, Jen Oxley is a major force in preschool animation and has cemented that role as the in-house creative director of Little Airplane Productions, Inc., helping to shape such series such as *The Wonder Pets!* Clearly, one of the major reasons for Oxley's success is her willingness to take on freelance work, even during periods of long-term employment.

HOW TO INCREASE YOUR BUSINESS SKILLS WITHOUT REALLY TRYING

As a freelancer, you also get experience in business negotiations. Your time, fee, and the approval process itself are all up for negotiation. With freelance, you learn to estimate the length of time required to do a job. Knowing how to judge time goes hand in hand with knowing what to charge as your fee. Freelancing puts you in contact with a larger variety of people and personalities. One of the most important ingredients to a successful career in animation is the ability to work harmoniously with all kinds of people. It's the mother of all business skills: people skills.

CONTINUE TO NETWORK: MAINTAIN CONTACTS IN SICKNESS AND IN HEALTH

Let's call sickness "unemployment" and health "steady employment," for the above heading to make sense. People do notice when you only contact them when you need something. It says something about how you view the relationship and communicates that you're only interested in speaking to people when you have to. It suggests that you are not interested in what they are doing or what is going on in their lives.

At some point you'll be busy with full-time work and dirty dishes will pile up in the sink and you may easily fall out of touch with your friends in the industry. The good news is that e-mail makes it easier than ever to stay connected. While you may not always have time to do lunch or say hello by phone, e-mail takes no time at all. Make it a point to stay in touch with people every couple of months. Tell people how you're doing and where you're working. Ask them how they're doing and where they're working. Make plans to meet up for drinks, lunch, or at industry events.

In addition, continue to network to create new contacts. Make it a point to attend animation events and talk to at least one new person per gathering and bring business cards. However, be forewarned, most of these informal animation events are geared towards the social and community ends of the business. It's probably a bad idea to thrust portfolios and other samples into people's hands while they're socializing. Make the connections first and then make a plan to meet up and show your samples at the appropriate time and place.

Joining volunteer organizations like ASIFA is a terrific way to network and connect with contacts new and old on a regular basis. Linda Simensky, known in the animation industry for her roles as a development executive at Nickelodeon, Cartoon Network, and PBS Kids, has said that she owes much of her people and business skills, not to mention many industry connections, to her time as president of ASIFA-East (1990–2000). Volunteer groups are fragile. People who are donating their time and energy have the option of walking away at any point if they aren't appreciated, challenged, or having a good experience. Successfully leading such a group of volunteers over a ten-year period taught Simensky more management lessons than she could have learned exclusively from being a TV network executive.

Despite Simensky's busy schedule as a senior director of programming at PBS Kids, she remains an active ASIFA-East board member today.

HOW VOLUNTEERING GOT ME WORK DOWN THE ROAD!

In 1996, I was working full time at Michael Sporn Animation, Inc., and I was a member of the ASIFA-East board of directors. The volunteer work was anything but glamorous. Often it involved me sitting on the edge of my bed processing checks as part of my membership secretary duties. I remember my roommate telling me how I was wasting my time. I knew better. Volunteering made me feel good while providing me with lots of opportunities I wouldn't have had otherwise.

At one of our monthly board meetings in 1996, I met Nancy Keegan, who was working as a storyboard artist and animator for the brand new show, *Blue's Clues*, not yet a household name. At that time, Keegan was writing a column for the ASIFA-East monthly newsletter in which she would introduce the animation community to some new faces on the scene. Having only a year in the business underneath my belt, I soon became the subject of one of her columns. Over a dinner/interview we became fast friends. From that point on we stayed in touch and reconnected at ASIFA meetings and events each month. Later in the year, I was looking for work and Keegan was kind enough to introduce me to the producers at *Blue's Clues*. With her help I was able to get a job interview, which led to a seven-and-a-half-year job on the production!

My volunteer work with ASIFA-East gave me connections to a wider body of people than I would have met working on any one particular job, while also providing a means of staying in touch with them at monthly events. The encouragement of members inspired me to stay focused, and create my own films to screen at ASIFA-East's annual animation festival. The organization also enabled me to meet (and discover) so many of my animation heroes, including Paul Fierlinger, Ray Harryhausen, Shamus Culhane, Jerry Beck, Michael Sporn, John Canemaker, Tissa David, R.O. Blechman, Yuri Norstein, Al Brodax, Richard Williams, and many others. Who said volunteer organizations such as ASIFA don't pay anything? What you can get in return for your time is priceless.

Hedgehog drawing presented to me by Yuri Norstein, which can be found gracing my bathroom wall. From the author's collection.

THE REEL WORLD

"If you are working on a project it is very easy to get wrapped up in it and forget about the next one. Then before you know it, it's over and someone asks you for your reel. Then the mad scramble begins, locating the footage you want to use to update your reel with your latest work. If you stay on top of it, whenever an opportunity presents itself, you'll be ready."
—*Justin Simonich, animator*

At the end of every week on the job, round up your designs, layouts, or storyboards. Save copies for yourself. Back up your animation on discs or portable hard drives. Later on, it becomes much more difficult to assemble all of these materials once the production wraps or you've moved on. Not everything you file away now will make it into your portfolio or reel later. Save the critical assessment of which samples are best for another day. Don't procrastinate. Your phone could ring tomorrow with a freelance job and they may need to see some of your most recent samples. At the risk of repeating myself: prepare for the unexpected opportunities and events.

In 2001, the stop motion animation crew of MTV's long-running *Celebrity Death Match* had over six months of animation ahead of them to complete the current season. Suddenly, the series was shelved by the network and the animators' work stopped abruptly with the frame on which they were working. It was like Pompeii, only without the lava.

This is a good example of how even so-called "guaranteed work" can end suddenly. Layoffs happen at the big studios as well as with the little guys. All one can do is try to prepare for the unexpected by continually updating reels and portfolios. You may need them sooner than you think.

The end of production of *Blue's Clues* played out very differently than its Viacom cousin, *Celebrity Death Match*. Since beginning production in 1996, *Blue's Clues* animation artists had never gone on hiatus. Seasons blurred together as work continued nonstop on the hit series. However, in the fall of 2001, our animation department of twenty-five individuals was told that *Blue's Clues* was going to cease production in two years. This was the most generous notice of time that I'd ever heard of in this business. Armed with this information, some employees prepared by utilizing tuition reimbursement offered at Nickelodeon to take classes in the 3D program Maya. Many others procrastinated and didn't really set out to work on their reels and portfolios until well after *Blue's Clues* ceased production. At any time during those two years, the network could have yanked away our jobs, leaving us with a fate much like *Celebrity Death Match*. A good motto to live by is, "Hope for the best, and prepare for the worst."

In your career, it's up to you to ensure that your first long-term job is the first of many. Make your own "fat years" regardless of what the industry throws at you. And don't worry about counting a single carb along the way.

Choosing Your Battles on the Job

"I had a low tolerance for stupidity and would get too easily frustrated by the legion of non-animator 'production pukes' (as I used to call them!) interfering with our efforts to get the job done. I've let myself get all bent out of shape over people who in the end weren't worth getting bent out of shape over. And I've done my share of complaining. I had a very 'military' approach to my work and my peers/subordinates/superiors. Most of the time it served me well, but sometimes it didn't."

—Jim Petropolis, animator and director

On a job, it's important to know the difference between choosing your battles and choosing to battle. Situations come up on a daily basis that can challenge even the best intentioned person. Yet, not all these situations are of equal importance. Before you do anything else, examine your needs or desires in any given situation. Next, look inside yourself to discover your role in the problem. Before looking for a change in others, you have to exhaust the possiblities in yourself. With self-examination you may even come to the conclusion that the problem is not even your concern. If you decide to go forward to battle you must first ask a lot of questions in anticipation: What are the stakes or risks? Is there a chance your reputation or job itself could be on the line? How healthy is your relationship with the person whom you're about to engage? How might she react? What is the best way to approach the subject? Can it wait until tomorrow, when you might have a more level head or a different point of view? These are just some of the many questions you should ask yourself before acting out a confrontation.

Of course, there are times when you may find yourself in a battle with little or no advance warning. In that case, you won't have time to go over the mental checklist of questions. In these situations, find out what the other person is feeling and thinking. Don't rush to your own judgments. Animation is a collaborative business. The relationships you have with your co-workers are just as important as the work itself. You can't succeed in one while neglecting the other.

The inevitable complication is that you're not going to get along with all your co-workers. Despite this, if you take the time to truly understand your own needs and the needs of others, you should have all you need to make a good judgment.

WHEN MOM DOESN'T KNOW BEST

It's usually advisable to wait a day to really think about a situation from all perspectives before taking action. It can be very helpful to use this time to consult a trusted and objective friend (preferably from the business). You want someone who will not immediately fall on your side in a knee-jerk reaction. Although the support would be nice, the advice that comes from this point of view isn't very useful. It may even be harmful. Mothers, fathers, siblings, and significant others can provide much needed support, but are not automatically our best counsel on matters concerning careers in animation. They don't know the industry, the circumstances, nor the way animation studios function. With that in mind, how can they provide the most imformed opinion? Use these home court allies for unconditional love and the strength that can bring. When it comes to advice we can trust, we need to lean on objective and experienced individuals. These people are not afraid to be critical or honest with us. In turn, we have to be mature enough to receive such analytical advice without taking it personally. If we're not ready for such honest criticism, this may be why we're having trouble at work in the first place.

THE DANGER OF BEING RIGHT

My greatest mistakes on the job were always caused by self-righteousness. I was right and I knew it. Feeling right gives one a sense of power, purpose, and entitlement. All of us need some amount of approval from our peers and superiors. However, the need to be right runs counter to everything that is most important. Our primary goal is to serve the production on which we're working to the best of our ability. Our second, equally important concern is to create and maintain the healthiest possible relationships with our co-workers.

Proving that you're right becomes a game and, as in any game, there are winners and losers. To be right means that someone else is wrong. Yet, for a production to be all it can be, everyone must be allowed to deliver their best performance. On the job, sometimes we're right and sometimes we're wrong. In a healthy studio enviornment, we're allowed to be wrong. It has to be okay to make some mistakes and have a chance to learn from them. If it's okay to be wrong, it follows suit that it must be okay to be right. In a studio, being right might mean having the best idea or the most experience with a particular problem. Okay, let's say you're right. So what? It's how we use being right that counts. When you're right, your task is to get the other person to come along to your point of view without making him seem wrong. There's an old expression saying that success has many fathers and failure has none. In today's workplace, no one need walk away feeling like a failure.

The long-term effect of blindly waging battles can take a huge toll on your reputation. Those you've squashed eventually get jobs elsewhere. Some of them will act as gatekeepers blocking your path to future opportunities. Ten years down the road, will it matter that you were right in any given battle? At what cost did you prove you were right? If you take the time to think about these consequences now, you can ensure that ten years from now you'll be greeted by your old collegues with good will. Those are the benefits of a good reputation. Sounds to me like a battle won.

LEARNING FROM OTHERS' BATTLES

Early in my directing career, I witnessed a battle between a lead animator and his director. The lead animator, recently promoted, had been promised that he would have some say over what shots he would work on. That pledge had come from the supervising director. Yet, when the lead animator began his position, his animation director decided not to honor the arrangement made by the supervisor and instead gave out the animation work according to his own needs. The supervisor had given his directors the right to organize the work as they saw fit, despite the fact that this might contradict previous understandings.

Thus began a year-long struggle in which the lead animator's enthusiasm waned to such a degree that his previously high-quality work suffered noticably. I did my best to intervene on the animator's behalf by speaking to his director, but he insisted on following his own plan. As a director of another team, it wasn't my call to make. Eventually, the director gave up on the animator completely and even recommended the animator's termination. As a last resort, the production assigned the lead animator to my team.

At first I was a little wary of working with this animator, but then I thought about why he was unhappy and what I might be able to do about it. The first thing I did was show the animator the storyboards of our next two shows. "Let me know what you'd like to animate," I said. He was stunned that I asked him that. Instantly he became the great lead animator he'd been before. In fact, he surpassed his past triumphs. If people are valued, challenged, and encouraged to do their best, the results can be spectacular. I was able to get the desired result with this lead animator by observing someone else's battle and ensuring that it did not become mine.

BATTLIN' FOR DOLLARS

Promotions and merit raises are given out by management in recognition of excellence in the workplace. These rewards are also mangement's way of solving problems. For example, when a department head suddenly gives her two weeks' notice, management will often look internally to fill that position. This allows them to groom key people from within the studio and offer an example to others on the crew that there is room to grow. Likewise, a period of expansion in operations may create a need for new positions and promotions. With such policies, management has good reason to believe that those promoted will be loyal and productive employees, encouraging others to follow their lead. On the other side of the equation, those who are promoted in this manner know they're likely to have the management's support, since the promotion was management's idea.

As an employee, anything you try to initiate in the area of promotions or merit raises is far more precarious. Even if you successfully battle or negotiate your way up, there can still be a risk of creating bad blood. If you threaten to leave if a promotion/raise is not offered, it can be assumed that you'd be willing to walk away at any time. Whatever gain you've made will likely be short term. You risk losing status and respect. Remember, good work tends to rise to the top. If you're stagnating at the bottom, think about what you might be doing or not doing that might be holding you back. Are you impatient? Do you lack faith that the company will recognize your hard work? Are you already being paid a fair price for your work but would simply like to be earning more? Most of us could use more money. Still, do the answers to your additional monetary needs really have anything to do with the company payroll?

The average merit raise tends to be anywhere from two to six percent. This is not an increase that you would even notice. Why go out on a limb to ask for a raise that will not even change your life? Instead of battling for bupkis, why not take on the occasional freelance job? As mentioned earlier, additional freelance work one or two months out of the year can nearly double your annual income! Remember, work relationships, like any other relationships, get strained over money issues faster than most anything else. Consider all of your options before proceeding. You may just find that the answer rests with you.

There are, however, occasions where the pay on a particular project may be unfair. Once I was offered a promotion at a lower percentage increase than others were getting in the same role. The reason? My salary was starting at a higher base than theirs. In an effort to be fair, the producers felt the right thing to do would be to bring everyone up to an equal level of salary, regardless of what their rates were prior to this. This didn't seem fair to me. I decided to battle. My argument, presented in a meeting with my supervisor and the producer, was that it was not possible to preserve fairness with this unfair practice because everyone comes to the table with different skill levels and varying amounts of years with the production. Not only did I end up winning this argument, the rest of the employees promoted along with me were able to have their increases raised too. Not a bad consequence.

On another occasion I battled over a low increase after my first year as a director. In that year, I'd helped the series meet their new goal of doubling production. I knew what I'd been able to achieve with my team and when I was presented with a six percent raise I felt dissapointed. "This raise doesn't acknowledge what I was able to accomplish this year," I said in the meeting. Later that day, they raised my pay another percentage point. It was a small gesture but it made me feel a lot better and more appreciated by the production. I thought that was the end of it, but it wasn't. Two weeks later, one of the producers called me into her office. "I understand that you were unhappy at your rate increase," she said. Then she told me that she was raising my salary again. This time by an additional one hundred dollars per week. Management's change of heart blew me away. I felt vindicated in speaking up. In this case, it was a battle well chosen, fought, and won.

There is one thing left to consider when it comes to "battlin' for dollars." What happens when they say no? Are you willing to leave if you're turned down? Try to set your own expectations somewhere in the middle of what you're asking for and what they are offering. Ideally, both sides should feel like they won.

GOOD JUDGMENT IS PRICELESS

"Once or twice I confronted superiors when I felt they needed it. Most of the time, I came away victorious but emotionally spent. I have since learned to be ever more patient and kind. I am amazed that patience and kindness often disarm those stress-puppies who otherwise make animators' lives miserable . . . and it is much better for team morale! I have also learned from watching others' mistakes. I have learned never to take my feelings out on someone else. Everybody has feelings, and nobody, not even the annoying person we all hate, likes it when they're hurt. Animation is supposed to be fun." —*Jim Petropolis, animator and director*

Early in my career, I worked on a four-month-long industrial video where I was the sole assistant to the director. Two months into the project, my director decided to move the production out of state to his neighborhood. For two weeks I helped him move into his new store-front office space. We picked up office supplies, furniture, and decorations for the new studio. The one problem was that we had deadlines to hit at the same time and the studio preparations greatly interfered with the time that I needed to spend on the work. On top of everything, the director's work style was very hands-off. Working solely on my own, I started to worry that I was falling too far behind. I wasn't very tactful when I brought up my concerns to the director. I managed to insult him by telling him my time was being wasted on non-work related business and the long commute out of state. He was so annoyed that he didn't even want to talk about it.

A day later, after the situation had cooled off, my director called me at home. He confessed that he almost fired me but instead decided to give me the option of splitting my time between working from home and working at the client's office. He also pledged not to distract me with business other than the work itself. In turn, I had to agree to work occasionally out of state, in particular for the final two weeks of production when the deadlines would be tight.

With this second chance I truly felt foolish and sorry for the way I had behaved. There is always a way to express yourself without hurting someone's feelings or challenging their judgment, authority, work ethic, or experience.

GO WITH YOUR GUT!

"I would say that I've learned to follow my gut. That's not to say that you shouldn't take time and think things through, but most of my mistakes could have been averted had I not second-guessed myself."
—*Melanie Grisanti, animation producer*

I don't know if you can teach good judgment. Like common sense, we all have it in different degrees. More of us should learn to trust that gut feeling when it tells us that something isn't right.

On one such occasion I was in the middle of a layoff period from a studio. It had already been two months since my job ended and there was no telling when the studio would be able to bring me back. The studio owner was a very supportive man and encouraged me to work on my personal film at the studio. This way I could use his video pencil test system, copier, and anything else I might need. It was a wonderful gift to me and my film. Plus it was nice to have someplace to go each day. For a couple of months I came into the studio each day and merrily plugged away on the film. After a time, my funds were starting to dry up. Unemployment insurance would only stretch so far. Occasionally I would slip away from the studio and go on a job interview or two. I tried to do this as discreetly as possible, although one friend at the studio had the habit of belting out "good luck" whenever I marched out the

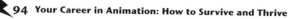

door heading for an interview. So much for total discretion. Despite going on several interviews, nothing seemed promising until I was offered to test for a storyboard position on a series. I jumped at the opportunity.

For the next three days I sequestered myself in my apartment, banging out the storyboard test. I even ordered cable television so I could watch the show to better understand its style. Each day I put in about twelve hours to do the best job possible. Everything was going on track until I got a call from an employee/friend at my old studio. The message was that a TV crew was going to be filming a segment on the studio the next day. My friend thought it would be super if I could come in and fill a chair at one of the work stations. Otherwise the place, smack in the middle of a layoff period, would look too empty. I really wanted to help, but I was torn because I had to spend the next day on the test. It would be due first thing in the morning the day after that!

"You can work on your test here," suggested my friend. "I don't know if that's a good idea," I answered. But, like a fool, I did go in and like an even bigger fool I did use the studio's facilities to work on a test for another employer! It was a very thoughtless and ungrateful thing to do (and I did it!).

At the end of the day, the studio owner came over to my desk and whispered in my ear. "It's very unprofessional of you to work on someone else's work in my studio." I could have died right there. Of course he was right. I'd allowed myself to go against my better judgment. I second guessed my gut feeling and I had only myself to blame. A studio is like the studio owner's home. As a guest in their home, we have to be considerate and remember our manners. Our actions define who we are as much as our work and our words. It only takes one mistake to damage one of your most important career assets—your reputation. As independent animator Paul Fierlinger says, "By people's manners I can tell everything about them."

NEITHER GOOD COP NOR BAD COP

I have learned, the hard way, to focus primarily on the duties within my job description. Each day is loaded with potential landmines that we can walk onto knowingly or learn how to avoid. At my recent job directing animation on a television series, I've been able to correct many of the mistakes I made while in a similar role a few years earlier. For instance, it's a given that some of the crew is going to have problems with tardiness. As an animation director my concern is with the creative end of things. I'm neither a good cop nor a bad cop. I don't dish out consequences for lateness. There are support staff such as the associate producer and coordinators who, by definition, deal with such issues. If my task is to direct animation then I must focus on that and on preserving good work relations with my animation team.

Sounds simple enough. Yet, in the world of animation, there is much variation as to what the job expectations are of any given position. On my previous directing gig, I was encouraged and expected to do as much staff managing as directing. This put me in both a creative and policeman position. That shouldn't be impossible, but it proved very difficult on several occasions. My authority was a soft power. As a subordinate to my supervising director and all of his superiors I was living many layers below the decision-making area. I allowed myself to think I had more influence over employee issues than I actually had. Trying to manage a team in this fashion was a road I shouldn't have walked on.

RIGHT BATTLE, WRONG TIME AND PLACE

We may have the best possible justification to fight a particular battle and still end up choosing the worst way to wage it. When this happens we dilute our message and risk making our error in communication the issue on the table.

Animator Justin Simonich found himself in just this type of situation while working at a studio as a freelancer. "The majority of the people who worked there were full-time employees and received benefits, 401K plans, the works. The few freelancers, as recent hires, were not eligible for any of these. This policy created some tension between the two groups. I worked side by side with and did the same job as a full-timer but didn't get any of the perks. The network decided to give out hats to the staff as 'thank you, job well done' on the project. They didn't provide any for the freelancers, only the full-time staff. We had all worked just as hard on the project and were considered by the network as not deserving of a small token of thanks. It wasn't that I wanted a hat, I just wanted to be treated the same as everyone else there. It wasn't easy to take.

"A few weeks went by and I thought that I put it behind me when the director came by with a card to sign. It was for a group of VIPs from overseas making a surprise visit. They wanted me to sign the card which would be given to the VIPs along with a bunch of hats. The very same hats which they didn't have enough of to give to me just two weeks earlier. This was the proverbial straw that broke the camel's back. I blew up at my director on the floor of the studio, telling him I couldn't believe he was asking me to sign a card and give someone the hat I wasn't worthy of receiving myself. I then walked out and took an early lunch. It may have felt good at the time, to let it all out, but the time and place I chose to do so wasn't the best. I frightened a number of my co-workers around me, as well as seriously strained my relationship with the director.

"The animation community is a very small one so be careful not to burn any bridges. I have worked a number of places since then, and with many of the people with whom I shared that early job. If I didn't make sure to mend fences before I left that studio, that incident could have come back to haunt me. Your reputation is very important; good or bad it will precede you wherever you go."

CHOOSE YOUR BATTLES CHECKLIST

Our success in the workplace is tied to how effectively we choose our battles. We may not always choose our battles correctly, but we can choose to always learn from our mistakes. Use this choose your battles checklist to prevent tomorrow's mistakes today:

+ Think before you act. Ask yourself questions like, "What do I want out of the situation?" Examine your role in the problem. Confide in a trusted, objective person who is knowledgeable about the industry.

+ The goal is not to be right or to make others be wrong. Everyone should walk away a winner or a least a participant in figuring out the plan to get there.

+ Learn from the battles and mistakes of others without having to make those mistakes yourself.

+ Battlin' for dollars: seek other alternatives for money (such as taking on freelance work) if the production is already paying you a fair wage. If you must battle, aim to compromise with your employers somewhere between your number and theirs.

+ Listen to your gut. Learn to not second-guess your best judgment.

+ On the job, look after your duties first and foremost. Be sure you clearly understand your role on the project.

"Your reputation is everything. Guard it with your life."
J.P. Dillard, animator and director

 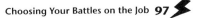

Making On-the-Job Criticism Your Friend

The first story I ever heard about "getting the message" came from my dad. He had an employee to whom he gave assignments, which the employee would put aside and say, "There's plenty of time for that. I'll do that later." Then the employee would show my dad a personal project he was working on during company time—for example, plans for the world's greatest clock. The "clock maker" not only ignored his work assignments, he blatantly spent time on his personal projects instead. All the while he tried to reassure my dad that there was plenty of time to get the assigned work done. Each time this scene played out, my dad asked the employee to put the personal work away. Each time, the employee ignored the message.

Frustrated with the "clock maker," my dad complained to his boss. Understandably, he didn't wish to continue working with the employee. "I don't care what you do with him, but I'm not going to work with that guy," my dad said. The boss went one better and fired him. In a scene that played out like a movie script, the "clock maker" gathered up his clock-parts in a box to make his final exit. Along the way he bumped into my dad and snidely commented, "I suppose you had nothing to do with this." My dad blasted back at him, "Don't think you had nothing to do with it." The story stayed with me over the years as a classic example of someone who didn't get the message in time. To "get the message" is to understand its implications and then react or change your behavior accordingly.

GIVING THE MESSAGE: DEFINE SUCCESS, MAKE IT ACHIEVABLE, AND RECOGNIZE IT

It seems to me the above heading is one of the keys to succeeding in a leadership role inside an animation studio. Let's assume that you are a studio department head, or supervisor, or director. You are directly responsible for your team hitting their deadlines, keeping the quality of work high, and jumping all types of daily hurdles along the way. In terms of your authority over administrative issues, you have no real direct power. You may recommend hiring, firing, or promotion, but it is not your call to make.

The good news is that within your own limited authority and job description, you can still help create the best possible work environment. Imagine a workplace in which everyone is given the tools and support they need to succeed. Every day is another chance to get it right.

A secure and confident leader knows that success can only be achieved if the expectations are realistic. Part of the leader's worth is to know what can get done in the allotted time with the available resources (crew, equipment, time, and money). If we temporarily expect our crew to go beyond what is reasonable we have to own up to that fact. We have to define the increased expectation and make the duration clear. In all fairness we should be prepared to appreciate the extra effort through whatever means we have available. When overtime pay isn't available, even something as simple as a sincere "thank you" can work wonders. Anything less and we risk losing good will and respect from our crew.

In a healthy studio environment, success is earned and shared by everyone on the crew. The tone of a studio is set from the top on down, so it's up to the leader to set a clear and consistent good example. Share credit with all of the authors. Publicly acknowledge individual achievements as well as those of the entire team. We want to encourage people to do their best every day, while at the same time demonstrating that it's okay to fail in pursuit of those goals now and then. Sure, as a studio department supervisor, you don't have authority to hand out raises or promotions, but there are still many creative ways to recognize good work. My favorite way to show appreciation is to involve the entire crew in the creative process and to delegate the choicest assignments as rewards for a job well done. At this point in my career I have directed more than forty hours of TV animation. In all that time, I don't think I ever turned in an animation schedule that didn't stretch or challenge each crew member to reach new heights of his potential.

Finally, the studio is where you and your team spend most of your waking hours. Why not have a supportive, rewarding, and creative work place?

REMOVING OBSTACLES TO SUCCESS BY SENDING THE RIGHT MESSAGE

A TV series animator I worked with was brilliant, but often missed deadlines. His work was regularly finished by his director, a routine in which the two of them worked for well over a year. When this animator was traded to my team I was aware of both his great work and his history of bad time management. I set out to remove what I saw as his obstacles to success. Unfortunately, the road to progress was bumpier than it needed to be. First, before winning over the animator's trust, I called him in to a meeting with our supervising director and laid out our expectations.

I used our first episode together, in which the animator's work was two weeks late, as an example of what needed improvement. Hearing this message for the first time and in the presence of the big boss, the animator felt justifiably ambushed. Unsurprisingly, he reacted defensively. The trust between us had been shattered. I had focused so hard on the deadlines that I forgot about the person. After all, my goal had not been to make enemies. The real prize I was after was to help enable all my animators to reach their full potential.

For a while the relationship between the animator and me was uncomfortable at best. At the breaking point of the crisis, the animator marched into my office to confront me. For almost an hour he cut me to ribbons: I was doing a lousy job as a director; he didn't feel supported or protected; he was used to having a lot of help. He had come to expect someone to pick up the work he couldn't finish and he resented me for personally not doing that.

As I listened to his rant, the real issue became clear to me. Having had unconditional support in a near consequence-free environment, he never had to worry about failing. It had been okay that his work was always late and had to be finished by others. He and his entire team had always worked in the same pattern: get a late start, get even further behind, and do a last minute rush to the finish line. The lion's share of the work was always taken on by the team's director, who, by picking up his team's slack, became his team's enabler. My very different leadership style frightened this animator. He wasn't sure he could succeed on my terms, but I was certain he could. By open-mindedly hearing out his complaints, I was back on the road to regaining his trust.

The animator and I ended up working together for another year and a half. In that time we both did our best work because we had grown and learned from each other. Long after the dust had settled he marched into my office again to tell me what a great job I was doing. I don't think I'd ever felt more successful than at that moment. It was a success that we'd both earned.

Yet, success didn't have to be achieved in such a rocky manner. The key is to consider *people* before anything else. It's true that issues come up that need to be addressed, but we can't blindly seek out objectives without respecting the needs and feelings of our crew. That's what separates good leaders from bad.

THE NICK OF TIME

A director I worked with had an animator under him who was argumentative, overly defensive, and occasionally rude. The problem dragged on and on. The director developed a strategy of ignoring the problem, instead of handling the situation head on. The director let the animator blow off steam and would then tell him to take it up with the supervisor. The animator never took his complaints any further up the chain, but fell into a safe routine of mouthing off to his director. To top it all off, the animator only worked half the day. The other half of the day was filled with reading comics, watching TV in the break area, or chatting with others. Time rolled on and one day this animator ended up on my team.

The animator's difficult personality emerged from week one of us working together. Every note I gave the animator was battled and negotiated to the point of exhaustion. Yet, my first real order of business was to get a fair day's work out of him for a fair day's pay. At a meeting with him in my office, I outlined the production's daily expectations of each animator. It seemed like the message was understood. Next, I explained why we needed to work effectively together so each scene could be its best. I also asked him to tell me if there was something I was doing to contribute to the source of his frustrations. "No, everything is fine," was his reply. No cajoling from me could get the animator to open up. Instead he reassured me that he'd do better and try harder.

As the weeks passed his problem with time management improved. To my frustration, I still couldn't get the animator to stop battling every single note, so I consulted with my supervisor. "Talk to him again," was his advice. Fair enough. Three more meetings failed to bring the desired result. Maybe the best solution would be to do what the animator's previous director had done: ignore the problem and give up. I tried to do just that.

One day I found myself sitting in a rough-cut review with my supervisor, who had a lot of notes on a sequence by my difficult animator. They were all good notes that would undoubtedly improve the animation. My stomach was filling with knots at the idea of having to relay these notes to the animator. Suddenly I wondered why I was being this animator's partner in a dysfunctional relationship. I was giving him a message that he wasn't getting, but he was also giving me a message that I hadn't been hearing. I had a plan.

After the rough-cut review I showed up at the animator's cubicle wearing my jacket. "Put your coat on," I said. "We're going for a walk." At first he laughed, thinking I was making a joke, and then his face filled with fear. "What's this about?" he asked. "We're going outside to talk," was the only information I'd give him and I wouldn't answer any questions until we got outside. The elevator ride down from the fourth floor was a short one, but I think it must have been the longest ride of his life.

I said to him, "You're difficult to work with. You argue every note on your work. I've tried to get you to open up and explain to me what is going on. You always assure me that everything is fine and then nothing changes. And you know what? That's okay. It's okay because we don't *have* to work together. You don't *have* to work here and I don't *have* to work with you."

He was shaken. He asked me if he was being fired.

"That decision is up to you," I answered. "If you want to turn things around, then do it now. If not, then you don't have to work here."

He finally heard me and subsequently told me about his trouble with authority and his insecurity about his work. After that, the change in the animator was the difference between night and day. He went on to finish out the season and return for the next one, his work improving by leaps and bounds.

I learned that, as a director, it's not enough to give a message; you sometimes have to find both the right message to give and the right way to give it. The animator and I remain good friends to this day.

GETTING THE MESSAGE

Feedback on the job comes in many ways, including officially, unofficially, verbally, in writing, from peers, and from superiors. The responsibility to fully understand the message always falls on us. Later, when it's too late, it won't matter that we wanted to hear the message more clearly, more often, or with the consequences outlined. As adults, we are responsible for ourselves and should assume that feedback won't always come to us in the most ideal or proper manner. If we accept that, we'll be more likely to recognize important feedback when we hear it and therefore have a chance to do something about it.

There are three stages to successfully getting a message:

✦ Understanding the message.

✦ Acting on the message. Results are what matter. Words mean nothing unless they are accompanied by actions.

✦ Staying on message. Following through for the long term without sliding back to past behaviors.

Desktop Dilemma

The setting: a corporate studio environment in which the entire senior staff is made up of women. The production: a preschool series. One day a male animation artist, fairly new to the job, decided to decorate his computer desktop with an alternating slide show of bathing beauties. Every minute or so his monitor would refresh itself with another scantily clad supermodel. In this way his computer screen became an inappropriate billboard within an office shared with two other people. Among those two was his department supervisor, a woman. She promptly advised him to change his desktop pattern. "It's bound to offend people around here," she warned. The animation artist with the questionable desktop could not be persuaded. He didn't get the message.

Over the course of a few weeks, various crew members entering their department made jabs about the bawdy desktop display. Eyebrows were raised. People shook their heads. Again, the department supervisor advised him to change the desktop. Instead of getting the message at this point, he took each person's complaint personally and left the images up to spite them, in a classic example of choosing the wrong battle. A few more weeks passed. One day this animation artist was out sick, but had left his computer on. It was the same day the all-female senior staff happened to have a meeting in this office. They watched as the desktop slide show played out and cringed in displeasure.

From that day forward, the artist's stock fell in the eyes of the senior staff—a judgment which proved impossible for him to erase. The small issue had big consequences.

We have to use common sense and understand the company's culture and the personalities of its key staff when making certain decisions. All of us want to be surrounded by things that communicate our interests and personalities at work. In fact, animation artists are known for displaying entire toy collections in their workspaces. However, if we're working in a corporate environment, we have to show some proper judgment and fully consider the feelings of those around us.

Lateness and the Silent Bargain

There are so many stories about chronically late employees that I don't know where to begin. In each case, the problem was exacerbated by the employee not getting the message to come in on time. One such animation artist developed a chronic lateness problem when working as production assistant on a TV series. She was a pleasure to work with in every other way, but she just wouldn't show up on time. It was an issue because she had key production duties to perform at the start of each day. She got several verbal warnings from two supervisors over a period of a few months. When the problem did not go away, she was finally written up and called into a meeting with the department head. At the meeting she was given the choice to come in on time for the next two weeks or not bother coming back to work after that. The message suddenly hit her all at once. Happily, she turned the problem around and was on time or early from that point on.

Not everyone gets a second chance. Allowing yourself to ignore important messages is akin to playing chicken with an oncoming car. It's a dangerous game. You have no way of knowing when your time will be up. How many chances will you get to hear a message? One should be all you need.

On the surface this all seems so logical. So why do so many people go down this path? The reason is what I call a "silent bargain." In a silent bargain, a person who is late, for instance, can think of a variety of reasons why it's okay, even if they've heard messages to the contrary. In a silent bargain, one justifies their own actions to themselves: It's okay that I'm late because I sometimes stay late, or I get all my work done anyway, or besides, everyone else is often late, too.

First of all, your employer doesn't want you to stay late. They'd rather you work the set hours of the day and anything you do beyond that is above and beyond their expectations. Besides, everything is set up, support-wise, for a set period of hours each day. Working late at night means you work without supervision, feedback, tech services, and so on. Second, the excuse that you get all your work done anyway proves that you could in fact be doing more work if you weren't late. Third, maybe other people are often late too, but you should assume that the problem is also being addressed to them. The bottom line is, worry about yourself and not what other people may or may not be getting away with. If you've been asked to correct your lateness, get the message the first time.

Employee lateness can be such an issue that one studio even resorted to creating a morning meeting scheduled fifteen minutes before the start of each day. Attendance of the early meeting was mandatory and after the cutoff time, the door to the room was closed. Any stragglers had to open the door and show their shamed face before the group while squeezing between tight rows of occupied chairs. One late arrival led to a warning. Two late arrivals meant dismissal. If more people could get the message the first time, extreme measures like this wouldn't be considered necessary.

Tuning In to All the Messages

Some of us have the tendency to hear what we want to hear and discard everything else. It's called selective listening. An extreme example of this scenario is the story of a terrific animator who blew all his deadlines while working on a TV series. The production was run very loosely with little to no consequences for late or unfinished work. In this environment, the animator, despite the fact that he always missed his deadlines, was promoted to a lead animator position. In his new role, the animator was supposed to not only finish his work but also take on work to help others. Instead, he always needed bailing out himself. His work had to be given away to other animators to finish time and time again.

For a while things continued this way, but like many long-running productions, the standards and procedures changed. Less than a year later, the production tightened its process and increased its expectations of each animator, and especially for the lead animators. This lead animator was warned verbally and then in written form to speed up many times over a period of a year and a half. The expectations were made clear, yet the results were still always out of reach. Generously, the production gave the lead animator a seemingly inexhaustible amount of chances to improve. In the end, the senior staff had to admit defeat.

Following a brief production hiatus, the lead animator's contract was not renewed when work began on the next season. The lead animator was stunned. The only message that had gotten through was the promotion he received a year and a half earlier. He had tuned everything else out, with major consequences.

Another lesson that can be learned from this experience is a lesson for management. Not everyone can fit our expectations. Some can do pretty spectacular work, like the case of the lead animator above. A smart and fast-reacting production should be able to find a way to work with such an animator to everyone's benefit. If the issue is one of speed, why not use such an animator in a freelance capacity where he is paid on a flat rate and given only the amount of work he can handle within a set schedule. Management has to get the message, too.

It's a given that communication on the job will not always be perfect. Yet, we should strive to understand each other sooner rather than later. Problems tend not to solve themselves. Like a marriage, a good working relationship can take effort. There is an automatic obligation on both sides of a message (the part of the communicator and the receiver) to make it succeed.

I've Got No Strings: The Life of an Independent Animation Artist

"I firmly believe that there will soon be nothing else left for an independent animator to do but to initiate their own projects, which means that the new generation of animation artists should pay attention to learning other survival skills than how to start or join a studio. They should learn social and interrelationship skills, and how to become a keen observer of the world both close by and very far away. The pursuit of originality should be of greater value than the scheming of clever strategies of one-upmanship."
—Paul Fierlinger, independent animator

Still from Paul Fierlinger's A Room Nearby. *Courtesy of the artist. I would describe Fierlinger as an animator's animator. If anyone is doing animation truly for adults, then this is it.*

O f all the career paths in animation, perhaps the most romantic is the notion of the truly independent filmmaker. However, the term independent is a problematic one. If we're going to get anywhere with this chapter we need to first establish ground rules for the term "independent." We can agree that independent animators make some of their yearly income profiting from personal projects. It is also agreed that even the world's best known independent animator, Bill Plympton, takes on commercial or sponsored work to help fund his personal projects.

For Plympton to cut off this source of money would be to cut off his cartoon nose to spite his cartoon face. So, when we talk about the "independent animation filmmaker," we must be referring to a sort of creative independence. Bill Plympton makes the films Bill Plympton wants to make. He answers to outside influences only on his terms. On his personal projects, Plympton is truly creatively independent. Still, gray areas creep in. Bill Plympton runs a studio. He employs a staff that makes some degree of artistic contributions to his independent work. As an independent filmmaker, he is beholden to others in a variety of ways. For instance, on his feature, *Hair High*, the background paintings were assigned out to various artists. In addition, Plympton has frequently collaborated with musicians Hank Bones and Maureen McElheron, who have written songs and scores for most of his films.

"Hair High"   Bill Plympton ©2003

Still from Bill Plympton's fourth fully animated independent feature film, Hair High. *Courtesy of the artist.*
John R. Dilworth on Bill Plympton: "Is he not our God?"

At the end of an interview I did with Oscar-nominated independent animator Michael Sporn, he asked a question to himself that I hadn't asked: How dependent are you on others? This was his answer: "It would have been impossible to do what I've done without some enormously helpful and faithful people. There were a number of folks who worked their butts off for my projects, and I'm totally, completely, wholly grateful to them. I am my films, but my films would not have been anything without the brilliant work of a lot of other artists."

Still from Michael Sporn's Champaign, *which takes the animated film to often unexplored territory to tackle a serious subject: Champaign, a young girl whose mother went to jail for committing murder.*

Okay, so we know that while independents may be making the films they want to make, it doesn't mean that they work completely alone or without creative influence from others. So, the term "independent" is really a matter of how much and how often. In my animation career to date, I've produced an independent animated film of my own every two years. While that sounds like a lot, it has really only been a partial commitment in my life, taking third and fourth place to the priorities of a full-time job, freelance work, and (most importantly) time with family and friends.

There are many other animation artists, like me, who are part-time independent filmmakers. There are far fewer independents, like Bill Plympton, who have forged a unique voice in filmmaking while making a total commitment to their own brand identity. By comparison to most of us part-timers, the independents covered in this chapter seem all the more heroic for their devotion. Whether that entrepreneurial spirit is in us or not, there is still much we can learn from the creative examples and business models outlined in this chapter. Our hats off to the independent spirit.

ORIGIN STORIES

"I found that when I made my first film, *Your Face*, which was nominated for an Oscar in 1987, it made a lot of money. I thought, 'Wow, this is great! I don't need to work for Disney or Warner Bros. I could work for me and still make a living.' It is possible to make a living doing independent films. Besides, I had made a living as a freelance illustrator for fifteen years before that. That was a similar lifestyle, but now it's moving drawings instead of still ones."
—*Bill Plympton, independent animator*

Elvis wasn't born The King and neither are animation artists born independent animation filmmakers. Most of them have cut their teeth working for years in the animation industry or other related commerical arts fields. Like

Still from Debra Solomon's multi-award winning first film Mrs. Matisse. *Courtesy of the artist. Mr. Matisse, eat your heart out.*

Bill Plympton, Debra Solomon had decades of success as an illustrator before making her first sequential animated drawings. Stop motion wunderkind PES labored for years in advertising, acquainting himself with short, punchy films that hold your attention.

PES on How He Got Started as an Independent

PES is quickly becoming one of the world's most sought-after directors and stop motion filmmakers. PES's success owes as much to his talents as a filmmaker as it does to his marketing savvy. But, before I spoil all the fun, I'll let PES explain how he got started, himself:

"I shot my first film when I was twenty-five. It was live-action and it was a short film, precisely forty-eight seconds long. It was more like a commercial than a traditional short film, with fast-paced editing and a surprise ending.

"I spent seven hundred dollars on it and called in lots of post-production favors. I had to figure it out from the ground up. I wrote it, directed it, produced it, cast it, did the costumes, built models to create my own effects in-camera and I even borrowed a 16mm camera to shoot it. My goal was to discover, in a relatively low-risk scenario, whether or not I enjoyed the process of making a film enough to continue doing it.

"At the time I was working in a large advertising agency in New York City. It was my first job after college. I was a 'creative assistant,' in other words, a glorified secretary, to an ad executive on the creative side. This meant I had gotten my foot in the door in a fun place to work, but that was about it. I was at the bottom of the totem pole. My days were spent doing menial tasks like booking flights and making popcorn in the reception area. Stuff you could do with your eyes closed. But at least I was getting paid, and I had lots of time to devote to developing some of my own ideas.

"The advertising agency was great for many things, one of which was resources. There were people, machines, tape stock, and tens of thousands of dollars worth of goods and services.

"Another interesting thing about being in the advertising agency creative department was that I was surrounded by creative content from all over the world: commercials, short films, music videos, print advertisements, and posters. I looked at everything in my spare time and was definitely influenced by it. I was drawn to the short storytelling format of commercials. A simple idea, you're in and you're out. Leave a viewer with a thought, make them laugh, but more than anything: get their attention. Show them something they'll never forget. The big lesson I learned from advertising is that short can be powerful.

"After I made my first film (the forty-eight second *Dogs of War*) I promoted it to advertising press sources. I slapped a logo on the end and called it a "spec commercial," a term used in advertising to refer to commercials that were not commissioned but are useful in getting a director paying work within the industry. The press ate my film up, even though it wasn't a commissioned job.

Still from PES's breakthrough stop motion short, Roof Sex. *Image courtesy of the artist. Don't try this on your roof.*

"Calls from agents and commercial production companies looking for up-and-coming directors started coming in: What else do you have? And when can I see it? What's your next project? Can you send me your reel? Unfortunately I had only those forty-eight seconds to my name.

"I planned my next films. The second was another live-action short film shot in a desert that could also function as a 'spec commercial.' I called this idea *Whittlin' Wood.* The third film was a little idea about two chairs that have sex on a New York City rooftop. It was to be an animation with objects. Two life-size chairs would need to be moved inch-by-inch on a real rooftop. I knew immediately I had to quit my job in order to make these films because I would need lots of time to shoot the second one, *Roof Sex.* On top of that I had to teach myself how to animate.

"I took out eight credit cards and quit my job. This was a scary leap, but necessary for me. It was the moment I placed all my faith in myself and my own ideas."

THE INDEPENDENT ANIMATED FEATURE FILM

"My long-term goal is to make a feature film. While I'm doing that I'd like to build a body of short films."
—*Pat Smith, independent animator*

Perhaps the earliest best known independently made animated feature film was Lotte Reiniger's *The Adventures of Prince Achmed* (Germany, 1926). But, for sheer body of work, nobody can touch Ralph Bakshi, who created a string of nine animated feature films beginning with the groundbreaking *Fritz the Cat* (1972). Bakshi's achievements are all the more remarkable because his films scored distribution deals with the major studios. Also, Bakshi was making feature films before the days of computers, which have since led to quicker and cheaper production models. With the accessibility of cheap technology, it's a wonder that we still haven't yet seen a boom in the production of independent animated feature films. Perhaps, even with the falling costs, the still somewhat slow production flow and limited distribution potential stifle the possibilities for the time being. Still, it seems like only a matter of time before indie animation features pop up the way indie live-action features have since the advent of the digital camera.

Until then, indy hero Bill Plympton remains one of the few examples of an independent animator building up an impressive roster of feature productions. Plympton described his transition from making short subjects to feature films at an ASIFA-East event on the making of *Hair High*:

Independent animator Pat Smith at the drawing board. Photo courtesy of the artist. Smith is committed to finishing a new independent animated film every year and a half.

"I started doing feature films in 1990 with *The Tune*. Feature films were something I've wanted to do since I was a kid and saw Disney feature films. I always thought that was something that was a corporate affair. You need a lot of money, talent, and time. I found out in the late eighties that you didn't have to be in Hollywood to make a feature film. People like Spike Lee were making independent films right here in New York. I was inspired by that and realized that I could make feature films by myself. Another inspiration was my 1989 collection of short films. As I put it together I realized that I did over an hour of animation in four or five years. If I could do that, I could probably do a feature.

"My feature films haven't been that successful. In fact, dollar for dollar, my shorts have made much more money. But, the feature films bring a certain amount of respect or branding. After I finished *Mutant Aliens* I started work on *Hair High*. The whole process of writing this film took about a year. During that time I was doing concept, character, and background sketches.

Bill Plympton, the most celebrated independent animator in the world. Photo courtesy of the artist.

"Martha Plympton, a distant relative of mine, and I were hanging out and I told her I was having trouble getting my films distributed because there were no big (voice) names involved. She asked around to see if there was anyone she knew that would want to work with me. We ended up with a really good cast: Ed Begley Jr., Beverly D'Angelo, David Carradine, and Sarah Silverman.

"The whole process took two and a half years: a year to write, a year to draw, and half a year for post-production. The budget for this feature was $400,000. You try to get people to work for you as cheap as you can. My budget breakdown for *Hair High* was:

- ✦ My duties (I do a lot of work myself to keep the budget light): Director, animator, character designer, storyboard artist/layouts/screenwriter.

- ✦ Backgrounds: $100 per BG—$20,000

- ✦ Voice-overs: Used Screen Actors Guild actors—$20,000

- ✦ Cel painters: $100,000

- ✦ Camera: $50,000

- ✦ Cels, stock, and supplies: $80,000

- ✦ Editing: $20,000

- ✦ Music: $15,000

BRANDING AND PROMOTION

In the wrong hands, an independent animated film is an expensive paperweight. In the right hands, the film is a calling card shouting out your name, brandishing your reputation, and blazing a trail of success beyond your wildest expectations. PES explains why branding and promotion are so important to the independent filmmaker: "If you have something new to say, it's only half the job to make it: you have to get it out there. Otherwise, you don't give it a chance to have an impact and you lose out on the opportunity to experience any benefit the film may bring you. Promotion is a very important part of the equation.

"This weird thing happens when people get familiar with your work. For better or for worse, people start seeing you as a kind of brand: your taste, the ideas you have, the way you tell a story, the pacing you set. This is your fingerprint. People latch onto your name as a symbol that stands for the combined identity of all these things. 'Have you heard of this guy, PES? Oh, he's the guy who did that Nike thing,' or 'Oh, the chair guy,' or 'that's very PES,' stuff like that. I believe it's very important for artists to carve out their identities in the marketplace, really develop a distinct voice. When advertising, music video, television, and film people know about you, they not only enjoy your films but they also keep you in mind for future commissioned projects. Unless you have a trust fund and/or are happy getting paid outside the industry, this is valuable turf for you. Do not underestimate the value here. It's only a matter of time before they bite."

DISTRIBUTION STORIES

Nobody makes a film intending for it to sit on the shelf, but that is where many end up. How do independent filmmakers get their work out there so it can be seen and recognized by their peers and potential clients? We are talking about distribution here and films are generally distributed the following ways, via:

✦ The Internet on sites such as Atomfilms.com

✦ Personal Web sites

✦ Film festival screenings

✦ Representatives: companies, or individuals that rep your film for a set contracted percentage fee and length of time.

✦ Self-distribution: self publishing on DVD

Xeth Feinberg pioneered Internet animation with his Bulbo *cartoons, pictured here. Image courtesy of the artist.*

Web toon pioneer Xeth Feinberg explains how he has utilized the Internet to secure distribution and receive income from his shorts: "As an independent animator and cartoonist with a background in CD-ROM animation, at the dawn of the new millennium I had been mastering the potential of Macromedia Flash (the miraculous little computer application that makes Web toons possible) for a bit over a year—which practically made me a wizened old expert in the field.

"In 1999 I was already making my pseudo–silent era black and white *Bulbo* films, cutting my teeth on a series of children's interactive storybook Web toons, and creating the first more or less fully animated Web toon series for Scifi.com, *The Existential Adventures of Astro-Chimp*. I also did enough other freelance Flash production work to have learned a lot about how not to efficiently produce Web toons. I worked solo and was able to turn out a finished 'Webisode' in a week or less. All this work was getting seen, and though I was making a living at it, Web animation still seemed more like a fluke than a career.

"At the start of 2000 things started heating up. New Web portals and 'destination sites' were being touted (and funded) as the 'next television.' Because Flash animation files (unlike video) were small enough to be easily viewed by the average Web surfer, demand for them exploded.

"Infamous, never-was pop.com wanted to get *Bulbo* cartoons on their site. Luckily, currently existing San Francisco–based Mondomedia.com presented a more intriguing Web toon syndication plan that also preserved all my rights while providing production funds upfront. (I was frankly lucky in signing the *Bulbo* deal in the summer, when the world of Web toons was still near its peak.) By 2001, the well-documented dotcom meltdown had clobbered Web animation along with many of the entertainment sites that sponsored it.

"In some ways, the Web animation scene has come full circle. Just like in 1999 there's still work and opportunity out there but the crazy boomtown mentality is gone, at least for now. If you got into Web animation like I did, as a way to make your own stuff cheaply, creatively, with minimal outside interference, taking advantage of the Web's miraculous worldwide distribution system, then there's still a lot to be excited about."

PES's primary method of distribution is self-distribution via his personal Web site, eatpes.com. PES explains: "An early important decision I made was to create a Web site where my films could have a home. Sarah Phelps, then my girlfriend (now my wife), was key in this process. She learned basic HTML and we put it up ourselves in a couple of weeks. I called it EatPES.com, and I offered my films up for free. The idea was to do something simple, focusing on the work. On my Web site I posted my short animations along with *Roof Sex*. *Roof Sex* drew thousands of people to my site instantly, since it already had a life of its own.

"Traffic on my site began to climb over the following months, completely by word of mouth. People came to the site looking for *Roof Sex* and discovered a body of work, lots of ideas, and executions. Films I had made two years before were now seen in the context of everything else I had made. This is very valuable to people out there because you suddenly leap from being a one-hit wonder in the public's eye to an artist with a particular style and distinct point of view. This 'fingerprint' is really the most valuable asset you have. It's what makes people want to work with you."

Animation festivals can be called the lifeline of the independent animation filmmaker, providing opportunities for films and filmmakers to get noticed. If we were brick layers, we'd all attend the annual Brick Layer Jamboree (if there was such a thing). As animation artists, our people can be found at animation festivals! Festivals provide a common ground and point in time in which filmmakers from all over the world can gather to share ideas, inspiration, and complaints. To the independent animator, festival play can lead to distribution deals, funding to complete projects, and commercial job offers. Not surprisingly, festivals play the most important role in Bill Plympton's career: "For me, most of my money comes from selling the films to the markets in the different countries. The buyers go to the major film fests such as Toronto, Sundance, and Annecy. I go to these fests partially as a business opportunity."

For independent animator Michael Sporn, festivals have an allure because they are generally the only place his films can be seen on a big screen. "In the early days it made a large impact. Lately, festivals have become too political and it's gotten harder to get into them. Film production has gone way up and the festivals are inundated, so it's understandable." Sporn continues, "A bigger part of the festivals, now, is the conference part. You meet up and

Still from Michael Sporn's recent short, The Man Who Walked Between Two Towers. *Image courtesy of the artist and Weston Woods.*

reacquaint with others you haven't seen in a while. It's important to communicate with others about the art."

For PES, festival success was fast and furious: "Annecy 2002 is when my life started to change. *Roof Sex* took a top prize for best first film at Annecy. Overnight it became one of the most talked about films in the world. When we returned home to New York the fax machine was flooded with papers and my first instinct was, 'What the hell happened here?' But it turned out to be licensing agreements for *Roof Sex*. Television stations all over the world had seen *Roof Sex* at Annecy and wanted to run it. Better yet, they were offering to pay. I was dazzled by the requests; there was a genuine desire out there for short content. It confirmed everything I had been feeling when I first decided that short and memorable was the way to go."

PES on the set of his short, Roof Sex. *Image courtesy of the artist.*

Some filmmakers use representatives; companies or individuals that rep their films for a set contracted percentage fee and length of time. Independent animator John Canemaker has found successful film distribution through Phoenix Films, Bernice Coe, Charles Samu, Jane Balfour, and most recently on DVD by Milestone/Image Entertainment. "So I have made money over the years, but I really don't know how much. The films were never made for money anyway, but for my own personal expression and satisfaction," says Canemaker.

You might think that success and recognition should make it easier for established filmmakers, like Bill Plympton, to secure future distribution deals. As Plympton tells it, it isn't necessarily so: "I always thought the distribution deals on films such as *Mutant Aliens*, which was a pretty big success, would carry over to the next films. We took a trailer with press kits and went to Sundance and showed *Hair High* to a lot of distributors and they really liked the project. IFC Films was interested. We thought we'd get some money to

Still from John Canemaker's Oscar-winning autobiographical film The Moon and The Son. *Image courtesy of the artist. In addition to his films, Canemaker is a successful author of many animation books as well as being a professor and director of the animation program at New York University Tisch School of the Arts.*

start it off and pay some of the bills, but none of it came through. We only got one pre-sale in France. They gave us some money for pre-production."

Plympton continues, "Over the years I've learned things to look out for and be aware of and afraid of. I think one of the things you should be aware of is if someone buys the rights to show your film and they don't release it within a year, you should get the rights back. They may have paid you some money, but it's very disappointing to not have your film out there. Before making a deal with someone, ask who else they've made deals with. Then call those people up to get feedback. Did the company pay their bills and honor their agreements? If they are a reputable company they will give you names of their clients. Also it's good to be a member of ASIFA. In ASIFA, there are a lot of other animators that you can confide in. Ask them, what's a fair price for a film?"

Independent animator Breehn Burns, of Lone Sausage Productions, self-distributes his films via self-publishing on DVD: "We put out shorts and DVDs on a strict schedule of whenever we get around to it. My first experiences in animation were directing a couple of independent films and then animating at Nick Jr.'s *Little Bill* for a year before launching into the realm of pitches and pilots which, for me, amounted to hours and months and years of

my work sitting on some executive's desk somewhere with a sticky note on top reading, 'maybe.' I realized that if I kept going at that pace, nobody real would ever actually see my work. So instead of pitches I make short films, instead of TV deals I make DVDs."

One of the most interesting success stories in independent distribution resulted from a coming together of various independents. Maybe we should call them, in this case, "co-dependents." It all began when eleven independent animators met in a large Chelsea artists' loft in New York City. Eleven went in, *Avoid Eye Contact* came out. *Avoid Eye Contact* is a DVD containing some of the best independent films from New York City's thriving animation scene. This DVD is the first product of an inspired group of artists, whose vision goes even further.

The poster from Here Comes Dr. Tran *from Breehn Burns, Lone Sausage Productions. Image courtesy of the artist.*

On *Avoid Eye Contact*, young animators joined seasoned masters in the unique program. Included were legendary animators such as George Griffin and Academy Award nominees Bill Plympton and John R. Dilworth. These masters were accompanied by industry heavyweights such as John Schnall and Patrick Smith, and the latest up-and-coming animators like Mike Overbeck and Jesse Schmal.

In addition to the films, each artist contributed making-of documentaries, commentary, or pencil tests, giving the viewer a rare insight into the artist's thoughts and methods.

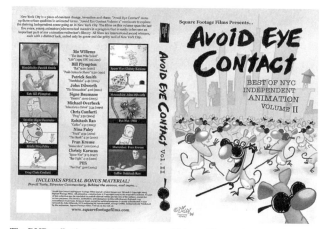

The DVD collection Avoid Eye Contact Volume II *contains some of the best independent films from New York City's thriving animation scene. Don't avoid this DVD! Image courtesy of Square Footage Films.*

Beyond the art form, *Avoid Eye Contact* is truly visionary in terms of commercial distribution. Animator and contributor Signe Baumane states, "The entire production of this DVD has been done by the animators themselves." She continues, "The look and quality of this volume would not have been possible without the animators taking complete control." The artist-run Web site www.squarefootagefilms.com features in-depth information about each animator, as well as a convenient online store for purchasing the DVD and other products. The animators have named their distribution hub Square Footage Films, an ode to the perpetual plight of animators cranking out animation by the foot on studio jobs, and have already garnered several other distribution deals world-

wide. "Obviously it would take more than one DVD to survey the best of New York animation," adds Baumane. "We've recently released Volume II, and are preparing three other animation compilations right now."

Why New York? Animator and *Avoid Eye Contact* contributor John R. Dilworth answers, "I need New York City. It's a cynical place. It's a skeptical place. I guess I'm tuned into that."

Still from John R. Dilworth's The Mousochist. *Image courtesy of the artist. This gem is available on* Avoid Eye Contact *Volume II.*

New York City contains the world's largest, most prominent, innovative, and successful group of independent animation filmmakers. There, a close-knit community has formed, fueled by small screenings, studio visits, local festivals, social events, and by the monthly events presented by ASIFA-East.

BILL PLYMPTON'S THREE RULES FOR SUCCESS AND WHAT MAKES A BREAKTHROUGH SHORT BREAKTHROUGH?

With two Academy Award nominations to date, four independent, fully animated feature films, and numerous screenings of his work on television and at festivals under his belt, Bill Plympton knows a thing or two about being a successful independent. Go to an international festival such as Ottawa or Annecy and you'll see how Plympton's reputation goes way beyond these shores, ensuring his place as the world's leading independent animation filmmaker. To help us capture some of that lightning in a bottle, Plympton offers up his three rules to follow to be a successful independent:

"One: Make short films (less than five minutes). It's weird to say, because I also do long feature films, but when you do short films you really have to make them short. For some reason ten, fifteen, or twenty minutes is very hard to sell. Film festivals don't want to show films that long. Theater owners don't want to show long short films. Buyers don't want to buy short films over five minutes. Why do a big opus short film when you can do a short film in half the time and it will be easier to sell?

"Two: Make them cheap. Keep the budget under $2,000 a minute. If you're gonna use a lot of fancy digital effects or fancy music it will be harder to make your money back.

"Three: Make them funny. I don't know why, but when people see animation they want to laugh. Certainly there are exceptions. A film like *Father Daughter* won an Oscar and was fourteen minutes or something and did a lot of sales. But, generally speaking, if you do a funny film it will be a lot easier to sell it. The classic example I bring up a lot is [Marv Newland's] *Bambi Meets Godzilla*. He did it in a weekend. There were twelve drawings in the film. It's a minute and a half. It cost five hundred dollars. It's gone on to make $100,000. It's still making money. It's in like every compilation."

If Plympton's three rules can be taken as a business plan to become a successful independent, what about the content of the films themselves? Just what is it that makes a breakthrough short breakthrough?

As veteran filmmaker Candy Kugel of Buzzco Associates, Inc., says, the recipe for a breakthrough short can be rather elusive: "Is it luck? Timing? The audience? We don't know if we've made our 'breakthrough short,' since they're all different. *A Warm Reception in L.A.* premiered at Annecy in 1987 where it was in the last half of the last showing. We got no feedback from it at the time, and, although we liked the film and were proud of it, it took a few more festivals before we heard the compliments. When I was at Annecy two years later, I

Still from Buzzco Associates, Inc., short A Warm Reception in L.A. *Image courtesy of the artist.*

kept on being introduced as the director of the 'classic' short, *Warm Reception!* Since all the films are different in style, tone, and message, we have had a variety of successes and failures and at this point I'm not sure what it is that compels us to continue making films since both recognition and prizes seem so unpredictable and quirky. Don't get me wrong, they're nice, but they can't be the motivation for making a film."

Michael Sporn adds, "A short has to entertain an audience for it to break through. Usually, if you try to do this, it doesn't work. If you have fun making it, the audience can usually tell, and this comes back in some success. An Oscar nomination for my short *Doctor DeSoto* brought a lot of international success, but not the most pleasure in the end. *The Hunting of the Snark*, which still hasn't been sold to television, and *The Marzipan Pig* are my favorite films to watch over again."

INDEPENDENT PROJECTS. COMMERCIAL RESULTS.

There are many good and obvious reasons to make your own films. Having this creative outlet allows you to put the commercial work you do in perspective and helps you establish an individual identity in the industry. Ironically, an independent film, which often comes from a very personal place within the soul, can have very outwardly commercial results.

Bill Plympton recalls immediate commercial success from his first short, *Your Face*: "My first Oscar nomination made me, all of a sudden, very desirable for the ad agencies, and for three years I was inundated with commercials, and invited to festivals."

Candy Kuglel and Vincent Cafferelli, of Buzzco Associates, Inc., were asked by clients to replicate the look of their independent film *Snowie and the 7 Dorps*, which became the CTW series *The Further Adventures of Zook and Alison*. Another Buzzco film, *Nothing at All*, became an anti-smoking PSA. Designer Dagan Moriarty has had a similar experience: "Clients tend to respond to your own work, I think, because it comes straight from the heart. You are showing the uncensored version of your work, what you think it should look like. People really notice it, and want to get some of that into their own projects, so they hire you!" Independent animator John Serpentelli adds, "With the freedom of making an independent film, you can explore approaches and techniques that can become an invaluable resource for doing commissioned work."

Michael Sporn has created his own unique blend of the independent and the commercial: "I feel no difference between the independent shorts and the commercial shorts I do. They all have a place in my heart or I wouldn't work on them. They all have thoughts to deliver and something to see. Animating them is the fun part. Independent projects are the only reason for being in this business. Fortunately, I've been able to do a lot of self-initiated jobs for clients. Francis Ford Coppola did *The Godfather* as a job and *The Conversation* as a personal film. He cared for both equally."

Commercial results aside, John R. Dilworth felt compelled to make independent shorts: "I just needed to do them because I fell in love with the independent filmmakers from the seventies and eighties. I really believed in the art, but I also wanted to be famous. I believed that animation was a special vehicle in which to communicate ideas and I still do. You make films to learn how to make films. I don't know how to do them still! When you're making a film you're not deliberately saying 'this is what I'm going to explore.' The problem in my animation is that it is too much attached to my own life. Of my commercial work, the only thing that I can say that is close to my life in a personal way is my *Courage the Cowardly Dog* series. In *Courage* I was able to explore a lot of themes . . . and we did it so rapidly! How many short films can you make? What an opportunity!"

Pat Smith's successful independent films enabled him to secure two representatives, who have been able to consistently land him commercial work.

Animation drawings I made for a film with Dale Clowdis called Scout Says. *Image courtesy of the artist. This independent project helped me land two jobs: one, a sheet-timing job on a pilot, and the other, a directing job on a series.*

INDIES FOR DUMMIES

"On independent films you give *yourself* a deadline . . . it could be flexible to some degree, but if you don't give yourself a deadline you could work forever on something . . . or never start it. But it's hard to finish. You can start something, but how do you keep going? That's one thing I'm proud of. I can do that."
—*John R. Dilworth, independent animator and creator of* Courage the Cowardly Dog, *Cartoon Network*

I've noticed a trend. Most folks that make independent animated films do so because it's in their system. Chances are they start experimenting with animation early in life, before film or art school. These are the filmmakers who were making films (or something quite like films) before there was a grade attached to it. It's easy to see how these folks go on to make their own independent productions in their post-school years.

After talking to many independent filmmakers over the years and going through the struggles myself, I thought I'd round up some helpful hints that

Still from John R. Dilworth's independent film, Life in Transition. *Image courtesy of the artist.*

might give you a leg-up in sticking with a project and making it as smartly as you can. The list below focuses mostly on the rigors of making a narrative film, but I think much of this would still be applicable to experimental work.

Work Smart!

If you've got a traditional narrative film, do an outline, thumbnail sketches, a board, and an animatic. In short: follow a production process. As you move forward to the meat of the project, employ studio techniques such as numbering your drawings and organizing your scenes in folders.

Make Your Project Doable!

When I was at the School of Visual Arts, there was a fellow student who was going to make the *Citizen Kane* of animation. He was going to get smoke bombs and fire under an oxberry to help pull off the realism needed for his twenty minute opus. All of this, before he knew how to animate a bouncing ball. Guess what? The film was never made and the student vanished from the animation department altogether. Keep your project manageable (the longer your project will take you, the less likely it is that you will be able to see it through). Life has a way of throwing up obstacles.

Know When to Say "When!"

Remember the classic Walter Lantz short in which Smedley the dog kept offering Chilly Willy the penguin "more butter . . . more syrup" on his pancakes? Well, Chilly didn't know when to say "when," but you can. Since, ultimately, you're the one you're trying to please, you must also be the voice of reason and be able to move on after completing something. You could work on something in one stage forever, so set your standard or goal for a particular phase and recognize when you've reached it. Also, film festival deadlines work as great incentives to complete your film by a certain date.

Utilize Your Natural Improvement Curve When Working
Unless you are Michelangelo, chances are, you will have room for improvement and will get better as you go. So, avoid the trap of having to redo all your previous work by not working start to finish. Work this way all through production (even in stages like inking or creating backgrounds), and you will end up with a much more unified piece.

Collaborate with Others to Improve Your Production
Just because you can do everything yourself doesn't necessarily mean that it would be best for your production. On the same note, don't do your own voice-over work unless you are the best possible choice. I can do as many funny voices as the next guy, but that doesn't make me an actor. When you animate to a great voice track it gives you lots of ideas for the animation. Remember, you can't hang a good performance on a bad track.

Show Your Work to a Circle of Friends at Each Stage of Production
Make sure these friends are professionals whom you respect, not your family cat or your hairstylist. Your circle of friends will have a fresh eye that only distance can ensure. Chances are they can find areas that you may have taken

for granted in being so close to your project, although not everything you hear will be useful to you or in the direction you want to go. Don't forget that you're still making *your* film. You don't want to end up with a film made by committee.

Use the "Little Elves" Production Style
I think many projects get abandoned when one realizes the huge amount of work required to complete a film. It can be very daunting. However, if you whittle away at it for a few hours, a few nights a week, you'll be surprised by how much you can accomplish. I call it the "little elves" production style because the next day, when you look at last night's work, it

An animation drawing from my animated film seems like little elves must have worked on
Stand Clear, *which was written by Debbie* it through the night. If real little elves
Staab and Cara Cosentino. The film, although actually show up in your apartment, con-
only running a little over a minute, was created tact an exterminator right away.
over a period of six months by lots of little elves.

Test the Specs of Your Finished Film Early On

Don't go too far in finishing your animation drawings until you do a small test. Ink a small scene and take it all the way through color and composite with a final background. Take careful note of what works and what doesn't.

Don't Listen to Hype About Better Software

It's common to hear, "You could do your film faster in another program." Yet, you should do what works for you. While there are time savers around, animation is, by its very nature, a tedious and time-consuming thing. Exploring software or programs takes time too (not to mention additional expense). That may be a venture best undertaken when you're between projects. Then, you can start a project specifically to test your new software skills. I just blew your mind, didn't I?

Show Your Final Cut to an Editor Before Calling Your Film Finished

This is your last chance to get an objective and trained eye on your work in key areas like continuity, screen direction, pacing, etc. You're going to have to live with this film for the rest of your life, unless you're George Lucas. Speaking of Mr. Lucas, avoid the trap of wanting to go back and redo/revise your earlier works (student or otherwise). Your older works represent where you were at the time and there's nothing wrong with that. Now you are in a different place as a human being and a filmmaker. What will you gain by revisiting an old ghost? You have much more to gain by doing something new.

Collaborate with a Composer/ Sound Designer

This can be more or less critical depending on the nature of your film. But, usually you will benefit greatly by working with a pro to compose a score specially made for your film. Go to any animation festival and after a while you'll experience a feeling of disconnectedness watching the films on the screen. I suspect that occurs because a lot of filmmakers use public domain/library music in their films. It just doesn't support what's on the screen. Sound is half the experience. So much of the pathos, humor, storytelling, and drama will only come out with the correct score.

One of my animation drawings for the signal film Dale Clowids and I created to open the ASIFA-East animation festival, in which the music and sound design was provided, once again, by the fabulous Mr. Chris Jones.

Exploit Your Connections and Cash in Old Favors

In big Hollywood moviemaking, no one spends her own money. Our indie equivalent to that would be to develop mutually beneficial relationships with other craftspeople who can work on our projects for free or below cost. Hey, one day you'll help them too, right?

9 Surviving Unemployment

"Time off is actually a mixed blessing. In the beginning I used to think of it too much as being about whether money was coming in or not. But when you're in the midst of a production you often have too little time for some of the other things you also want to do, whether it's making an independent film or taking a trip. Over time I've learned better to plan ahead before a project finishes to make sure I get to do some of these things when I finally have the time!"

—Ray Kosarin, animation director, producer

 No matter what you call it— layoff, downtime, in-between jobs, sabbatical, hiatus—an animation artist is bound to experience multiple lags in employment. This chapter is like a sister to chapter 5, which can be read as preventive medicine to help ward off downtime, or at least reduce it by the following ideas:

Still from Ray Kosarin's independent film, Uncle. *Image courtesy of the artist.*

+ Initiate your own creative projects (films/paintings/sculptures, etc.) Not only can these projects open doors and opportunities to you, they can also help you avoid being creatively stereotyped.

+ Engage in self-promotion (Web sites/mailers/business cards, etc.).

+ Enhance your marketable skills; learn new software, improve your life drawing.

+ Take on freelance. The idea is to work when there is work.

+ Network: attend animation events, maintain connections, and make new ones.

+ Volunteer: Join up with volunteer animation organizations like ASIFA.

+ Build up your reels/portfolios on a weekly basis.

In an interview for this book, Ray Kosarin told me, "You can never change factors outside your control, such as how many shows the networks are looking to buy one year, or which ad agencies have lost which accounts." Toni Tysen added, "Most of the time you know how long projects will last, but the only downer is when a company pulls the plug on a production and you get no warning time to plan your next move." In the summer of 2005 an animated series for a major network was cancelled after eight months of production had been done. The animation crew was given one hour's notice to pack up their desks and leave. While these events are rare (I've only seen it happen twice) it does happen. On the other side of the coin, it is empowering to think how much you can control. You can control how much effort you put out there, where you focus that energy, and how it all pushes you forward into the career of your choice. As the old song goes, "Let the rest of the world go by."

One of the primary goals of this book is to paint careers in animation as realistically as possible. Realistically, you can expect to experience some amount of downtime sooner or later since much of the work in this industry is short-term freelance. For this business that's normal. Now try explaining that to friends and loved ones working outside of the field.

By November 2004, I had just been through a ten-month blitz of freelancing for five different clients on TV pilots, series, DVDs, and a feature film documentary. I worked many seven-day weeks and lots of late nights. At the end of this whirlwind of work, I landed a year-long directing gig, complete with health care benefits. A few weeks into this new job, I was having dinner with some old non-industry childhood friends. At dinner, they congratulated me on "finally" getting work. It was odd because the last ten months of freelance sure felt like work to me.

In the animation industry, we are gypsies going from job to job, sometimes town to town, or country to country. This year, all of us animation artists should make a point of educating at least one loved one about the nature of our careers.

DRY SPELLS

At the time of this writing, I have been working for ten consecutive years straight since my last "break," not even with one week between jobs. I thought that was a long run until animation director Jeff Buckland told me he was currently enjoying fifteen years in a row of steady work. Needless to say, Buckland and I will welcome our next breaks with a sigh of relief. So far, the downtime I have experienced was all within my first two years in the industry. During that time I was without work for a total of four and a half months. It's a given that there will be more periods of downtime in my future. On average, animation artists seem to spend one to three months out of the year unemployed. While this is a common average, there are many different reasons why downtime occurs. I asked some experts on downtime (typical animation artists) to find out how long they were unemployed and why.

For animation artist Rachel Peters, there were three major factors in her four months of non-work: "It began as a gamble with contracts. I ended one job when I could have gone on longer with that company, and likely eased into the next project, but I wanted to move on to something else that didn't pay, but gave me a great creative experience. I had been getting a decent amount of job offers up until then, so I took a chance and assumed it would be easy to jump back into work after my volunteer job was done. That was the first factor: gambling.

"The second factor: I didn't know Flash, and was quite defiant about learning it. I think there was a little bit of pride involved there. I was a snobby, purist, classical jerk. I was getting Flash offers, but didn't know the program (but I also didn't realize it would only take me a week to learn).

"The third factor: ethics. Halfway through my big dry spell, I got a couple of offers that would have been great, creative opportunities, but on very 'adult' shows. For my own reasons, and for the integrity of some of my other independent work, which screens at churches and summer camps, and is aimed at young teens who are, in their nature, very impressionable, I just couldn't have my

A still from Fran Krause's recent independent film, Moonraker. *No, it has nothing to do with 007. Get over it. Image courtesy of the artist.*

name show up in something like these late-night, cable, 'adult' shows. I had to make some tough decisions. So some of the lack of work was by choice."

Animation artist Amanda Lattrell experienced downtime as a result of moving from New York to Boston: "I was out of work for about three months and was learning how to use Flash while waiting for something to open up at one of the two animation studios in Watertown."

Animator and cartoonist Nina Paley is planning to be primarily unemployed for the next two years to free up time to work on her as-yet unfunded feature, *Sita Sings the Blues*: "Who's afraid of debt (gulp!)? Right now I'm living on savings from last year, when I had a lot of good freelance work. I hope to raise money for *Sita* in the near future. Maybe grants, maybe investors. Who knows? I intend to make my movie even if it means debt. Also, I will take high-paying short jobs to fund my project, if any come my way."

Fran Krause, Danny Kimanyen, and Toni Tysen were among the many animation artists affected by the aftermath of the terrorist attacks on September 11, 2001 and their devastating blow to the economy. Krause recalls, "I think I went about ten months without significant work. There wasn't any work to be found. I survived off of savings and unemployment, and living very cheaply. It was my first big dry spell, so I had no idea that it would ever end."

Tysen's downtime lasted nine to ten months: "As far as I knew, there weren't any productions or even commercials that were being greenlit. It was basically a drought in the biz. I ate a lot of grilled cheese sandwiches and just stayed indoors so I wouldn't be tempted to spend money. I didn't really try looking outside of animation, thinking that some project would pop up sooner rather than later, of course not knowing that it would take nine months for things to turn around."

Kimanyen adds, "Most of the productions in town were already halfway through the season. When it's like that the production is pretty much tightly weaved and there are no openings."

Ray Kosarin wisely notes that downtime is unfortunately part and parcel of this industry. "In bad times, I've gone several months without a project, and in good times I've had to juggle overlapping jobs. In lean years you may go months at a stretch without a project, and other times work several years at a time on one series without a break."

USING THE TIME OFF EFFECTIVELY

My second dry spell lasted three and a half months and came during the worst possible time: My job suddenly ended with only a two-day notice. Happily, I was eligible for unemployment. Unfortunately, the unemployment office put a hold on my claim and as a result, I didn't get any checks from them until two months later. The layoff hit two days after moving into my first apartment. On top of everything else it was my birthday and just days later the girl I was seeing dumped me. Oh, and I burned the roof of my mouth on some hot pizza and for a few minutes it was really uncomfortable.

Each week I went on several informational interviews and the timing was always terrible. Positions had either recently been filled or studios were just finishing projects. My only salvation was in working on a personal film, my first post-school project, *Snow Business.* Each day I'd wake up at eight and be hard at work on my film by ten in the morning. Working on the film gave me something productive to do between making calls and appointments for more interviews. The film also provided me with fresh samples to show.

In a job interview you inevitably get asked what you're working on now. *Snow Business* allowed me to answer that I was working on my own independent film project. That sounds a lot better than saying that you're waking up at noon and munching potato chips while watching *Oprah.* However good it sounded to mention my own film, it felt even better to do the work. It was the perfect way to keep my skills up while getting a psychological boost in morale. Animator and cartoonist Nina Paley agrees, "Make a film. Or do something else creative that you love. There's making a living, and then there's living. Making art is living. Self-initiated independent films have been virtually my entire career."

Still from Nina Paley's feature film Sita Sings the Blues. *Image courtesy of the artist.*

Toni Tysen uses downtime as means of picking away at her film project little by little, although she has additional plans for the future: "I may look into taking classes in a different medium to get me thinking in a different direction."

Initiating your own film project is only one of the many ways that you could use time off as effectively as possible. For instance, animator Amanda Lattrell learned a new software: "I knew I wouldn't have trouble getting an animation job once I learned Flash, so after that I started focusing on my illustration skills and did my own artwork."

Ray Kosarin strongly recommends setting up a Web site, which, more and more, will come to represent your first contact with a prospective employer or client.

Animator Mira Scharf advised, "Many friends of mine have had the experience where they had taken studio tests (like an animation or story board test) during a non-hiring period only to get called months later for the job."

NETWORKING

Networking is like your own shadow; you can't escape it. Chapter 10 covers networking from top to bottom, but we'll do a quick review because networking is something that should be done year 'round, in times of work and times of unemployment. Since the most effective networking happens all year long you should not wait until you are unemployed to begin. Ray Kosarin adds, "Probably the best precaution you can take is consistently to follow up your contacts so that more of your legwork has already been done when it is time to land the next job." Animation artist Danny Kimanyen agrees, "I maintain relations with people even when I'm working, which is very important; people usually get a job and disappear. That definitely doesn't work for me. I also always let people know if I'm interested in a project; if you don't tell people then how are they supposed to know?" Downtime affords us the luxury of having time available to devote to networking. Why not get creative and have some fun experimenting in new ways of self-promotion? There will never be a better time to try something new.

Rachel Peters got inspired by treating finding her job, through networking, as her job: "I had a lot of fun marketing myself, mailing creative things to companies, fine-tuning the art of being memorable but not annoying. If anything, some companies wanted to interview me just to talk to me, whether they had work or not. That was fun, and it built some relationships. You never know when that will come in handy in the future. And, if not for a job, new friends are nice, too."

Animator Fran Krause recommends networking through animation organizations: "ASIFA has kept me from going stir-crazy by providing job leads and good friends. I think just meeting people that you can find work from in the future is a good idea." Toni Tysen agrees, "On one or more occasion, an employer has recognized my name through said organization, and this helped give me a leg up on my competition. You never know who's hiring."

Perhaps the most fun networking suggestion comes from Mira Scharf: "Some friends and I once had a big party since we were unemployed and had the time. It turned out to be a great networking event and some people found jobs."

Rachel Peters did the occasional minimum wage "normal" jobs to get by, sold some artwork, and worked at a donut shop for one and a half days, before quitting to go to an animation studio's Christmas party, where she found her next animation job: "I wouldn't advise that people quit their 'normal' jobs for animation parties. This just happened to work for me."

Still from animator Mira Scharf. Courtesy of the artist.

Downtime is something you shouldn't experience alone. Networking keeps you close to the action, which is not only helpful mentally, but can also help you land your next gig.

UNEMPLOYMENT INSURANCE

"Never gotten unemployment. I've never worked anywhere long enough."
Nina Paley, animator, cartoonist

Unemployment insurance is a lot like the social security benefits we'll get upon retirement. It's nice to know it's there, but it's tough to live on it exclusively. Unfortunately, the greater problem is one of eligibility. As we have discussed, animation artists work much of the time on a short-term, freelance basis. In order to be eligible for unemployment insurance, you must work in a staff position (with all the necessary taxes coming out of your paychecks each week) for a set amount of months in a row. As pointed out in chapter 5 of this book, wise animation artists take on extra work even in times when work is plentiful. They know that it is just a matter of time before another lull in employment comes along and the extra money earned today could make all the difference tomorrow.

It's in our best interest to keep our cost of living maintainable. Rachel Peters agrees, "I live in a city just outside Toronto, where rent is much lower. I live with roommates. I eat cheap. I buy clothes when my old ones have biodegraded off my body (I used to think I had a 'bohemian' look . . . but I've recently decided that it's more of a 'hobo' look), and I don't do fancy things like dye my hair or get manicures.

"Although there are things that I really enjoy buying, like old movies, toys, and Swiss Army knives, I don't buy a whole lot of stuff (there are only so many Swiss Army knives you can justify having at one time). I ride the bus. At one point (for no real reason, apart from my being weird) I was sleeping in a tree house, so being in a house is a luxury in itself. So, I'll survive. I'm trying my hardest to consciously lead the same lifestyle I did when I wasn't making much money. I don't want to get used to a lifestyle I can't maintain."

Danny Kimanyen sees unemployment as helping to buy him time until his next job comes around: "It also prevents me from tapping into my savings. If you play your cards right you can actually live off unemployment for a couple of months. I always figure that somewhere out there someone is surviving off of the same amount that I am getting for unemployment, so why can't I?" Toni Tysen was able to live off of unemployment as well, but warns, "I was able to live off it because I didn't have a family or other serious obligations. That would be a different story."

HOW TO PREVENT ANOTHER DRY SPELL

Preventative medicine doesn't always go down easy with some people. Some need to learn the hard way, when the chips are down for the first time. However, by then you're already dealing with the situation from a disadvantage. A career implies that there is some planning involved in our journey that goes beyond our job-to-job existence.

Ray Kosarin advises, "The best advice probably starts *before* you're out of work—which is to prepare for the downtime. Don't spend your entire paycheck like a sailor on furlough while you're working, but save some cushion. Update your reel or portfolio even before you absolutely need to look for your next gig, or you may find yourself caught out when you need to get samples together."

Once again, networking rears its head, this time as Rachel Peters's preferred method to ward off future downtime: "I've been continuing to build contacts while working, I keep in touch with people in the industry, and I've just generally kept an ear to the ground over knowing when different projects are starting, or in development. There's not much of a strategy there. I'm basically just talking to friends and keeping in touch."

Danny Kimanyen works to create his own opportunities: "I'm constantly trying to pitch something to somebody and even if they don't like my idea they keep my design work in mind for future projects. Most of them are projects that never see the light, but it still pays the rent. I try to never get settled into a job, and keep my phone ringing. I love the hustle of it all; however, I must admit that it's not for everybody. You've got to put in work to get work; that's just the way it is."

EBONYC (E'bon-ic)

Danny Kimanyen's comic strip, EboNyc, a project he has initiated to open up further opportunities. Image courtesy of the artist.

PEP TALK CORNER

Everyone experiences downtime sooner or later, from recent graduates to seasoned and successful show creators. Those with years of experience in the business become inadvertent experts on how to best deal with a bad situation. However, a pep talk, from anyone, would be flat without some concrete applicable advice. As usual, the animation artists donating their expertise to this book did not let us down. Here's what the experts had to say. It may just put a little pep in your step.

"Don't panic! Have confidence in your talents and actively pursue job opportunities. It's important to find out about every animation studio or project in your area and send them your resume. Even if the studio says they're not hiring, send your resume anyway because usually they'll hold onto it in case they need to hire in the future. Alumni networks can also be useful. Treat each day as work, even if you don't leave the house. Go online, make phone calls, and when you're not doing that, make your own art or animation that can be used in your portfolio."
—*Amanda Lattrell, animation artist*

"Learn to expect downtime. It happens, and if you stick to it, work will come back eventually. It could take a long time, though. In the meantime, keep animating independently to stay sharp. Try to learn new skills."
—*Fran Krause, animator*

"Don't give up. If animation is really what you want to do, no matter what, then it'll happen because you'll make it happen, whether you're conscious of it or not. I've seen a lot of people give up or opt out of the business when times get rough. Perhaps animation wasn't what was coursing through their veins and that's fine. Some need stability more than anything else, and they won't find that in animation. Everyone needs to be happy, in whatever capacity works for them."

—Toni Tysen, animation artist

"If you're not working, practice. If you don't keep your hand loose, you'll find it difficult getting back up to speed when you get work. For 3D folks, a great website is *www.10secondclub.org.* They have monthly competitions where you animate ten seconds of dialogue. It keeps you loose, and helps you build your reel. Keep brainstorming for short film or TV series ideas. Even if you don't have time to produce them, pitch opportunities come up all the time. Another fun realm to delve into is comics. There's a huge crossover between animators and comic artists, and it really helps your skills as a director. Your downtime is a great time to develop your artistic identity."

—Mike Overbeck, animator, director

Still from animator and director Mike Overbeck.
Image courtesy of the artist.

"It can be very psychologically stressful to not have work. Find your identity outside of what you do. Know that even the best of us have lulls. I've seen it many times, and sometimes it's just due to bad timing. Even if prospective employers say they don't have work for you, believe them if they compliment your work. They don't have to be nice, or even respond to you, so when they give you compliments, they're probably being sincere. Don't be too proud to work a 'normal' job, but don't get too comfortable in it."

—Rachel Peters, animator

"I would say to just calm down and compose yourself. Then I would say go out there and make something happen; nobody's going to hire you if you sit at home feeling sorry for yourself. I would also say to study your competition and play to your strengths."
—*Danny Kimanyen, animation artist*

THE INSPIRATION DEPARTMENT: KNOW YOUR HEROES

Each of my School of Visual Arts Animation Career classes begins with a little thing I like to call, "Know Your Heroes." I encourage the class to learn the rich history of animation and the names of those who continue to help shape the craft, the art, and the industry. To play "Know Your Heroes," the students are asked a series of questions, the answers to which may help them discover their own heroes. Correct answers are rewarded with prizes of posters, DVDs, toys, books, etc. Some sample questions and answers:

QUESTION: George Lucas produced this paper cut-out animated feature in 1983.
ANSWER: *Twice Upon a Time*

QUESTION: Who is the director of the Ottawa International Animation Festival?
ANSWER: Chris Robinson

QUESTION: What is the name of the animation organization for women, which was founded in 1994?
ANSWER: Women in Animation

QUESTION: What studio made *Robots* and where is it located?
ANSWER: Blue Sky in White Plains, New York

QUESTION: What illustrator is the creator of Disney's TV series, *Teacher's Pet*?
ANSWER: Gary Baseman

QUESTION: Which Disney animator is credited with the redesign of Mickey Mouse that is still in use today?
ANSWER: Freddie Moore

This sort of "game show" got the blood pumping at the start of each class. Knowing the history of your medium is not just a trivial pursuit. To be inspired to create something new and meaningful in this industry we need to know the achievements of the past as well as the innovation of today. Downtime might just be when we need this inspiration most. None of the animation artists interviewed for this book had any trouble naming their heroes.

The author, still a student at SVA, and flanked by two of his biggest heroes. On the left, his dad; on the right, Mr. Howard Beckerman.

"In 1998 I worked with Bruno Bozzetto, an Oscar-winning Italian director who lives in Milan. He was hysterically funny and brilliant! He created a series that was like the Euro version of *The Simpsons* called *The Spaghetti Family* (modeled after his own quirky family). It was the most fun I have ever had writing. I wrote the pilot script and a second episode in hopes that he could get a broadcast deal. Despite the distance and language barrier we were totally in step from day one. I only wish I had saved his story note e-mails; not only were they hilarious, but they also demonstrated how brilliant he was. Bruno Bozzetto is a true visionary."
—*Erika Strobel, animation writer*

"I was taught by Bretislav Pojar in Prague, who was Jiri Trnka's animator, and one of the great Czech animators. That was a great experience."
—*Elanna Allen, stop motion animator, character designer*

"Don Bluth, Gary Goldman, and John Pomeroy, the producing team for the old Bluth studio, were tremendous influences on me. They self-sacrificed, fought for a vision, and rallied a team to often do the impossible. They gave many people opportunities, including myself. Those are unsung heroes of this business. I hope that they find their rightful place in the history books for reinvigorating a great American art form that almost died thirty years ago."
—*David Steinberg, animation producer*

"Some of my favorite board artists are people I've worked with and I keep copies of my favorite boards that they've done to use for inspiration. Barry Caldwell is one of them, a great board artist that I worked with on *Pinky and the Brain*. Sharon Bridgeman, another brilliant board artist, has worked in TV and features. Sharon is incredibly funny and talented. Rob Davies, who I worked with at Warner Bros., is hysterical and just such a great artist. Rob is one of the creators of Atomic Cartoons animation studio in Canada, and the show *Atomic Betty* on Cartoon Network."
—*Diane Kredensor, storyboard artist*

"With patience, persistence, and determination, I got a job with John Hubley, who was my idol as a youngster. That job lasted on and off for about five years until John died. Within the first day there, I met Tissa David, who I consider my mentor, and John Gentilella, an expert animator of *Popeye* cartoons. It was a great five years. I've met, and for the most part, worked with all of my animation heroes: Art Babbit, Bill Littlejohn, Barry Nelson, Richard Williams, Emery Hawkins, Ed Smith, Jack Schnerk, Corny Cole, Gerry Potterton."
—*Michael Sporn, Michael Sporn Animation, Inc.*

"My storyboard heroes are Bill Peet, Brad Bird, and Ted Boonthanakit, and my comic heroes are Albert Uderzo, *Asterix the Gaul*, and Walt Kelly, *Pogo*."
—*Scott Cooper, storyboard artist*

"I am very fortunate in not only meeting my top two animation heroes, Frederic Back and Richard Williams, but I also maintain regular correspondence with both of them. I actually encourage my students to write to their heroes and try to strike up conversations."
—*Dean Lennert, freelance animator, director*

"Well I think my all-time hero would be Hayao Miyazaki. This guy has such subtle creativity. Sergio Aragones, just because of his simplicity and humor."
—*Aaron Clark, storyboard artist*

"I'd have to say that the most fun I've had in my freelance years was working with Ralph Bakshi on the two cartoons we did for Cartoon Network's *What-a-Cartoon* series in the nineties. Imagination is virtually unfettered when working with him."
—*Doug Compton, animator, director*

"I worked in animation before I learned anything about the field. By the time I knew anything, I had already been side by side with many of the people whose work I loved. One artist in particular, Ron Barrett, did a book called *Cloudy with a Chance of Meatballs*, which I thumbed through one hundred times as a child. One page in particular I would stare at for hours. I didn't remember his name . . . what five-year-old looks at the author? It wasn't until digging through some old books that I rediscovered it and saw Ron's name. We already worked on a number of projects together, but I had no idea his work had such a seminal influence on my psyche."
—*Richard O'Connor, Asterisk*

"The old Disney guys were my heroes when I studied animation at Cal Arts. I was thrilled to have them for teachers or have them come in to lecture. Ultimately though I feel I learned more from my classmates back then, which is exactly how the school was meant to work. Might not have fully appreciated it at the time, but many of the students later became the new animation heroes. I still get inspired by time spent with Joe Ranft, Brad Bird, Henry Selick, or Peter Chung, to name a few."
—*John Hays, co-founder, Wild Brain*

"Jan Svochak was my mentor. I fought diligently at Perpetual Motion Pictures to be his assistant exclusively at a time when this process was no longer done. I've also been so lucky to work with artists, designers, cartoonists, and illustrators who are also my heroes: George Booth, Don Martin, Neal Adams, Garry Trudeau, Maurice Sendak, on and on . . . "
—*J.J. Sedelmaier, co-founder, J.J. Sedelmaier Animation*

"I have a lot of heroes, but T. Hee, who I wrote with, was my teacher and mentor. Also Marc Davis and Cal Horward."
—*Bob Kurtz, Kurtz and Friends*

"I had the incredible experience of working side by side for years with two of my childhood heroes, Bill Hanna and Joe Barbera; two of my three favorite cartoon shows growing up were *The Huckleberry Hound Show* and *The Flintstones.* Joe and Bill were real-life examples of how the cartoon business kept one young. They were forty years older than I was, and somehow I always felt they were smarter and working harder than me. Most of all, I've uniquely been able to meet my future heroes, the dozens of creators we've made short films and series with over the past fifteen years."

—*Fred Seibert, president and executive producer, Frederator*

"For several years I was fortunate to work as an animator and later animation director for Michael Sporn—a true modern master. Michael has mastered his craft with such integrity and discipline as to reduce animation almost to its purest form. His films are beautiful, funny, sad, and smart. He directs and animates with the leanness, and almost nonchalance, that can only come from a lifetime of experience, and I have learned a tremendous amount from him."

—*Ray Kosarin, animation director, producer*

"I know he's practically my age, but I would have to say, I've always wanted to work with Lou Romano. Over the last seven years I've been lucky enough to collaborate with him on various projects. He really is a genius. Not only has Lou taught me bundles about design, he constantly surprises me with his versatility and ever-widening range of talents. I was so impressed with him, I wrote and produced a film revolving around his life."

—*Teddy Newton, character designer*

"I loved and admired Craig Bartlett from *Sesame Street* and *Pee Wee's Playhouse* and we both ended up having corresponding shows on Nickelodeon."

—*Traci Paige Johnson, co-creator of* Blue's Clues, *Nickelodeon*

"Jules Engel single-handedly taught and inspired countless independent animators. When I was thirteen I went to a Tourney of Animation and saw *The Killing of an Egg* by Paul Driessen. That film made a lasting impression on me. Richard Condie's *The Big Snit* has got to be one of the greatest indies ever."
—*Stephen Hillenburg, creator of* SpongeBob SquarePants, *Nickelodeon*

"I was a big fan of *Doug* before joining Jumbo Pictures (now called Cartoon Pizza). It was smart, fresh, and easy for people of any age to relate to. Getting to work with Jim Jinkins has been and continues to be a great learning experience. He has a very intuitive understanding of how children think. There is nothing contrived in his process, which speaks for his continued success. Getting to share and create in the visual development of *Pinky Dinky Doo* and other projects with Jim has been an amazing opportunity for my personal growth as an artist."
—*Paul Zdanowicz, background painter, art director*

"Matt Groening is my brother-in-law. I enjoy walking through the ComicCon with Matt, because that's a world where every single person knows who he is. The guys who started drawing *The Simpsons*, David Silverman, Wes Archer, and Brad Bird, were just a bunch of guys at Klasky Csupo once upon a time, when we were starting *Rugrats*, and now they are big shots. Brad's career has been amazing. If you go to festivals, you can meet the international animators like Plympton, Newland, Preistley, Dreissen. These indies are always very nice people."
—*Craig Bartlett, creator of* Hey Arnold!, *Nickelodeon*

"When I was young I got to work at the National Film Board of Canada. I met so many fantastic artists like Caroline Leaf, Janet Perlman, John Weldon, Derek Lamb, Kai Pindel, Sheldon Cohen, Ryan Larkin, and that whole 70s era of great NFB artists. Later, when I went to film school in England my fellow students were Nick Park and Mark Baker, who became close friends, and of course Alison Snowden."
—*David Fine, co-creator of* Bob and Margaret, *Snowden Fine Productions, Nelvana Limited*

"At Wild Brain, I'm working with Phil Robinson, John Hays, and Gordon Clark, whom I'd never heard of before I got here. I work with them every day and we bounce ideas off each other. Then I see their reels and see all the commercials from the nineties that got me really excited to be an animator. Just the thought of working with many of the guys who did Liquid Television makes me giddy."
—*Mike Overbeck, animator, director*

Networking: People Who Need People

"Attending festivals is always valuable, especially from the standpoint of knowing what's out there, making new relationships, or renewing old ones. Of course winning awards always helps a career, but the competition turns out to be more of a sideshow to the constant creative interaction surrounding a festival."

—John Hays, co-founder, Wild Brain; senior creative director

The front "self-portrait" side of John Serpentelli's thaumatrope, an innovative animated offering and "the perfect fidget toy."

The back side of John Serpentelli's thaumatrope showing a light bulb, showing that he brings good things to life.

f I could sum up this chapter in one word it would be, "people." Maybe it made you cringe when Barbra Streisand sang it, but when it comes to the animation industry we are people who need people. Networking, for our purposes, is the art of making new connections and maintaining old ones to ensure we stay connected. Sometimes to become effective networkers we have to fight our own solitary natures. Many who gravitate to careers in animation are shy and private people who do their best work at the end of a pencil or pixel. The work we do tends to be isolating, especially when you're freelancing on a job at home. In spite of this, healthy relationships with colleagues, employers, and potential clients are undeniably important. In fact, you can't have a successful career in animation without them.

BURNING BRIDGES

"I have burned a few bridges in the past and the plumes of smoke still waft in to choke me occasionally . . . it's a very small industry. Word travels fast. So if you have a great reputation, it will travel faster. Learn to balance 'creative integrity' with 'professional etiquette.'"
—*Erika Strobel, animation writer*

Savvy animation artists are careful not to burn bridges, or put more bluntly, permanently sever a relationship. The animation industry is so small that it's really not possible to burn a bridge and not have it come back to haunt you at some point or another. We're all connected by default. Bridge Burners beware: you're not just closing one door with one company and its employees at the time. Nothing happens in a vacuum. An unprofessional act of rudeness or dishonesty will haunt your career. The door you close today will close others for you tomorrow.

Word of mouth is how most animation artists find work. Habitual bridge burners narrow their employability over time. Is it worth the small amount of temporary satisfaction you gain by telling off your boss? While damage can be done in one single event or action, you can also burn a bridge with an accumulation of smaller things over time, possibly without realizing it.

If this is all obvious, then why are there bridge burners in the first place? The answer is that it's all too easy to trash relationships and move on. Bridge Burners emphasize the importance of the work, systematically undervaluing interpersonal relationships and seeing themselves as the smart people trying to navigate a studio full of idiots or, at best, competitors. These "idiots" are the real challenge for a habitual Bridge Burner. If the Bridge Burners didn't see people as obstacles to success they might appreciate that they are surrounded by people as excited about animation as they are.

Bridge Burners also make the mistake of thinking that the only bridge that they can burn is with the boss or management. Each relationship in a studio, from the boss on down to the intern, is a bridge to future connections. Stop motion animator Eileen Kohhlepp adds, "It helps tremendously to get along with your co-workers. You never know where they will wind up. Your co-workers will sometimes notice more about you than a producer or supervisor can. If you're a slacker, always coming in late, and always checking your e-mail, they'll remember."

THE INTERNATIONAL SCENE: FESTIVALS AND EVENTS

"Much of my knowledge of independent animation comes from
festivals. And that's where I meet many of the people I've worked
with, even those who are not independent animators.
Animation industry people who love animation tend to be
very motivated: they go to festivals, they go to events, they meet
people, and they also pitch. So it goes together that you'll meet
the people most eager to get themselves and their projects out
there at these festivals. It's the same for emerging live action
filmmakers and festivals such as Sundance."
—*Linda Simensky, senior director, PBS Kids*

Those in a major animation hub city like New York City, Los Angeles, San Francisco, Toronto, and Vancouver have it easier. Newcomers and veterans can plug into the animation community through monthly events, screenings, and industry parties.

If you don't live in or near a major animation hub city, fear not. You'll just need to do your in-person festival networking in a few bold strokes a year by traveling to animation festivals such as Ottawa, Annecy, and Hiroshima, which not only present the best in international animation excellence, they also offer ample opportunities to schmooze. Ironically, there were numerous New York City animation artists that I hadn't met until I attended festivals in Canada and France. Sometimes you have to travel far away to make connections on a local scale.

NETWORKING, OUT OF THE BOX

"One day I taped a day's worth of Nick Jr. and by watching the credits
I figured out whom to contact at the network. I wound up as an
administrative production assistant on the *Little Bill* animated series."
—*Eric Weil, writer, creator (with designer/director Jennifer Oxley)*
of Janie and Jerome *on* Sesame Street

One drawback to attending international animation festivals is the expense involved. Happily, festivals aren't the only way to network. Try a search online for animation studios in your city to find out where they are and the names of the major players. Arrange to pop in for an informational meeting. Then stay in touch from that point on!

Keep your eyes and ears open because networking opportunities can present themselves at the oddest times. Not so long ago, I was watching a local TV news report about Callaway Press, which publishes Madonna's children's books and the successful line of *Miss Spider* books, now a hit 3D cartoon animated at Nelvena and airing on Nick Jr. I looked up the company's Web site and a week later I had a nice informational meeting with the president of Callaway Press, Nicholas Callaway. It turned out that the company needed a CGI animator to capture illustrations from the animation files so they could be used in print work. I recommended a CGI animator, Doug Vitarelli, who landed the job.

Another great networking opportunity began as result of *Blue's Clues* animation artists Paul Beard and Michael Lesko founding a *Blue's Clues* softball team. They designed and ordered special hats and T-shirts for their team and organized official games with other television productions across town. Scores of people that would otherwise never have met were suddenly thrust together on the ball field. The games would inevitably be followed by a fun evening of dinner and drinks for all.

I once used the occasion of finishing my film, *Snow Business*, as a networking opportunity to wander around the floors of Nickelodeon setting up impromptu screenings with various creatives. Out of this afternoon blitz, a relationship was forged with Carol Forsythe, then head of Nick's Creative Lab. Seven years later, we played a role helping each other land full-time jobs outside of Nickelodeon.

Another off-the-cuff meeting at Nickelodeon led to talks of a development deal to make more shorts based on *Snow Business* for Nickelodeon International. The executive believed that the visual storytelling of my film could translate across many languages and cultures. While nothing came to fruition, it still showed me the power and potential of networking a project and myself.

A couple of years later, while listening to the commentary track of a favorite science fiction film on DVD, I noticed the film's director give out his personal e-mail address. I quickly dashed off a message to him praising his film and describing its impact on my life. This started an e-mail exchange, which serves as a reminder that the creative heroes in this business are accessible and that certainly makes networking easier and more fun!

The most joyous networking experience I've had is a Sunday animators brunch that my friends and I have been enjoying for almost ten years. Over eggs and toast, we discuss the latest animated films, books, and TV shows. We talk shop: sharing war stories and offering a sympathetic ear to one another. We learn from each other. We support each other. We're like the women on HBO's *Sex and the City* only without the expensive shoes.

UNUSUAL ANIMATED OFFERINGS

Animation artists use a variety of "leave behinds" as a means of networking. These are usually simple, cheap, and fun items that can be given to a potential client or employer at the conclusion of a meeting. Animation artists are supposed to be semi-eccentric, creative types. So why not think out-of-the-box when creating a bit of self-promotion? Independent animator John Serpentelli did just that: "I think the best piece of self-promotion I've come up with was at the very beginning of my career. I decided to make a business card that was a thaumatrope with an image of my shaved head (unusual in 1997) on one side and a light bulb on the other. Of course, when the thaumatrope was spun my bald head and the light bulb became one. This turned out to be big success, as Brown Johnson (Executive Creative Director of Preschool Television, Nickelodeon) told me 'this is the perfect fidget toy' and because of this gimmick many people remembered me for years."

Bill Plympton turned a lemon into lemonade, creating a unique animated offering: "For *Mutant Aliens* we ended up with an out-of-synch film print. I clipped up frames from that film print and I gave those away inside those tiny little plastic photo viewers. I made 1,000 of them with my name and contact info printed on the side. It was a good way to attract attention and get my name and film out there."

Rachel Peters likes to make personalized gifts for her top desired job picks: "People like candy. For one of the companies I worked at, I had decorated a little bucket (in a style I knew they'd appreciate, because it was reminiscent of their work), and I filled it with chocolate kisses. The sign on the bucket read, 'Rachel Peters kisses up.' Then I meticulously tied a note to each kiss, which read, 'Hire me??' and gave my name and contact info. By the end of the next two days, I think just about everyone in the studio knew my name. I got work one week later."

Showtime's *Queer Duck* director/designer/animator Xeth Feinberg bought cheap wall clocks at K-Mart, and replaced the paper face of the clock with a design heralding his characters and MishMash Media company logo. It made a shrewd animated offering. I've seen Xeth's clocks hanging in offices from New York to Los Angeles. This "leave behind" ensures that people see his work all the time.

I recently hired a storyboard artist, Otis Brayboy, to help create boards for some pitches. Brayboy did a top-flight job and at its conclusion he gave me a complimentary T-shirt with the logo for his company, Chick'n Skratch

Animation, on it. Now Brayboy will always be one laundry cycle away from the top of my mind. Clever man.

THAT TRUSTY STALWART, THE BUSINESS CARD

"I like making paper dolls or something fun to play with, with my business info on the back, instead of typical business cards. I want them to want to keep my information."
—*Rachel Peters, animation artist*

Drink Ghostmilk for strong ghost-bones and teeth. Snazzy glassware from the folks at Toronto's Ghostmilk Studios, given to the author as a house warming present.

Outside of the offbeat approaches to the animated offering, there is always the trusty, stalwart business card. This is the equivalent of tagging a person with your information. In the animation industry, your card should display not only your area of specialty, but also your personality. The four-inch-by-two-inch surface of a business card is a mini canvas on which to display yourself. The former head writer of *Blue's Clues*, Adam Peltzman, gives

"Happy New Year rocks" from legendary animation artist Don Duga. Who said it's bad to get rocks in your stocking? Image courtesy of the artist. Rocks courtesy of the Earth.

out a very unique business card, designed as a miniature three-hole punched script cover page. The card screams, "Writer!" The sheer simplicity and imagination of this card would be enough to make me want to call Peltzman in for an interview. Remember, this is a creative field. There is no reason that your business card should look like that of an accountant. The only standard rule to follow is to include your name, phone number, e-mail address, and area of animation expertise.

The Rachel Peters Paper Doll

IN ABSENCE OF RACHEL, PRINT DOLL,
CUT AROUND DOTTED LINES AND CARRY IN
POCKET AND/OR SHOE.

NEW! ACTION DOLL! RUNNING FROM NEIGHBOURHOOD DOGS!
JUST LIKE IN REAL LIFE!

CAUTION: CHOKING HAZARD. MAY CONTAIN TRACES OF NUTS (AND/OR SHARDS OF GLASS).
DO NOT PUNCTURE OR INCINERATE.

The Rachel Peters cut-out paper doll, soon to be available in all fine stores near you. Image courtesy of the artist.

Gallery of animation artists' business cards.

My dentist's business card. If a dentist can be creative with his card, why can't you?

HO-HO-HOLIDAY CARDS

"I always make up little Christmas cards and promotional cards for clients."
—*Bill Plympton, independent animator*

An interior spread of a Bill Plympton original holiday card from the author's collection. Plympton's Christmas cards helped to inspire his half-hour animated special, now airing perennially on Cartoon Network, 12 Tiny Christmas Tales. *Courtesy of the artist.*

After the ever-present business card, the next most common networking aid is the holiday card. The holiday card is a great opportunity to design a greeting that only you could create in any size or style you can dream up. In a creative field such as ours, store-bought cards should not even be a consideration. Fear not, no one is advising you to make 100 handmade cards. That would be a career unto itself. Instead, copy your original creation onto cardstock and fold it. You can still add little hand-made touches like bits of color and accents. Holiday cards are pretty special because outside of their networking application, they serve as a well-timed "thank you" to your contacts, clients, employers, and friends. Each year we receive a lot of support and this is a great way to show our appreciation. I like to include a personal message inside each card I send out. Add names to your holiday card list each year. It's a great end-of-the-year checkpoint to see how effective your networking has been. How many new contacts have you made in the past twelve months?

Rachel Peters recently found out that she was hired for her job at the insistence of the receptionist, who had enjoyed the Christmas card she had sent them: "I had taken a picture of myself in my donut shop uniform (where I worked for a whole day and a half), and the outside read, 'Season's greetings from Tim Horton's newest part-time relief employee! She's going places!' . . . Then, on the inside I begged them to get me out of that place, and complained about how the uniform made me look like a potato. There's no formula there. I just really enjoy making things and mailing things."

Multiple Emmy-winning *Sheep in the Big City* creator Mo Willems gives an illustrated, limited edition miniature bound sketchbook to all his contacts every Christmas. The little sketch-books are so attractive that Willems' clientele keep them displayed in their offices and homes long after other, more seasonal Christmas offerings are packed up, put away, and forgotten. One of Willem's sketchbooks featuring a pesky little pigeon was seen by a children's book agent and helped launch Willems into an additional successful career as a top children's book illustrator and author. Go into your local bookstore and pick up a copy of Mo Willems' *Don't Let the Pigeon Drive the Bus* and you'll be holding in your hand the awe-inspiring result of a simple offering.

"The Pigeon Tells A Story."

a mo willems sketchbook.

The Pigeon Tells a Story, *A Mo Willems Sketchbook, given as a holiday gift, which led to an additional successful career for Willems as a top children's book illustrator and author. From the collection of the author.*

GOOD NETWORKING IS TO NETWORK ALL YEAR LONG

Unlike the holiday season, networking is not something that only happens once a year. Keep in touch with people by writing to say congratulations on an accomplishment, or tell people what you're up to, when you start or leave a job, when you come across a book, TV show, or movie that they might like. Always inform your contacts of any changes of address, phone number, or e-mail.

Another sure-fire method of staying in touch is to have one or two lunches a week with contacts outside your immediate circle. This keeps you plugged in to all the gossip and goings-on in the industry around town.

These simple and easy ways to network all year long can have an enormous impact on a career.

VOLUNTEERISM AND MEMBERSHIPS

"I belong to ASIFA, the Writer's Guild of America, BAFTA (the British Academy of Television Arts), and a few others. Some of them are absolutely necessary (if I didn't belong to the WGA, I couldn't write for live action TV), and some are just lots of fun to belong to."
—*Allan Neuwirth, animation writer*

When it comes to networking potential it's hard to beat volunteerism. As a volunteer you give time, energy, and expertise and end up receiving the satisfaction that only comes from such generosity of spirit. It's not about money, but it can be the most valuable way to spend your time.

There has been a direct correlation between my success and my volunteerism with ASIFA-East. As a member of ASIFA-East's volunteer board of directors since 1996, I have forged many wonderful relationships that grew opportunities that I wouldn't have had otherwise. As the current president of ASIFA-East, it's a thrill to see the next generation of volunteers emerge to help keep our organization "surviving and thriving."

Find out what creative clubs and organizations are in your area by searching for animation clubs online or at the local universities. Contact the schools and talk to the instructors. There may be an animation club at the university. If not, help start a club of your own. Take out an ad in the animation trades in print and online, to find people in your area with a similar interest in animation.

NETWORKING DON'TS!

Just about the worst networking mistake you could make would be to make another person feel uncomfortable. For instance, a contact of mine once showed up at my office to see if we were hiring. When I told her that I would be in touch about it later that week, she persisted in talking to me about it right there and then and trailed me right into a closed-door meeting with my producers. I stepped outside with her to diplomatically ask her to stop by again when I was not busy in a meeting. This guerilla-networking tactic is wrong on so many levels. It's pushy, inappropriate, and reads as desperation.

Sheep in the Big City creator Mo Willems told my class that one of his pet peeves is having portfolios shoved in his face during a party. Wrong time. Wrong place. Yes, there may be people at the party who could hire you, but you need to remember that they are there to enjoy themselves. It's not fair to shove your work under someone's nose while he's drinking a beer and engaged in conversation.

Proper networking at a party or event is simple conversation. Don't push past someone already engaged in conversation so that you can cut in. Instead, stay calm and talk to someone else; you might just make a new connection you hadn't planned on. Be loose and spontaneous, but have a stash of business cards handy to exchange cards at the conclusion of each successful encounter. Add the e-mail addresses to your database and then follow up in some of the ways suggested in this chapter.

Excessive name-dropping is another thing to avoid. You don't need to fill the span of a two-minute conversation with a list of all the names you know. Keep your knowledge relevant to the conversation. Namedroppers come across like our industry's used car salesmen: slick and oily. Namedroppers try too hard and reference other people's achievements to boost their own status. These people seem to be trying to jump to instant relationships, but like the process of animation itself, relationships take time.

Also sharing a place in the networking hall of shame are the "Know-it-alls." Know-it-alls crave attention and approval, so they try to be "experts" in everything, constantly spitting out dates, titles, and bits of trivia. The problem is that they are often wrong. Even if they're right, they're assuming you don't know what they're about to tell you. In this business we are all experts of a sort. Anyone with a reasonable bullshit detector will eventually start to keep the know-it-all at a distance.

Take it down a notch. Talk on topic. By the way, it's okay to not know something. Remember, Richard Williams opens his master animation classes stating, "You don't know what you don't know." Rock legend Paul McCartney recently confessed to a journalist that he really doesn't know where his songs come from nor does he know how to make an album. Each time is new. By comparison, why should the rest of us think we've figured it all out?

Networking is not people collecting. Not everyone we encounter will be people we can build relationships with, nor would we want to in every case.

No matter how you network, avoid becoming a pest or a nuisance. E-mail is the modern method of choice to keep in touch with contacts because it's fast, easy, and respects people's comfort zones. People can respond or not respond at their leisure. Once, at an art opening I met a new contact with whom I had lunch a couple of times and later worked with on a freelance job. Before I knew it, he was calling me every couple of weeks, on every holiday, and for no reason at all. I tried to keep up for a while but the constant calls quickly became a nuisance. Pestering is not networking. These same calls would have worked better as e-mails, but you shouldn't flood anyone's inbox either.

PATIENCE

In the course of a career, you plant networking seeds and nurture them over time. A string of recent great jobs with some of the top animation talents in the industry resulted from relationships I had forged ten or more years ago. If

I had thought of networking as people collecting, I might have expected instant results of immediate job opportunities and I would have been sorely disappointed.

Adrian Urquidez, the author, and Felipe Galindo at the art opening of a gallery exhibiting Galindo's work. Networking is about nurturing relationships and supporting each other's endeavors.

NETWORKING ISN'T EVERYTHING

I know some folks who are great networkers, who can schmooze till the cows come home, but still have difficulty breaking into the field and landing a job. Successful networking by itself is not a means to an end. It's supposed to serve a career, not create one. The best networking in the world will not make up for a weak portfolio or a lack of experience or employability. In a few sad examples in the workplace, I've seen a few workers value networking in the office above job performance itself. These "mayors of the studio" buzz around and prioritize social relationships above all else. Another case featured a worker who pooled all her energy into creating employee raffles and contests. The outwardly creative worker showed little of the same energy when it came to the work she was paid to do. Needless to say, these types don't survive on the job very long, showing that networking, in this sense, isn't everything.

BALANCE

Networking, when it's done right and often, doesn't feel like work. It's making new contacts and maintaining old relationships with like-minded people, other animation artists. This is something we should want to do, right? It's not about what other people can do for you. To network effectively is to network sincerely. The people you meet become a part of your life and the players in your career to whom you should give back as much as you receive.

All Grown Up and No Place to Go: Starting Your Own Business

"The desire to have my own studio was one of the reasons I wanted to get into animation. Like many others I was following the mythology and success of Walt Disney. When it's your studio, you have immediate contact with your clients. When you work for someone else, the clients look on you as a piece of furniture."
—Howard Beckerman, co-founder of Beckerman Animation

Still from Pat Smith's film Handshake. *Courtesy of the artist.*

THE THREE CAMPS OF ANIMATION ARTISTS

There seems to be three major camps of animation artists. One camp's long-term goal is to create, sell, and produce their own television series or feature film. Another camp's long-term goal is to create their own studio business. The third camp consists of people who are happy simply excelling as workers for hire. No matter what camp you fit into, most animation artists that have worked as off-site freelancers get a taste of freedom that is similar to what it must feel like to be your own boss. You get to set up your workday your own way. You can take a double lunch or catch a movie in the middle of the day and have the option to resume work again at night. Animation artists, by the nature of our careers, sometimes work alone for hours or days at a time to complete a job. It's not surprising that many of us dream of opening our own studio where we could live and work in the ultimate example of independence.

Paul Fierlinger sums up the allure of owning your own studio: "I don't have to spend any time working with people I don't like; the commute to work is easy; it's easy to work anywhere from an hour to sixteen hours a day; the pay is anything but regular; industry news and trends pass me by and I live in fear of where the next job is coming from instead of having to live in fear of when I'll get sacked."

Some create their own studio business more out of necessity than from passion. Large studios tend to hire a lot of artists fresh out of school. They seek out this inexperienced youthful labor because they can pay less and expect more time and loyalty in return. Some companies believe that it's easier to train young workers who are free of the bad habits that years of experience can sometimes bring. Older workers will likely have family commitments, which pull them away from working late nights or taking on extra work for the weekend. Those who are forty years old and older either gravitate towards studio supervisor jobs or risk competing against an ever-growing crop of recent graduates for some of the same jobs. To stay competitive, the older people in the workforce must often lower their hourly rates, despite the wealth of experience they inherently bring to each project. It's easy to see why some older animation artists feel that going into business for themselves would be the best way to continue a career in the industry.

A STUDIO STARTS WITH AN ASSIGNMENT

"Build the studio second, find the job first. Having a studio is a product of need, and you go from there. It's not an 'if you build it they will come' situation."
—*Pat Smith, Blend Films*

Howard Beckerman made attempts to go out on his own at various times, but realized that he lacked a clear idea of how to get work. He recalls, "Surprisingly, one day everything came together. I was working at a key commercial studio and knew that I was only days away from being laid off. I bumped into an old friend of mine, producer, director, and editor Bob Braverman, who was at that moment the head of production at Xerox Films. It was a time of great interest in educational film production, what with the arrival of the *Sesame Street* TV program and also when major corporations, such as Xerox, were putting their considerable muscle into the production of specialized materials for schools. We were walking along Fifth Avenue in Midtown and, without breaking stride, Bob offered me three one-minute educational spots to produce. A few days later, when I attended a meeting at Xerox corporate headquarters, a fourth production was added. I began work at home and in a few weeks, July fourth to be exact, I moved into a rented space on 18th Street off of Irving Place. The next day the phone started ringing."

For Michael Sporn, his experience dealing with all the clients while working for R.O. Blechman's Ink Tank studio made him realize it would be a small change to do it for himself and he could make as much (or as little) money as he was making from staff positions elsewhere: "It took a very short time for me to get a short film from the Learning Corporation of America, *Byron Blackbear and the Scientific Method.* This led to a second one for them and a first for Weston Woods, who were planning to do their first film in the United States. I made it: *Morris's Disappearing Bag.*"

Bill Plympton advises that the next generation of studio owners first gain experience working for big studios such as Dreamworks, Blue Sky Studios, or Nickelodeon. He continues, "I'd start with an entry level job, make a lot of contacts, meet a lot of people, and put a lot of money in the bank. I'd learn all the programs, build up a good portfolio, and then after six to seven years, I'd have a good basis for starting up a studio. People coming right out of school don't have the right background to start a studio right away. It's really important to have connections with industry people so you know the work will come in. It's tough starting out, trying to get the jobs when no one knows who you are."

Ron Diamond, president of Acme Filmworks, went into business for himself partly because at the time no one was doing exactly what he wanted to do. He says, "I felt I'd be able to achieve a more satisfying experience by not going through the mailroom approach into animation production. My goal was to be connected to work where directors could do their thing."

AGENTS, REPS, AND LAWYERS . . . OH MY!

Just as creating a studio is a project of need, so is acquiring legal representation. Jim Arnoff, a TV packaging agent and entertainment lawyer specializing in animation, says there are many kinds of agents: "There are agents that represent authors for publishing, playwrights for theatre, and casting agents that represent talent, etc. As a TV packaging agent, I represent TV production companies. I don't represent individuals. If I do represent an individual, she'll be capable of ramping up for production (if needed) or I'll arrange to help bring in partners."

Asterisk animation studio co-founder Richard O'Connor explains: "Commercial agents are supposed to get you leads from advertising agencies. Entertainment agents are supposed to help you get meetings to pitch your projects and to negotiate your deal."

Agents get paid a percentage of the production budgets. Arnoff continues, "As a TV packaging agent, I get 10 percent of budget for the development stage and I get 5 percent of production budget of series. In addition to that I would get 10 percent of all the ancillary action." Lawyers are paid hourly. With a new client, a lawyer will ask for a retainer, which is the amount you pay before you start your services. If a lawyer is working for $250 an hour, they'll need a retainer of $1,250. Arnoff warns, "The retainer isn't a prediction or estimate of the billing hours. If every single point gets negotiated it can rack up hours. Your lawyer should keep you posted on the hours." The cost of a lawyer depends on their experience level. In New York $350 an hour is about average. A lot of lawyers who are considered "deal makers" will bring an added value to a project so it could be worth paying more for their services.

When does an individual or a company doing business need the services of a lawyer? Arnoff answers, "You need a lawyer anytime you're talking to anyone about working together. You need what is called a collaboration agreement. Handshakes aren't enforceable. Friendships don't apply. Keep it professional. It's like with a doctor, you see a doctor before you get sick. You want a lawyer before you get sick."

What makes for an effective partnership between a lawyer and a client? It's important to find someone you trust, who will return your phone calls. Arnoff offers, "You have to assume that person will be your cheerleader or ally. Don't lose sight of the fact that your lawyer or agent is a key to your success. Work that relationship like a spouse or best friend. Although a lawyer can be far away, an agent should be in your backyard. As a New Yorker, I can't represent someone who lives in Los Angeles."

"Clients should stay involved in the whole process and educate themselves as to the business side of things," Arnoff concludes. "You collaborate with your lawyer/agent. That's your team and you pick them. It's a reflection of you."

KEEPING THE PHONE RINGING

"Most of our work comes through recommendation, word of mouth. Some comes from picking up the phone and making calls and sending out reels and making contact. Right now we have six projects in house. Five came from personal recommendation or are repeat collaborators. The sixth is a pilot we sold together with a writer. To generate work, we've distributed postcards, trade ads, and buttons. We're tagging the walls of ad agencies and TV networks with our logo. An animator in the sixties once had his assistant dress up as Wonder Woman and hand out promotional material on Madison Avenue; we plan on emulating this."
—*Richard O'Connor, co-founder, Asterisk*

Still from the animated sequence created by Asterisk for the live action feature film The Stepford Wives. *Image courtesy of Asterisk.*

Howard Beckerman recalls a successful accountant giving him the following advice: "You must be able to get the work, you must be able to do the work, and you must be able to get paid. Most people can only do one or two of these." The easy part was ordering some stationery, renting the space, and slapping some paint on the wall. You amassed the necessary resources, people, and equipment to complete your first job but now that's over. Next is the hard part. How do you keep the phone ringing after the first job?

J.J. Sedelmaier, co-founder of J.J. Sedelmaier Productions, Inc., utilizes two reps, one on the East Coast, Andy Arkin, and one for the Midwest, Liz

Laine. Sedelmaier adds, "Most of our work comes from our reputation, however. Our reel gets updated about once or twice a year. It's the same with the press kit. We have a master DVD that is broken into several categories. We basically use that now, and add additional work that seems specific to whatever might be needed for a specific project. Our press agent arranges for me to do interviews, seminars, and presentations. We've also published a self-promotional comic book that showcases the studio's design and print work, and created a Web site."

The title card for The Ambiguously Gay Duo, *a familiar staple of* Saturday Night Live, *animated by J.J. Sedelmaier Productions, Inc.*

Mark Simon, founder of A & S Animation, Inc., agrees on the importance of creating press to help drum up business. Simon reveals, "We make sure our Web site ranks on the first page of search engines. We do press releases regarding our big projects and festival wins. I held a press event to showcase our technology one year and got on multiple TV stations. I write books and articles in Animation Magazine and AWN to keep my name in front of the industry."

Like many small independently owned studio owners, Michael Sporn is his own agent, business representative, producer, and janitor. While most of his work comes from repeat business, he has had some modest success pitching his own projects. Sporn adds, "Reviews of my films have helped; a lot of the HBO shows have gotten good exposure. The more your studio name is mentioned, the better. Once or twice I've hired a publicist to help promote particular shows I've loved and wanted promoted."

Breehn Burns, of Lone Sausage Productions, agrees that most opportunities come from exposure, people seeing his independent films and contacting him. "Conventions and animation or film festivals are great ways to get your work seen."

Bill Plympton lands fifty out of sixty of the commercials he gets because he has a name and a style. "The rest of the jobs come in because I'm around and they know I can produce. For some people it's appropriate to be stylistically diverse. There are not a lot of animators that get work for style. The rest of them are factory."

Cartoon rendition of Mark Simon, drawn by Travis Blaise. Courtesy of the artist.

An image of Dr. Tran from Roybertito's :60 Second Spot *(2005) by Breehn Burns, Lone Sausage Productions. Courtesy of the artist.*

FINDING YOUR CREW

"I look for responsible, mature people with good drawing skills, and a willingness to learn. Studios are not always working on the subjects that appeal to recent animation students, but a responsible person will dig in with the proper enthusiasm anyway. After all, animation production is all about problem solving whether you're animating a dinosaur or a box of cereal. Planning a production schedule or figuring out how to move office equipment from one studio space to another calls for practical skills not always learned in art school."
—*Howard Beckerman, co-founder of Beckerman Animation*

Animation artists working in small independent studios tend to wear many hats, being flexible, versatile, and willing to help out wherever they are needed. Mark Simon describes good employees as willing to do more than their job and to think ahead. Simon adds, "To succeed, they need to already be working towards their next position and learning on their own."

Richard O'Connor looks for "commitment, but not to the extent of a stalker, and a level of technical accomplishment and artistic ability that hasn't been hampered by poor work methods or stylistic crutches that are impossible to throw away."

Today's studios look for a mix of traditional skills and a mastery of new technology. Michael Sporn starts by looking for good drawing: "If they know Photoshop and After Effects so much the better. The more knowledge they have of real animation, the better."

Bill Plympton describes the ideal employee as having a passion for working in animation: "I've had a number of people who didn't care about animation. They don't last long. They should be personable, like to laugh, joke, and get along with people. Starting out, there should be an eagerness to work for not a lot of money. New hires tend to look at me as a stepping stone to working for other bigger places. Working for me is more prestige than money. Yet, if someone shows a lot of talent and skill I will want them to stick with me for the long haul."

FAMILY STYLE (DYSFUNCTIONS AND ALL)

Often the small studio takes on a family-like dynamic, with the studio owner as the parent. At a glance it would seem that the small independent studios would be a model for efficiency and good communication. The idea is that fewer people mean fewer stages for approval. Yet this is not always the case. Just as often, the small studio uses its size to a disadvantage because the bosses are too busy acting as workers themselves to properly delegate, explain, or manage the workflow. In this way, they are both their own problem and solution. The danger is that the lack of delegation keeps them shackled to the desk at times when they should be looking after the business. Someone has to keep an eye on where and when the next job will come from, and sometimes the small studio does not have the financial means to hire an agent or representative.

Ironically, large studios tend to have better communication and a more efficient approval process. They document workflow and the progress of individuals to make sure projects run as smoothly as possible. Process becomes regimented and training becomes standardized across the production.

In some ways, the family-style atmosphere of the small studios can make for a very desirable work environment. For the staff, there is immediate access to the number one person. At a large studio the boss may not even get a chance to learn your name. Large studios function in a far more compartmentalized way. There, employees are hired to perform specific jobs that typically have very little chance of variation. At small studios, employees, by necessity, wear many hats. Today you may be animating, next week you're coming up with designs, and the week after that you may be asked to create storyboards. Working at a small studio can give a greater understanding of the entire process of production or filmmaking. Often those who have worked at small studios are the ones who gain the confidence to open their own business down the road, make independent shorts, or parlay their valuable production knowledge into senior staff roles at the large studios. All of these potential outcomes make cutting your teeth at a small studio an ideal way to start a career.

Large studios offer a different set of advantages to the worker, most commonly health benefits, life insurance, and 401K plans. Large studios also tend to offer greater job security, due to long-form projects such as features, TV, or Web series work, and often the length of employment is known at the start of a job. This is in sharp contrast to the way work can suddenly come to a close at a small studio. At a small studio, a client check that's only a few days late can halt the weekly payroll. When layoffs come they can often be without warning.

REALITY CHECK

Create your own studio and the romantic fantasy can quickly yield to harsh realities. For one, as a studio owner and boss you are responsible for the welfare of all your employees. John Hays calls this the hardest part of the business: "You have to be prepared to lose good people when the time comes, tear it all down, and then rebuild everything over again. It's a delicate balance between quiet optimism and the sheer terror of financial ruin."

Ron Diamond agrees, "In our history there were some lean times with no work and we had to lay people off. I know that all my workers are talented and capable so if someone leaves it can affect the business in various ways. If you take a perfect circle and take a divot out of it, every angle of that circle is now affected by it."

Howard Beckerman didn't enjoy the business side of running a studio: "It bored me, and I was pleased to give it up for that reason. To be good in business you have to be able to decide at some crucial point that you are going in the wrong direction and make changes in how you run your company or what type of product you create. Most people lack this intuitive capability."

Dealing with problematic clients is high on the list of negative experiences for many studio owners. It can be doubly frustrating to have to educate clients about the process of animation and its costs. Mark Simon reveals, "The worst thing is dealing with clients who have no money or concept of what it takes to produce animation; shortening deadlines, smaller budgets, and budgeting against start-ups who don't know how to budget." Simon also complains about inexperienced studios that lead clients to believe they can get away with low budgets. "That hurts us all," says Simon.

Richard O'Connor points out, "When something goes wrong, it's up to you to fix it. When clients don't pay, you have to hound them." Many animation studios survive paycheck to paycheck, keeping their costs as low as possible, including small paychecks for even the owners of the company. Michael Sporn thinks that to survive it takes a stubborn attitude, a strong stomach to fight the lack of financing, and fortitude to lay off those you care about when you run out of money.

In conclusion, John Hays sums up the plight of the independent studio owner: "If you feel that the true joy of artistic creation can only be fully experienced when everything you have is at risk—money, family, friends, reputation, career, etc.—then starting an animation business is the way to go."

CLIENTS AND CONTRACTS

"Our contracts with clients are exceptionally formal. It's important for everyone to know exactly what the expectations are for delivery. The advertising agencies, our clients, impose those on us. We use three different lawyers: one lawyer is for contracts, one for employee labor issues, another lawyer is for visas and international issues."
—*Ron Diamond, president, Acme Filmworks*

A contract is nothing more than an agreement between two parties, outlining their mutual expectations. Contracts describe the job, revision and approval process, the deadlines, and pay schedule. Howard Beckerman explains that for commercials there are typically three payment periods, "One at start, another at pencil test, and the final at completion."

Mark Simon warns you should never assume anything with clients and be sure to do it all in writing. "Remember, it is a business. Not handling it in writing leaves too many things up to memory or false assumptions or not getting paid for revisions, changes, and additions. Learn to budget properly. Don't undercut others to the point where you can't afford your own business; it hurts the entire industry. Make sure you charge enough for not only your labor, but also for yourself, profit for the business, overhead, and taxes. It adds up quickly. Every job will take longer than you expect and every client will cause delays with late approvals and still expect the same delivery date."

On the other hand, Paul Fierlinger's favorite contracts were the informal ones. In his forty-seven years (and counting) of being in business he found himself, just once, in serious conflict with a producer for his attempt to breach their agreement but, as Fierlinger says, "He couldn't get away with it because in his anal distrust of others he had written an iron-clad contract."

CAREER CORNER: ADVICE ON RUNNING YOUR OWN STUDIO

What can you do to ensure the survival and success of your own business? Howard Beckerman recommends, "Don't buy fancy equipment. Or even paper clips. Get an assignment first, and then buy stuff, as you need it. If you make some money, don't splurge it on a yacht . . . animation is an up and down business. 'Nuff said."

Ron Diamond agrees, "Invest in people/ideas more than technology. Who cares about the technology? You'll use what you need when you need it. It's all about relationships. You should enjoy what you're doing."

Patrick Smith adds, "It helps to have a head for business, and a desire to have your work in front of a lot of people. You also have to be able to talk to people and work well with them in stressful situations. You need to be fearless about going into debt, taking chances with money."

Bob Kurtz, of Kurtz and Friends, offers the mantra, "Love what you do, stay open, and be honest to the project. Let go of your ego."

J.J. Sedelmaier warns against accepting projects, even well-paying ones, that won't reflect well on your reputation.

Mark Simon explains, "If you want to be a creative studio, you have to produce original content.

Kurtz and Friends company logo, courtesy of Bob Kurtz.

Shorts are the best way to do it." Bill Plympton adds in agreement, "It's important to do a short film every year or two and take the film to all the festivals. That's where potential clients will hear about you and pursue you. You must keep the creative side busy by producing new things. It's like our version of research and development. You get to create a brand identity."

For Sean Waimstein, co-founder of Ghostmilk Studios, it's about balance: "Find the time to manage all the projects, keep in touch with clients and communicate with staff, and find time for yourself as well. Recharging and personal time are important to avoid burnout. Stay positive and keep the work fresh. Time management skills are definitely necessary. That being said, you should be ready to work a shitload of hours . . . but for love. . . . "

Waimstein continues, "Think long and hard about it before creating a studio because it's not easy. It takes time and financial commitment and, in many cases, a sacrifice. Ensure that you choose the people you are going to be working with very carefully and outline everyone's roles, responsibilities, and ownership. Remember to have fun."

Ghostmilk Studios company logo, never past its expiration date. Image courtesy of Ghostmilk Studios.

Oscar-winning filmmaker Jimmy Picker advises, "Don't turn down an opportunity for your animation to screen on television, even if the pay is low. Put out your work just to get exposure."

Animator and director Mike Overbeck offers, "It's tempting to promise the sun and the moon when you're bidding for jobs, especially in those times

Jimmy Picker checks in on his puppets from his Oscar-winning Sundae in New York. *Courtesy of the artist.*

when you're hurting for work. Instead, always look for ways to work smarter, not harder."

John Serpentelli suggests, "Take some business classes and write a business plan. Then expect everything to take twice as long and cost twice as much as you think it will. Also, if you are interested in making money you should look to diverse businesses for clientele; not all jobs come from the entertainment industry. Oh, and hiring your friends is not a good idea unless they really are the best choice."

> "Is your main interest in the creative side or the business side?
> Either way you have to be very clear about your goals. If you
> want to do something entrepreneurial you have to be very
> adventurous and unafraid of risk. On the creative side it's much more
> complicated. You have to be aware that at some point artistic
> integrity will be in jeopardy simply because of the natural conflict
> between running a business and creative ideals. It's like having
> one foot on the gas and the other on the brake."
> —*John Hays, co-founder and senior creative director, Wild Brain*

The Horror! Pitching and Selling a Pilot or Series

"We get pitched hundreds of ideas each round and end up moving ahead in the paper development stage with probably only five or six."

> —Alice Cahn, vice president of development and programming, Cartoon Network

Character designs by the author for his preschool pitch, Owl and Rabbit *or* Neighbors, *shown to six networks and rejected by all . . . for now.*

There has been a lot written on pitching an animated series in the last ten years. Articles usually collect a handful of the top executives and ask them questions like, "What were the best and worst pitch meetings you've ever taken?" You end up with the dos and don'ts of pitching according to the development executive point of view. I find this information helpful, but it paints a limited picture of what really goes on in the pitch process.

Before we get bogged down on details here, we can boil this chapter's message into one of supply and demand. On the creative side, there's lots of supply. Suppliers are creators peddling their wares to the networks. The buyers are the networks. Each year there are limited funds available to develop new shows and even more limited air time on which to launch product. The demand is therefore far less than the supply, where the creator's only limitations are time and talent.

DON'T QUIT YOUR DAY JOB

"I don't know exact percentages, but I'd say that very few pitches make it to the next step. It's been different wherever I've worked. Nevertheless, I think the ratio of pilots to series is much better in animation than it is for prime-time network sitcoms," says Linda Simensky, senior director, PBS Kids. The percentage of those working (earning a living) in animation is so much greater than the number of people who have created and sold a pilot or series. It must be more than a 1,000-to-one ratio. The reality is that pitching shows, and in some cases selling shows, is no way to make a living. If you sell your idea, here's what you can probably expect:

◆ Prepare to wait up to three months for network legal to get you a first draft contract.

◆ Prepare to wait for another three months to have the contract revised and approved by both sides.

◆ Your contract probably only covers a "paper development phase." This means you only have approval to write a script, create character designs, and maybe a storyboard. This stage can last six months or longer.

◆ Most projects are cut off after the paper development stage. Your chances of going forward are likely fifty to one. Did I mention that this year of work creating, writing, and developing can pay as low as $2,000? Networks don't throw a lot of money at paper development.

◆ If your project goes on to pilot stage, this means you will be repeating steps similar to those above. This process will take one to two more years. It ends with the completion of your pilot that will likely never make it to air after being killed by focus group testing. In fact, most animated pilots are not intended for broadcast at all.

> "Pilots have to be perfect; it sometimes stifles your creativity because you're worried about taking too big of a risk or trying something too different."
> —*Traci Paige Johnson, co-creator of* Blue's Clues

Design by Traci Paige Johnson, a co-creator of Blue's Clues, *from one of her first animations,* Pumpernickel Puss. *Image courtesy of the artist.*

ALL THE PLANETS ALIGN

Fred Seibert, president and executive producer of Frederator, told the students in my SVA animation career course, "To succeed in this business you have to be ignorant that it is impossible." Yet, occasionally, the impossible does happen. Why is it that some projects manage to break through above all others? It need not be a mystery. While ignorance may be bliss, there's no reason why we shouldn't understand this business to the best of our ability. Towards that end, here's a round-up of why some projects are awarded that coveted prize of prizes, the green light!

You Are Someone Who the Network Wants to Work With

This is due to your reputation or track record of working on highly visible commercial projects in a senior role. Networks usually buy creators, not ideas. The reason that networks go with known creators is a good business practice. An established creator or top creative talent working in the animation industry has the chops, know-how, and proven ability to deliver. Even short pilots take money to produce and development executives can't spend the entire year's development booty on a bunch of unknowns. Their jobs are on the line. Somewhat understandably, they play it safe. This is a "business of animation" reality. Our focus, as potential creators, is to control what we can control. We can develop and pitch shows as often as possible; improving and amassing experience with each try. In the meantime, we can ready ourselves for future opportunities by working for others to learn how shows are created and produced. It's up to us to put ourselves in the position where we become the creators that the networks want to buy.

Sheep in the Big City creator Mo Willems agrees, "You could have the best idea ever and I guarantee that a network will not be interested in it unless they are interested in you. Fortunately for me, there was a logical progression in my cartoons from doing everything (producing, writing, animation, voice, camera, negative cutting, ink, and paint on *The Man Who Yelled* to farming out camera and ink and paint (the *Sesame Street* films) to directing other people's animation (*The Off-Beats*) to supervising direction (*Sheep in the Big City*).

"There was also a progression for me as a writer. I started with very short films that were essentially just sketches, and moved on to creating a character who could remain viable over several shorts (*Suzie Kabloozie*) to a full cast (*The Off-Beats*) and then a series. Working in short form for a long time was a great help when it finally came to assembling longer projects. It wasn't until I'd made over forty animations shorter than five minutes that I wrote and

Sheep in the Big City creator Mo Willems attending the ASIFA-East animation festival. Photo from the author's collection.

directed the twenty-two minute *An Off-Beats Valentine's*. Also, the discipline of writing for *Sesame Street* with a demanding head writer helped me evaluate the strengths and weaknesses of my cartoon scripts. Every previous animation experience provided equally vital lessons that I drew upon while working on *Sheep in the Big City*."

Rob Renzetti, creator of Frederator/Nickelodeon's *My Life as a Teenage Robot* agrees with Willems. "It helps to have some kind of track record in the industry. Work well and hard on other people's shows. Gain a reputation. If you go in as a rookie, you will need to be much more brilliant and fantastic."

If you are new to the industry, have never helmed a series or project, or are an industry outsider, chances are slim that your ideas will sell. There are, of course, exceptions to the rule.

Trey Parker and Matt Stone (*South Park*) and Mike Judge (*Beavis and Butthead*) were outsiders to the animation business before they sold their respective projects to wild successes. However, *South Park* was almost a pre-sold project because of its underground success as the *Spirit of Christmas* short, which had been produced as a made-to-order video Christmas card for TV executive Brian Graden. Pirated video copies of the crude and funny little short swept through the industry and public alike. With such a successful national "focus group" test, it was inevitable that *South Park* would score a green light somewhere on the cable spectrum. *South Park* found its home on the struggling cable station, Comedy Central, becoming the network's first hit, and, some say, its first funny show.

Beavis and Butthead began as the homemade garage short, *Frog Baseball*, from outsider, Texas-based, amateur animator Mike Judge. The Generation X antics of its two anti-heroes was picked up by MTV after first scoring a hit on the festival circuit as part of Spike and Mike's *Sick and Twisted Festival of Animation*. Like *South Park*, *Beavis and Butthead* was a pre-sold proposition. MTV had so much success with *Beavis and Butthead* that they built a studio around it. The New York–based animation studio, MTV Animation, housed hundreds of animation artists cranking out such shows as *The Head, Daria, Celebrity Death Match*, and *Downtown*.

Nickelodeon's *Hey Arnold!* creator Craig Bartlett was able to launch his series off of pre-established shorts as well. Bartlett recalls, "My *Arnold* shorts

Still from Craig Bartlett's Nickelodeon cartoon, Hey Arnold!, *which began as a couple of clay shorts for Sesame Street. Copyright 2005. Viacom International Inc.*

got it all started. I think everyone who wants to create a cartoon should try to make their own short to get the ball rolling. Your own short reveals your sense of art, story, timing, humor, tone. It tells much more than just pitching your idea ever could. Make a short!"

You Are a Celebrity

"I'd been working for Moby on a few projects. He wanted to do some animation. So I thought that maybe the Nick Jr. project I was proposing could be musical. So I brought in Moby to meet with them and they really liked our idea for a short film. It's always a good sell to bring in a celebrity. I'm sure it helped having Moby there."
—*Elanna Allen, character designer, stop motion animator*

Elanna Allen's creation for Nick Jr, called Bing Can Sing! *featured music by Moby, who was also at the pitch meeting, adding a touch of celebrity razzle-dazzle to this terrific project. Copyright 2005. Viacom International Inc.*

Savvy would-be creators might consider utilizing the power of celebrity by attaching some name cachet to a pitch project. Hollywood has functioned on this system since the breakup of the studio system began in 1948. For example, Charlton Heston's name was attached to star in *The Planet of The Apes* when the project was shopped around to various studios. The offbeat tale of an upside-down simian society may not have made it to the screen without the actor who lent his name at the earliest, most crucial, stage. Creators seeking celebrity involvement should contact the celebrity's management and send along a script and some artwork. You never know who will say yes.

It's a much safer venture for networks to greenlight projects initiated by or involving a celebrity. The idea is that celebrities provide built-in audiences and that makes advertisers happy. In the lean budget years of 2001 and 2002, where development was extremely scarce, Nickelodeon still managed to scrounge up money to develop and produce animated projects created by celebrities such as Wesley Snipes, Spike Lee, Whoopie Goldberg, Rosie O'Donnell, and Bill Cosby. While celebrity involvement is certainly helpful to sell a show, it doesn't guarantee success on television. Which of the celebrity-centric shows above went on to be the next big hit? Insert cricket noise here.

Your Idea Fit the Network's Development Agenda

"There is usually a network strategy, formulated by several key people involved with the programming, branding, on air, online, and marketing areas. The programming piece usually fits in with that strategy."
—*Linda Simensky, senior director, PBS Kids*

Each year, networks set a creative agenda that at times asks its executives to find shows with "break-thru-ocity" and "pixie dust." Other terms that are thrown around include the "uber-idea" and something that is "left-turn." Often, what networks are not looking for is more specific. One major network issued a memo warning creators to avoid pitching shows featuring "rainbows, trees, clowns, or dust-bunnies." Some networks won't consider your idea starring a bunny because there's already a successful bunny out there by the name of Bugs. One major network recently reversed a short-lived ban on animal ideas. During the days of "no animals" they said, "We believe kids won't relate to shows with animal characters. They want to see other human kids on the screen." When asked how they explained the success of *SpongeBob*, "We can't," was the reply. So, how can creators navigate through these waters? Happily, these network bans and buzzwords change with trends, marketing reports, shuffling personnel, and hostile company takeovers. Your great idea about a clown and his pet dust-bunny living in a tree in Rainbowtown just might sell yet.

My character designs for my preschool pitch, My School, *which turned out to be lacking "uber idea," "break-thru-ocity," and "left-turn," but, still had plenty of "neat-o-rama." I made up that last term, but I give my permission for networks to use it freely.*

But just how do networks go about setting their development agenda each year? Eric Coleman, vice president of animation, development & production at Nickelodeon answers, "My boss, the executive vice president of original programming and development, and I will generate a new development agenda each year that outlines our goals for the upcoming season. It's a pretty simple process where we consider what we have on our air, what we need on our air, what we're personally interested in exploring, and what we believe our audience wants. We then finalize four or five categories to develop for and we hit the streets in search of appropriate material and talent."

Eric Coleman, vice president of animation, development & production at Nickelodeon.

Fred Seibert adds, "Often an executive works off of development parameters decided by his or her network for that season. Others work off of what he or she believes a superior is interested in."

Madeleine Lévesque, director, original production, Teletoon (Canada), answers, "Setting a development agenda is a group effort that comes from many departments and evolves throughout the year. The most difficult aspect of this endeavor is to line up the timing. When production takes eighteen months on average, development is, more often than not, over two years, and projects circulate for years and years before they get greenlit, it's really tough to respond in the short term. This is a constantly moving target."

Creator Elanna Allen describes how network mandates effect pitching: "Networks have a mandate as to what they're looking for and it's usually pretty narrow. For instance, at this moment Nick Jr. is looking for shorts about 'food.' If you don't know that you're at a disadvantage."

So how does one learn what the networks are buying at this particular time? The most common answer executives give to potential pitchers is to "watch our channel and see what we're doing." This makes for fairly easy research, but what will you really be seeing? You'll be watching what they bought and developed two or more years ago. Recently, one network broadcast a string of new programming that was made up of mostly space and comic-hero type shows. Behind the scenes, the network had already decided to move away from such subject matter in their next development round.

Still, watching the channels as research is not a waste of time. At the very least you should be able to detect the network's intended audience. To find out the current development agenda, nothing beats asking a development executive for that information. I have found development executives to be very helpful in that area. Often there is a one-sheet, a short summary of the network mandate, they can forward to you that outlines what they're looking for.

Eric Coleman explains, "If you're interested in pitching to a network, just call up the development executives and ask your questions. They want you to know the answers because they want you to come in and pitch what they're looking for, when they're looking for it."

Today's TV networks see themselves as on-air destinations. Each aims to create a unique programming environment. This shows up most clearly in the look, feel, and sound of what surrounds the programs; interstitials, bumpers, and even on-air-hosting devices like *Face* on Nick Jr., *Clay* on *PlayHouse Disney*, and the *Total Request Live (TRL)*–style live action hosting of cartoons on Nick and Cartoon Network. Things get a lot grayer when you actually watch the programs. There has been too much cross-pollination of network executives and show creators for there to be much of a distinction.

Networks developing animation for kids try to distinguish themselves from their competitors by skewing more or less toward girls or boys and skewing action or comedy. Yet all this is thrown to the wind as hits emerge on other networks and result in similar projects being greenlit elsewhere. Think about Cartoon Network's *Powerpuff Girls* giving rise to competitor network shows like Nick's *Fairly Odd Parents* and Disney's *Kim Possible*, and coming full circle with Cartoon Network's own *Atomic Betty*. As Fred Seibert says, "The hits on the network, or at another network, have a great influence at a given moment." Madeleine Lévesque adds, "There is a danger of being bogged down by all the other networks' hits and turning into a follower."

Using their network's most recent development mandate as their guide, development executives look out for the needs of a network. The network, in turn, caters to a particular audience in

Madeleine Lévesque, director, original production, Teletoon, Canada.

order to secure that audience's spending power, which will attract advertisers. All of this aside, how much does the personal taste of a network development executive come into play? What, if any, impact does that have on your idea getting sold?

Eric Coleman answers, "To get a series into production I need to sell it up the ranks at the network, so of course I'm most passionate about the projects that I would want to watch myself. Development is a very subjective process so I can't help but gravitate toward the projects with a sensibility or design that appeals to me. At the end of the day, though, it's crucial to develop shows with the audience in mind. I pick projects that I love and I think kids will too."

Fred Seibert, president and executive producer, Frederator.

For Fred Seibert, his taste is a critical and necessary factor in deciding to greenlight a project. "It's not the only factor—we're making cartoons for an audience—but for me, it's a necessary factor. I want to believe in the project and the creator, and my taste affects those feelings directly."

Linda Simensky also uses personal taste as her guide. She adds, "I tend to believe that a network that hires a development person hires her partly for her ability to factor in what their network is looking for, and partly for the network's taste. The most talented network development people tend to have very good judgment and confidence as well. It's a great feeling when you can go around telling people you've just seen a project you really love. That gets people excited."

Alice Cahn reveals, "It's not so much how much your own personal taste influences projects, but your ability to put yourself inside the mind/heart of your target audience. Certainly my own interests, likes, and dislikes come into play, but it's

Linda Simensky, Senior Director, PBS Kids.

more about your professional and personal connection with the audience than it is about what you like."

Madeleine Lévesque believes, "Personal taste should never be a factor in making a decision. Responsibility is to the network, not to yourself. Extracting personal taste is difficult but certainly attainable if you understand that you're not programming for yourself. We're programming for an audience. By the way, using your own kids as a test audience is also a big mistake since it's impossible to be objective when it comes to your own kids."

Alice Cahn, vice president of development and programming, Cartoon Network.

You Arrived at Just the Right Development Window

In 2004, Cartoon Network announced a return to its *What A Cartoon* program, creating a need for twenty new original shorts. In 2005, Frederator announced a fourth season of *Oh, Yeah! Cartoons*, beginning a search for thirty-nine new original shorts. Such announcements herald a pitching bonanza, but outside of these situations, do networks buy only in specific cycles of the year? If so, is there a better or worse time to pitch? Or does this have any effect at all?

Linda Simensky advises not pitching around holidays. "If people are out of the office, you may miss the one person you need to meet." Outside of this, the primary buyers of animation, including Nickelodeon, Teletoon, Cartoon Network, and the Disney Channel, are open for pitches all year long. While pitches are taken all year long, there may be specific rounds of development. For instance, Alice Cahn reports, "In preschool we currently have two rounds of development each year; once a set of projects are identified as possibilities, we bring our multi-disciplinary team together (development, scheduling, acquisitions, enterprises, new media) and discuss how the project fits within the Cartoon Network environment and how it might play in the larger children's media environment. The process can be anywhere from three to six months from initial pitch to greenlight decision."

You Have Network Cheerleaders Rallying for You

It's critical to have development executives be your cheerleaders to the network. They're the ones who will sell you to their superiors once you leave the room and you probably won't be in the room when your project is greenlit. Madeleine Lévesque adds, "I do often remind creators that I and a lot of other people in the company must 'sell' the title internally. That's why it's so important to be really excited about it."

It all comes back to relationships. Get yourself out there and meet industry people outside of official pitch meetings. For anyone serious about selling their shows, attending animation festivals are a must. All of the major networks send their development executives to the festivals as scouts. Festivals provide a great opportunity for creators and development executives to meet in a fun, inspiring, and social environment. The rest is up to you.

There is a word of caution to relay here. Network development executives are often encouraging of individuals. However, that doesn't automatically make them sincere cheerleaders once you leave the room. One friend of mine learned this the hard way.

He approached a development executive with a pitch for a live-action sketch comedy series for tweens. The network scheduled a meeting with him, but then they rescinded and said he must first send some writing samples. Like any self-respecting writer, he had samples galore and quickly sent them some funny scripts. After a month delay, they told him they liked his work and scheduled a new appointment for him to pitch. He used the opportunity to invite other writers into the project and for two weeks they brainstormed sketch material. Two of the writers were also actresses who readied to perform some of the material at the pitch meeting.

Character designs by the author and Dale Clowdis for their pitch, Mangoose. *After some interest at Cartoon Network, we attempted to retool this idea for Spike TV, a network still feeling its way to the degree that they replaced the entire development team along with the network president. Such upheaval always makes for a lousy time to pitch.*

The whole team was very excited until a day or so before the scheduled pitch when the network executive cancelled the meeting again. Now the executive wanted to read the new material in place of taking a meeting. Disappointed, the writer and his team sent in the scripts. Two months later, the development executive finally granted the team a meeting. Everyone mustered their enthusiasm once more. When they got to the meeting, the development executive, who had been their contact, had blown them off. In her place was a lower level person who opened the pitch meeting with the revelation that the team had just missed the development round by a mere few weeks. Imagine their disappointment.

My writer friend was very confused and saddened by the experience. He said that the executives' encouragement was why he'd put so much time into the pitch, rallied a team together, and sacrificed many weekends. He wondered why they would lead him on and ask him to do so much work if they weren't sincere about it. I thought about it for a moment and told him, "They did this because they're generous with your time."

It's no skin off a development executive's nose to ask you to keep working on your project. It costs them nothing to ask you to donate more of your time and energy to your own project. The onus is on us to cultivate relationships with smart and sincere development people. It's just like dating. Look at the warning signs. For instance, there's a very likable development executive that keeps asking me to pitch and then doesn't return my calls or e-mails. Is that someone who sincerely wants to work with me? An executive genuinely interested in working with you nurtures you through the process. They check in on you, return phone calls, and help sell your idea up the ladder.

PREPARING FOR THE PITCH MEETING

Near the end of *The Muppet Movie*, Kermit and the gang finally land a meeting with a studio mogul played by the legendary Orson Welles. Before you can say *Rainbow Connection*, Welles rings up his secretary and asks her to prepare the "standard rich and famous contract."

In the real world, pitching is a little more complicated. Before you enter a pitch room you have got to be able to say your idea in two minutes or less. In fact you should be able to sum it all up in a sentence. For example, if I were pitching the *Powerpuff Girls* (Cartoon Network), I could say something like, "It's about three pint-size superheroes that save the day before bedtime." You shouldn't have to talk about your idea for two hours to do it justice. If it can't be boiled down to a fun, simple, and captivating log line, it's probably not a good fit for an animated series.

With the above mentioned logline, I'd offer some samples of "show art" (finished color artwork done in the style of the show) illustrations of the main characters in action. The show art reveals characters and shows them interacting with their world.

After the logline, you still have nearly two whole minutes to fill. Next would be the set-up or concept for the show. In the case of the *Powerpuff Girls*, the next thing we might mention is, "Professor Utonium created the Powerpuff Girls in his lab from sugar, spice, and everything nice. Living as a family with the Professor as their father-figure, the Powerpuff Girls balance lives as preschoolers with the adult-sized task of protecting the city of Townsville." Next, I might talk about the main villain, Mojo Jojo. Then I'd explain how the girls spring into action when they receive a call from the Mayor on their special phone and that there will be a narrator opening and closing each episode and so on. I'd pitch all of this in one minute while displaying show art of each of the main characters.

Show art I designed for use in my pitch with Richard Gorey, called Tad and His Dad.

All of the above was about concept. Next, we would dig deeper and use the remaining minute to dive into character. If I were pitching a venue such as Cartoon Network's *What A Cartoon* or Frederator/Nickelodeon's *Oh, Yeah! Cartoons* then I'd probably reverse this order and follow my log-line by going right into character information. That's because *What a Cartoon!* and *Oh, Yeah! Cartoons* are seeking characters above all else. The concept or gimmick is supposed to be secondary or in support of the characters. This is the very definition of the oft-used network term, "character driven." Characters are the reason we care. *Buffy the Vampire Slayer* is about a high school girl who happens to be the chosen one, equipped with supernatural powers, to fight vampires and demons. That's a great log-line, but it tells us nothing about her character. Why would I care about Buffy? I have to prove to a development executive why Buffy is special. She's conflicted about the role she's forced to play. She's struggling to be normal in a world turned upside down. These are some of the things that start to make her a character beyond the concept of the show. Animation is no different.

Lastly, you would mention a brief synopsis of possible episodes to show off your characters and concept in action. This is really the last piece of the puzzle, tying all the elements together.

The combination of your strong characters, great concept, and fun episode ideas should be enough to show why this idea has potential to last for one hundred episodes, spin-offs, and several feature films. If your pitch is not a good fit for the network, no amount of verbal gymnastics will convince them otherwise. Besides, your two minutes are up.

When pitching with partners you should have a general idea of what each person will be contributing at the meeting. It would be a good idea to have one person take on the main duties of introducing the project. Another member of the team may take over to pitch the story, discuss the characters, or describe the technique of the finished project. All members should be sure to read the room and adjust their presentations as needed. In addition to this, partners must also read each other and be ready to step in and offer support/back-up to a tough or unexpected question.

SCENES FROM A PITCH MEETING

The first thing you want to do is introduce yourself and your team. Briefly discuss your background and what experiences led you up to this point. Follow this by asking the executive to tell her story. How long has she been with this network? What projects has she shepherded? What is she excited about? Everyone should already be feeling looser and more comfortable. I like to follow the executive's cue as to when it's time to start pitching at a meeting. This way I don't risk coming across as over-anxious. Besides, the "getting to know each other" portion of the pitch is a lot of fun. It's where I first get to show off my personality. This part of the pitch is as important as the pitch portion itself. This is the formation of a long-term mutually beneficial relationship.

During your two-minute blitz pitch, you don't want to rattle off your spiel like an automaton. You've got to read the room. Reading the room is being aware of how the pitch is being received (as you are giving it). You should be open to interruptions, questions, or switching gears along the way. Remember, good pitching is a conversation, not a monologue. Don't over-rehearse or worry about the exact wording of your presentation. Keep things loose, fresh, and spontaneous. Afterwards, you can make a note of what worked and what should be retooled. Each pitch is a chance to hone your presentation.

As the pitcher, it's your job to set the tone of the room. What if the executive just had a fight with her husband that morning? What if her dog died the night before? What if she just got a dressing down by her boss? All of those things and more can certainly start your meeting off on a sour tone. We have absolutely no control over such things. Instead, it's up to us to create a relaxed and friendly vibe. The first step is to dress casual. You're not an accountant. Men don't need to shave. Women don't need to wear make-up. I like to dress how I would if I were meeting friends at local neighborhood bar. I want to be comfortable. TV executives dress pretty casual themselves.

Be sure to throw in some well-placed sleuthing at the beginning or end of a pitch meeting. Don't leave the meeting without asking what they're about to debut on TV or what they've got in development. The information you learn will help you shape a follow-up pitch.

TAKE THE PRESSURE OFF

"I have been in development for years since I went to Cartoon Network at the end of 2001. I've pitched to them, to Nickelodeon, and to Disney. I've met most of the development people in that world. No development person is obligated to tell you when your idea is dead with them, in other words to put it out of its misery and allow you to move on. They just don't return your calls and e-mails and let you guess."
—*Craig Bartlett, creator of* Hey Arnold!, *Nickelodeon*

At the conclusion of a pitch meeting, you're not likely to hear a "yes" unless you're a celebrity or one of the top hit-makers in the business. Chances are you won't get a "no" either. In fact, I'm still waiting on the "no" from some pitches I gave two years ago. Of course, silence is in fact "no," and that's a good thing to understand and accept.

It's only when we fully understand the nature of pitch meetings that we can exploit them to our own benefit. For instance, if I know that I will not get a "yes" or "no" at the conclusion of a pitch meeting, that allows me to take the pressure off. If there's nothing immediately at stake, then I don't have to give the perfect pitch. That makes me feel relaxed. When you're relaxed, it puts others in the room at ease. People feed off each other's energy. Relaxed people come across as confident and stable. The executive knows that if your idea sells, she'll be spending a lot of time with you. It's not just the idea you're selling; more importantly, you're selling yourself.

The pitch meeting should be thought of as a first step, a valuable chance to make a new contact, get feedback on your work, and snoop around as to what the network is looking for at this particular moment.

The pitch, especially a first pitch, should be considered an informational meeting. Whether the experience is good or bad, there is always something to learn from it. How did your method of presentation work out? Was it a good thing to bring a series bible to the meeting? Did the executive become over-whelmed by too many details? Post-meeting, take stock of what worked and what didn't, and try something new next time.

You're not at the meeting to get the last word or to do battle. You're there to build a successful partnership between you and the network. Just be your-self and be sincere and the rest should follow. Like-minded people always find each other sooner or later. Pitching means that you've started to look.

The reality is that it will likely take years of pitching and repitching before you sell something. Therefore the pitch meetings you make along the way are to get you and your ideas ready for the day when all the planets align. The meeting you take today sets up the opportunity you may have ten years from now. Creator Elanna Allen adds, "Even if you're pitching stuff that's not that good at first, it's still worth pitching if your end goal is to have a show. The person you are pitching to will be at a new company in two years and now you'll have a contact there. It's scary, so to get over that fear, you've got to do it."

WHEN CREATORS ATTACK . . .

The surest automatic deal killer is a poor attitude. You may only have one chance to make a good impression. Even if you disagree with the development executive, you need to behave like a reasonable professional. There is always something to be learned from even the most seemingly off-base criticism. Give the development executive the benefit of the doubt.

Linda Simensky explains, "When you tell them why the property is not what you are looking for, they get angry at you, they tell you that you're wrong, and create a contentious environment. No matter what you think of the show, you end up disliking the person, and that never makes you want to go to bat for that person."

Character designs by the author for my preschool pitch, Keisha Catterpillar, *described by one executive as being very ordinary. I must have responded with dignity and grace because I was asked to pitch again for the next development round, by which point I'd found a more receptive pitch audience at Frederator.*

Fred Seibert has had many bad pitch meetings. "I guess the saddest are when someone has no skill and very little talent. But the most annoying are the so-called professionals who think number one, they deserve a pick-up, or number two, believe the audience is stupid, or number three, their 'talent' is enough to cover up a terrible project."

For Eric Coleman, the worst pitches aren't just bad—they're boring. "The biggest crime when pitching is being boring."

Madeleine Lévesque was pitched in a bathroom once, which she says was not very smart. "You need to have the proper environment and that does not qualify!"

PITCHING STYLES

"I don't know what the correct protocol is for a pitch meeting.
I try to just be myself. I like to bring a puppet in with me
to a stop motion pitch meeting."
—*Elanna Allen, character designer, stop motion animator*

There's a limitless number of styles or ways to present your material and to create a lasting impression. I would recommend that if you choose to be nutty, not to choose style over substance. The presentation cannot be more memorable than the idea itself. Yet, as a creator, it is you that is on sale as much as it is your ideas. Above everything else, be yourself.

After snagging his Oscar nomination for *The Chicken from Outer Space*, John R. Dilworth donned a space suit and pitched his heart out all across Los Angeles. John Kricfalusi threw himself into a sweaty frenzy, pitching the cartoon antics of *Ren and Stimpy* to Nickelodeon. After being asked, "Why should we hire you?" a writer auditioning for *Saturday Night Live* rubbed raw sandwich meats on his chest. Then there's the story of Gabor Csupo and Arlene Klasky, selling their show *Ahhh! Real Monsters* based on a simple doodle scrawled on a paper napkin. This approach might work for you, too, if you had directed award-winning commercials for over a decade, made three seasons of *The Simpsons*, and created the hit original series, *Rugrats*. Until your resume matches theirs, you should avoid presenting ideas on a napkin.

Cartoon Network's *Codename: Kids Next Door* creator, Mr. Warburton, described his pitching style. "I like to come up with a colorful ten- or twelve-page booklet that really describes the world I'm trying to pitch. Not too many words, not too many pictures. Short, sweet, and to the point. Once I finished them I just mailed them on down to the development people at Cartoon Network. The rest was all done over the phone and at my drawing desk and computer . . . but not

Still from Mr. Warburton's Codename: Kids Next Door, *Cartoon Network.*

quickly, mind you. Development always takes a long time, and generally, that's a good thing. Every show needs time to be developed."

Nickelodeon's *Hey Arnold!* creator Craig Bartlett recalls, "*Hey Arnold!* was pitched in August 1993 to Mary Harrington in Burbank, California when she was head of original animation for Nickelodeon, kind of by accident, after me and five other *Rugrats* writers had pitched several ideas we had come up with together. We talked for an hour or so and were out of ideas, so we pulled comics and other things out of our briefcases, just trying to find out what Mary liked. I showed her my videotape reel of old *Penny* cartoons that I had done for *Pee Wee's Playhouse*—at the front of the reel were three Arnold cartoons that I had made myself, in the claymation *Penny* style. That got Mary's attention. I then showed her some Arnold comics that I had drawn for *Simpsons Illustrated*, and it seems that one particular panel of Arnold screaming was the real clincher for her. She laughed and laughed. When the meeting adjourned, Mary buttonholed me outside and said that she wanted to pursue Arnold further.

"We six *Rugrats* writers then adjourned to a pizza place and debriefed about the meeting. The other five guys sensed that I had somehow gotten my own show out of the group meeting. Paul Germain said, 'Arnold is gonna go to series, mark my words.' I met with Mary over the next four months, refining a pilot outline, and the pilot was greenlit in January. The pilot was made in 1994 and the series was greenlit a year later."

Eric Coleman described two of his favorite pitches. "The pitch for *SpongeBob SquarePants* was one of the best I've ever had. Steve Hillenburg set the mood with a seashell that played Hawaiian music, he wore a Hawaiian shirt, and he built an aquarium with all of the characters living inside. But more importantly, he captivated us with his description of SpongeBob and his world. The pitch felt very simple yet very fresh at the same time. And very funny. He didn't just promise it, he demonstrated it. He had wonderful

Stephen Hillenburg's SpongeBob SquarePants, *Copyright 2005. Viacom International Inc.*

artwork and character descriptions and storylines that conveyed a very well-crafted vision for a series.

Coleman continues, "The pitch for *Avatar* was also one of my favorites. There's a great depth and complexity to the show and at the pitch the cre-

ators had not yet fully wrangled their vision for it, but they gushed forth with such energy and ideas and incredible artwork and compelling characters. After about twenty minutes the pitch was spiraling out of control and I interrupted them—we laugh about it now—I told them 'I have no idea what you're talking about anymore, but I love it.' I just knew it was something special, and that's a wonderful feeling for a development executive (and all too rare). We were all so excited to jump in immediately and start to figure it all out."

Cartoon Network's Adult Swim hit, *The Venture Brothers*, was created by Jackson Publick, who recalls, "I pitched it by writing a full half-hour script and putting together a little 'pitch book.' I mailed them off to Linda Simensky at Cartoon Network and a week later got the phone call informing me they'd like to make the pilot. The pitch book ultimately was comprised of a page describing the overall concept of the show, several pages devoted to describing the main characters, and about half a dozen episode concepts—illustrated with about two dozen color drawings."

Still from Cartoon Network's Adult Swim *show,* The Venture Brothers, *created by Jackson Publick.*

PARTNERS IN PITCHING

For a few years I tried pitching alone. First I developed and pitched some ideas as promos for MTV. Then I pitched a concept for MTV's *Cartoon Sushi*, which was a short-lived follow-up to the much more successful *Liquid Television*. Finally, Machi Tantillo, from the Oxygen Network, asked me to pitch them a cartoon from a woman's point of view. Never one to run away from a challenge, I attempted to do just that. In these pitches I primarily worked alone, doing the writing, design, storyboarding, and the pitching itself.

Show art for my ill-advised pitch to the Oxygen Network, designed by Bob Levy, my dad. Nice design, though.

The pitches didn't sell. Shortly thereafter, Linda Simensky asked if I would be interested in pitching at Cartoon Network. For the first time, I decided to approach a colleague, Dale Clowdis, as a potential collaborator on a pitch. Clowdis and I became fast friends as co-workers at *Blue's Clues*. Our careers on the show had a similar arc. We both became lead animators at the same time and were assigned to work together to create all the original animation for the show's new feline star, Periwinkle. A short while later I was promoted to an animation director, and Clowdis followed only a year behind. Most importantly, we got along well. Happily, Clowdis agreed to my offer to collaborate and we got down to work.

We quickly learned that we both had a lot of good ideas. Brainstorm sessions always yielded results. Before long we dashed off a pitch about two odd humanoid-animal brothers from another dimension called *Mangoose* and sent it to Cartoon Network. Good ideas aside, we both still had a lot to learn about pitching. The nice folks at Cartoon Network pulled us through three more attempts to develop and repitch our zany idea. In the final try, we fully scripted and storyboarded a potential pilot episode. In the end we didn't make the sale, but Cartoon Network encouraged us to try again with a new idea. So, we began the process all over again, this time, with more experience under our belt.

We began by submitting a two-sheet, which is a two-page rough proposal for a pitch. On it was a logline, brief character and setting descriptions, along with some sample plots. We called the show *Hard to Swallow*, and it was about a worm, a bird, and a cat engaged in an uneasy and unnatural friendship. Cartoon Network liked it and asked for more information. We eventually

repitched them three more times, writing and storyboarding two complete possible pilot episodes. In the third and final stage we provided a show bible, filled with fancy color artwork, possible plots, and full descriptions of the entire universe of *Hard to Swallow*. In the end, the network passed again and for the first time without really giving us a reason. We'd come so far that it was heartbreaking to stop there, so we hatched a new idea: we'd make our own pilot film and then

A still from Scout Says, *a film I made with Dale Clowdis for our pitch,* Hard To Swallow. *Backgrounds were by Bob Levy. Image courtesy of the author.*

use it as a pitching tool. Two years later, we repitched *Hard to Swallow* with our film, *Scout Says*, named after the plucky, bossy bird of our show, Scout.

With hindsight I can see that Clowdis and I drew strength from one another. We rallied each other on to keep trying. Neither of us could have gone on for so long without the other. So far, our film, *Scout Says*, has succeeded more in landing us new work than it did getting us a series. For five years I'd made a steady commitment to pitching ideas with Clowdis and some preschool ideas on my own. I was ready for a break. I settled into a new directing job at Cartoon Pizza and put pitching out of my mind. Then one day, Fred Seibert came to lecture at my SVA animation career class. In front of the forty-two students he expressed the sincere hope that I would pitch him another cartoon idea. His company, Frederator, was about to embark on a new season of *Oh, Yeah! Cartoons*. He had thirty-nine seven-minute cartoons to find.

Despite many commitments, I squeezed in time to pitch Seibert two ideas. This time I wanted to try several new things in my pitch plan. For starters, I wanted to bring in more partners than I had in the past. For one, I brought in writer Richard Gorey to help develop the idea I had called *Tad and His Dad*, which was the story of a father/son magic act. Knowing Frederator's fondness for pitches in storyboard form, I decided to make a monetary investment and hire a storyboard artist to board out the two ideas. Otis Brayboy created the pitch boards.

Tad and His Dad caught Seibert's interest off the bat and he encouraged us to make some improvements. Rich and I made changes to the script and I handled the board revisions myself. The second time we pitched *Tad and His Dad* we had near bulls-eye. Although a green light was discussed we were asked to toil through what turned out to be six months of revisions and repitches. During this time, I took a huge chance and contacted the management of former frontman of The Lovin' Spoonful, John B. Sebastian, to see if he would be interested in writing some music for our project. Amazingly, Sebastian enthusiastically agreed and within weeks he wrote a terrific song for our cartoon. In the words of Frederator vice president of creative affairs, Eric Homan, "Fred did back flips at the news of Sebastian being on board."

In the end, we didn't get our green light at Frederator, but Rich Gorey and I were left with a fully developed great project that we've begun to shop elsewhere. At a recent pitch meeting for *Tad and His Dad*, a top executive from a huge media company screamed, "I love this!"

In the world of pitching cartoon shows, there is no way of knowing if and when we'll ultimately be successful. Each pitch makes you a sharper salesman, creator, and storyteller. Each pitch is a chance to forge important relationships with not only your creative partners, but with the network executives as well. It's been an eye-opening experience for me to learn that my best and most successful work may not come out until I collaborate with others.

TEST FOOTAGE IN A PITCH MEETING

"Test animation won't override a poor concept. I don't care how good it is. It can provide the incentive to work on the concept. I can say with certainty that if it's not perfect: don't show it."
—*Madeleine Lévesque, director, original production, Teletoon, Canada*

There are pros and cons to making a film or a piece of finished animation for use in the pitching process. Many pitchers advocate showing off their ideas in a form closest to a finished production, a one-minute test film. The footage usually consists of a character showing off her quirks in a short self-contained sequence. The benefit of creating such a film or test footage is the executive doesn't have to use their imagination to visualize what is in your head. This can be a useful tool to help get across your vision. Linda Simensky agrees, adding, "Sometimes it's just fun to see the character come to life. We had a pitch here at PBS that was really funny, but the creator had made a short film that was even funnier than the pitch, and that really helped the project generate enthusiasm."

On the con side, creating a film or test footage takes time to prepare and this is time lost out in the real world. You don't want to take two years to get your pitch together. Attention spans are short, so you don't want to present anything that will take over a minute to watch. Eric Coleman adds, "It's most important for your pitch to make a strong impression about your project. You shouldn't just claim the show will be funny, thrilling, innovative, etc., you need to demonstrate it, whether you have animation or not."

If you decide to use test footage at a pitch, remember, the test footage is part of the pitch, not the pitch itself. Don't look for a way to keep from having to speak at the meeting. Don't avoid making a personal connection.

MERCHANDISE AND BUDGETS

The most common question I hear from people who are about to pitch for the first time is, "Do I need to know the budget of my show?" The answer is absolutely not. You are not the money person. You are the creative person with a project to pitch. The network holds the purse strings. Creators need to focus only on the pitch idea and how best to communicate it. If the network wants you and your idea they'll work out finances.

Keep your focus on the creative end, which does not include bringing merchandising ideas to a pitch and showing how your cartoon would look on T-shirts, mugs, and bumper stickers. You've got to sell and create your show first. Besides, of all the duties that a creator of a hit series takes on, merchandising is the least under his supervision or approval. Networks have entire departments devoted to marketing and merchandising their hit properties.

FOCUS GROUPS IN THE PITCH PROCESS

Focus groups are used by networks in the development process in a variety of ways. In Linda Simensky's experience, focus groups are sometimes used like Magic Eight Balls, enabling executives who have no programming instincts to make decisions. Simensky says, "The best way to use focus groups is to go in hoping to learn things about your show, to test the basic ideas, and to try out ideas to see what gets kids excited. If your network trusts twelve ten-year-old kids in a room more than they trust you and your department, find a new job."

Eric Coleman appreciates the brutally honest feedback that comes from kids during focus group testing. However, Coleman cautions, "This feedback is only one factor in the decision to pick up a series. Rave reviews certainly help a pilot's pick-up chances, but ultimately we're most interested in hearing feedback to guide us in the development process of projects we're already optimistic about."

Madeleine Lévesque reminds us, "We tend to forget that the breakaway hits always come from behind. *The Simpsons, SpongeBob, Family Guy*, these shows focus-group tested terribly."

MY EMOTIONAL ROLLERCOASTER

"Never let anyone try to psych you out of your dream. It's a long shot, it's tough, but if you truly care and have talent you'll get the opportunity to contribute in a meaningful way."
—*Madeleine Lévesque, director, original production, Teletoon, Canada*

Recently, I had the unique opportunity to pitch the same three preschool ideas to two separate divisions of one parent network in the same week. In one division, an executive said that my pitches were the best stuff that anyone had ever pitched them! Unfortunately, the network wasn't buying any more shows until six months later. I was told to keep in touch. For the next six months I stayed in touch through e-mail and phone calls. Unsurprisingly, the whole thing turned out to be a dead end. Still, it's always encouraging when someone likes your work, even if there's no deal at the end of it.

A few days after this encouraging pitch meeting I pitched the same three ideas to the network's other division. I knew the executive, so I was at ease and on top of my game, belting out my ideas with excitement and enthusiasm. The executive leaned forward at the conclusion of the first two pitches and asked, "Don't you think your designs are ordinary?" That was one question I hadn't prepared an answer for.

A little shaken, I showed the idea for the third and final pitch. My favorite of the three, I had saved the best for last. A solid concept, good storyline, strong designs . . . or so I thought. At the end of the last pitch she said, "Okay, now this one is good, but I'm looking for *great.*" The meeting concluded shortly after that as I gathered up my materials and my pride; I made a silent vow not to return. With all the networks out there, certainly we should, at least, exhaust the possibilities before pitching to a toxic executive again.

FANTASY VERSUS REALITY

Many of us want to create, pitch, sell, and make our own animated TV pilot/series, but it's not likely to happen as quickly or as smoothly as we'd like. Still, some creators do manage to break through. When that happens the fantasy of success yields to the reality of having to deliver what you've promised.

Blue's Clues co-creator Traci Paige Johnson's experience co-creating and helming a long-running series gives her a unique perspective. "In the first season I worked eighty hours a week, dreamed it, ate it; it consumed me and I lost myself, it was like giving birth. When getting a show off the ground, you need to be involved with everything to set the tone and vision. Once the second season comes around you can delegate more and if you're lucky enough to get more seasons you can delegate even more. When I first started, the time devoted to managing people was equivalent to the time spent on the creative . . . I wasn't expecting that. I sometimes felt like a kindergarten teacher."

Jackson Publick, creator of *The Venture Brothers* on Cartoon Network's Adult Swim, was so busy by the middle of the first season of his show that he only had time to write scripts on nights and weekends. He added, "The biggest challenges production-wise are time and money, as always. They're both limited, and they both keep you from being able to keep revising and embellishing and finessing your work, which can be a good thing—don't get me wrong. Another challenge was confidence. It's pretty alarming when you don't consider yourself much more than an average-at-best draftsman and you're suddenly forcing talented people to draw like you.

"Pretty much all of my time goes to making my show. I'm either writing or drawing or thinking/worrying about writing or drawing. An unexpected bonus of all of this is I don't have a lot of time to fall into the trap of watching bad reality TV when I get home at night and I rarely ever have to wonder 'whatever am I going to do this weekend?'"

Postcard announcing the premiere of Mr. Warburton's first pilot for Cartoon Network, Kenny and the Chimp, *from the author's collection.*

With *Kenny and the Chimp*, Mr. Warburton's first pilot for Cartoon Network, he suddenly found himself out in Los Angeles, being told what to do, and how to do it. Warburton recalls, "Every day I learned eleventy billion new things and then went home to bed and stared at the ceiling saying 'hooooly shit, what just happened?' When I went out to do *Codename: Kids Next Door (KND)*, it was so much easier because I kind of (slightly?) knew what I was doing. That of course didn't stop me from crying myself to sleep some nights due to sheer terror over whether it would turn out okay.

"I roughed out 80 percent of the animation for *Kenny* because I had never sent anything overseas before and I was scared about how it would turn out. It was really hard and probably pretty stupid. Korea would have done a better job. Don't tell anyone, but I'm not really that great of an animator. You're not printing this, are you?

"To be honest, I'm glad *Kenny* didn't get picked up back then. I wasn't ready yet, probably would have had to move out to Los Angeles, and ended up with a so-so show that I had no control over."

For *Bob and Margaret* co-creator David Fine, there were different challenges at different stages. "At first, the challenge was to write half-hour scripts. We didn't go anywhere until we were confident we could do that. Surprisingly, it was actually easier to write half hours than our original short *Bob's Birthday*, which launched the series, because the short was so precious that writing it was much more exacting. The series was also exacting, but because each episode was one story rather than *the* story, we felt more relaxed and could try different things.

"After the writing, certainly the big challenge was working with a big production team and working long distance with them, in many cases. We had some great people on the show, but we were also very demanding and wanted a lot of control, which didn't always sit well. Occasionally we would have a great deal of redoing to do and that put a lot of pressure on us and the production. When *Bob and Margaret* was in production, we worked insane hours. We were quite pleased with what we ended up with.

"In many regards, the show exceeded our expectations, but then we didn't entirely know what we were getting into. I suppose the only letdown was the technical problems with the line quality, which led to a ridiculous amount of reshoots throughout most of the first season and still never ended up right. It put such a heavy burden on the production and it was surprising because it was the last problem we imagined we would have."

KNOWING WHEN TO WALK AWAY FROM A DEAL

When it comes to what might be our big break opportunities, the last thing on our mind is to walk away. It was the last thing on my mind when I was suddenly offered a development deal at MTV Networks.

At the time I was working as an animator at *Blue's Clues*. After a chance encounter with a kind-hearted top executive at Nickelodeon, I was asked to consult on a few years old, unaired, *Heckle and Jeckle* revival pilot made by MTV Networks. He shared that although it was unsuccessful, there was the possibility to give the whole venture another try; after all, *Heckle and Jeckle* was owned by MTV Networks' parent company, Viacom.

A day later I received the pilot tape via inter-office mail and then spent a week studying it. After much thought and research, I wrote up a critique letter that also doubled as a proposal for a next try. A few days later the MTV Networks head sent an e-mail thanking me and commenting that some of my suggestions echoed the thoughts of the president of Nickelodeon. After this I started to get wind that they wanted me to be involved in the redevelopment of *Heckle and Jeckle*. Just before Christmas break in 1999, a network development executive called me with the good news that they were going to be offering me a development deal to help revive *Heckle and Jeckle*. "I'm just thrilled to be a part of this," I said. The executive replied, "Part of it? You are it!" We agreed to meet up right after the holiday break.

In our first meeting we talked classic cartoons and loosely brainstormed how *Heckle and Jeckle* could be brought up to date without sacrificing any of what originally made it great. However, the first cracks in the facade appeared when the development executive dismissed my request to create a project mission statement defining what were we trying to achieve. The development executive was very reluctant to lay out any parameters.

I was at no point given the impression that my role would be anything other than a creative director. After all, it was my vision for *Heckle and Jeckle* that led to this deal in the first place. So, imagine my surprise when the contract finally arrived and it defined me exclusively as the artist on the project. According to the contract, I would draw the ideas created by the writer (to be identified). In other words, the writers would conceptualize and I would be their pencil. The contract specified that I was to provide unlimited character models, color models, and background setups until they said "when." Then they would have the option to ask for unlimited revisions for an indefinite amount of time. The compensation for all this was so low it was almost nonexistent. I politely tried to relay these concerns to the development executive who used the conversation as a chance to remind me that I was "below the radar." He advised me to sign the deal and not mess with things.

On the issue of infinite artwork and revisions, he assured me that it was for my own benefit. "This way, you can create all you want and not have to limit yourself," he suggested. "It doesn't matter that the contract defines you as the artist. We both know you'll be creating the concept too, so it doesn't matter what it says on the contract."

"If it doesn't matter what it says, then it should list my role correctly as the creative director on this project," I replied.

"You're just naïve. You're nervous because it's your first deal," he insisted.

Staying as emotionally detached as possible I answered, "I'm just responding to a contract that originated from your office. I'm talking about what is written on this piece of paper."

After an hour of trying to coerce me to sign, he agreed to revise the contract. The next day he called me to apologize for his behavior. He'd thought about it and felt like he'd been a bully. I accepted his apology and we agreed to put it all behind us. The apology made me feel better and I opened my mind to making a fresh go of it. A couple of months later the next contract arrived and it was a near replay of the one before. Again, we negotiated the contract, but this time he advised me to get a lawyer.

He had his chorus. "This legal stuff is gonna get ugly. You should get a lawyer. This isn't the work. You should keep your eyes on the prize. You're below the radar."

I had my chorus. "I'll be happy to get a lawyer when we have a contract that reflects the original intention of this project."

It would have taken a forensic team to discover any differences between the next agreement they drew up and two that preceded it. When I rejected this third contract, the development executive refused to even speak to me about it. The only option left was to talk to his lawyer at the network. To the lawyer I explained my frustrations about the contracts and how none of them had come close to listing my role in this project correctly.

"Why am I listed as the artist? This development executive hasn't even seen my portfolio. How does he know I'm the right artist for this? This project originated because of my concept of how to revive *Heckle and Jeckle*. All of this was based on a letter I wrote. It was about the overall vision I had for the project. No contract I've received thus far has come close to putting this deal in the proper light."

The lawyer recorded all of my comments and passed them along to the executive. My words must have cut deep because he suddenly decided to grant me an in-person meeting after all. By this point, nearly a year had gone by since that first promising phone call in late 1999.

In anticipation of this meeting I got some good advice from a top development executive at a rival network. "This isn't your big break. Your big break will be with your own creations, not *Heckle and Jeckle*. A good development executive would be supportive and protective of you. You should walk away from this." That was the key. After this whole stressful unhappy year dealing with all this nonsense, the thought of walking away was a revelation. I felt lighter and happier just thinking about it.

At our final meeting, the development executive let me have it. "You've had your back up this whole time. Don't you know that you're below the radar? You don't have your eyes on the prize. This stuff that you're focusing on . . . it isn't the work."

"No," I said, "It isn't the work. It's the relationship."

With that, there was nothing really left to say. The meeting ended with him offering me one last deal, one final chance to sign. The contract came shortly after and, again, nothing of any importance had changed. I didn't sign. It was all over. I've never regretted my decision.

Ironically, in the span of the ten months when I was repeatedly told that I was "below the radar," my career blossomed in many ways. I was promoted to director at *Blue's Clues*. On the side, I illustrated at least eight *Blue's Clues* books for four major publishers. Linda Simensky named me as her successor as president of ASIFA-East. My latest independent film, *Snow Business*, secured a distribution deal, which led to paid television broadcasts in six countries. The success of my independent film led to invitations to pitch at the Oxygen Network and Cartoon Network.

In contrast to my experiences, the development executive was let go a short time after our experience together. The moment I realized my success was not tied to this man, this project, and this network, I was able and ready to walk away. You have to believe in yourself above any one opportunity. If you really want it bad enough, there'll be plenty of other opportunities.

PATIENCE

A certain amount of patience is required for a would-be creator waiting for network feedback on her pitch. The first thing to remember is that your network development contact is likely to be juggling many projects at varying stages of development. With this in mind, you should allow several weeks before you start reminding the contact you're awaiting the verdict. I prefer to shop my projects around to a few different networks at once. This way I'm not waiting on any particular network, plus I get to benefit from having pitched my idea more than once. It's good to get a broad sense of how your ideas and pitching style are being received. Each time is a chance to experiment with the presentation.

How much time should it take for a network executive to give an answer on a pitch? It's impossible to say. While it's natural to assume that if a network is interested in your show they'll tell you immediately, it may not be the case. The process by which networks pitch material up the ladder internally takes time. Some networks round up worthwhile pitches once a month to present to the top echelon of decision makers. These meetings don't always occur like clockwork. Delays can also occur because network development executives are juggling other duties besides their role in development.

In addition to her development duties at PBS, Linda Simensky produces pilots and series and works on the network's current series. Simensky also oversees kids programming so she works on strategy and closely with the other departments.

Eric Coleman described his many duties outside of development. "I also oversee the animated current series in production for Nickelodeon, so I get to stay with the projects as they evolve over time. And I am the executive in charge of certain series so after the development stage I continue to work closely with the creators, writers, artists, etc., to bring to life the vision that got us all excited in the first place. I also work closely with the other network departments (programming, marketing, consumer products, etc.) to represent the animation department and all of its shows."

LEGAL SPEAK

The average creator didn't get into this racket so they could nuzzle up to lawyers and accountants. Legal implications are the byproducts of success. There isn't much you need to know before you're in a position to get a deal. Once you're faced with a contract, ring up other creators who have sold pilots. Which lawyer did they use? Would they use them again?

Many would-be creators get bogged down on the issue of copyright protection. This book doesn't pretend to be a legal guide, but creators do have basic copyright protection the moment they put pencil to paper. It helps to sign and date all versions of your material. For official copyright protection, creators would be advised to file their projects with the Library of Congress and get official copyright protection, for a small fee, of course.

When it comes to deals I like to remind people that Madonna's current recording contract would have little in common with her first. The point being that no single contract is your final deal.

Happy Trails: Parting Thoughts and Advice

Still from Dean Kalman Lennert's independent film, Dear Anna Olsen, *his labor of love for over fifteen years. Image courtesy of the artist.*

he last time I had lunch with Jeff Buckland, I asked him if there was a typical path to becoming an animation director. Not only did he answer my question, he inadvertently summed up a key theme of this book: "I think there's a certain amount of chance involved in any career path, so no journey will be typical. But when you set out with a specific destination in mind, you want to be prepared. Study the language, learn the exchange rate, and pack sensible shoes. It's similar to working in animation. Start with the basics: learn to draw, paint, and write. The more skills you have, the better equipped you'll be for whatever arises as you move up."

Whether you've read this book as a newcomer to the scene or an industry veteran, *Your Career in Animation: How to Survive and Thrive* is now part of your animation arsenal. It is my hope that this book has given new insights into this business—at the very least the book is a lot cheaper than flying around North America to have lunch with the one hundred animation artists featured in these pages. I think I speak for everyone in this book when I say that we look forward to our careers in animation overlapping with yours. Until that time, your fellow travelers and I couldn't resist one more opportunity to pass along some words of wisdom to help inspire you on your way.

"Once, a long time ago, I met the animator Robert Breer and asked him if he had any advice for someone who wanted to be an animator. He said: 'Do it while it's fun, and then don't.' Not great advice, maybe, but over time, I've grown to agree."
—*David J. Palmer, animation director*

"As a beginning producer, I felt like I was carrying the world on my shoulders. I carried an intensity every day at the office that did not serve me in my job. One day, Maurice Hunt, a director, said to me, 'Enjoy the journey.' I repeat those words to myself often."
—*David Steinberg, animation producer*

"Make films, write scripts. Try, and fail, and try again."
—*Fred Seibert, president & executive producer, Frederator*

"The worst thing for any artist is to rest on their laurels. I think it's important to try out new mediums. Sometimes I try to change it up each week. Pen and ink, to clay, to cutouts."
—*Teddy Newton, character designer*

"Regarding career plans: I know I'm an artist, and find essential fulfillment in creative expression. I used to think I'd draw comics forever; then I burned out. I'll do animation as long as it makes me

happy. If it ever turns into a soul-sapping chore,
I'll have to find another creative outlet."
—*Nina Paley, animator, cartoonist*

"I do think it's incredibly important to have something of your own
to work on outside the studio . . . something totally unrelated
to work. It's inspiring, rounds you out as an artist,
and if nothing else. . . clears your head."
—*Sue Perrotto, animation director*

"It's easy in animation to make mistakes with your peers
and superiors because they tend to be your closest friends;
we're all around the same age, we share similar interests,
and when you've worked in the industry long enough you
start to know everyone pretty well. In the end, people
have their roles to play in the workplace and those roles
define who they are from 10:00 A.M. to 7:00 P.M. A very good
person and friend could be unreasonable as a boss, or could be your
difficult employee, and it's important to isolate the different
roles your friends play (as they relate to your life and your job).
Additionally, it's important to trust your instincts when you
feel that you're being taken advantage of and, though it's important,
to respect friendship, but not to be blinded by it."
—*Liz Artinian, background artist*

"I can't really speak for how my own independent work has
affected my career as I have been working on a single personal film
as a side project for most of my professional life. Although it
has made me slightly infamous in the New York animation
community: 'You haven't finished that film yet?' I will say that it is
very important to create your own work. This gives you a chance
to push yourself and your skills to the limits. It also helps you to
become established as a creator of content and property
and not just some kind of a fancy pencil pusher. You also never
know where your own films will lead you!"
—*Dean Kalman Lennert, freelance animator, director*

"Get sleep now! I can't believe how many late nights are involved in animation."
—*Scott Cooper, storyboard artist*

Drawing by animation director Jeff Buckland. Image courtesy of the artist.

"The best piece of advice I got was from my father-in-law. Remember it's show *business* not show *art*. Understanding that you are in a business providing a service may be the hardest realization to make, but once it is understood, it will be invaluable to your thought process. The final product is key; that should be your focus."
—*Paul Zdanowicz, background artist, art director*

"The job may be grueling and even unbearable at times, but it is in the end a more rewarding job than nearly any other on the planet. Above all, remember that you are helping to entertain those who might really need a laugh or other cathartic experiences through your efforts. Even the smallest, most seemingly insignificant contribution to a film is one without which the film would not be what it is. Remember that. You *do* count! Work hard and stand tall! Now have at it!"
—*Jim Petropolis, animator*

"Finding a position in a studio that lasts for more than a season or two is quite rare these days. You are always on the lookout for who's hiring or who's going to have a project starting up when you are available in six months. There is no such thing as a job you will work at for thirty years and then retire in the animation industry. Don't go into it planning to make a career out of it, go into it because you can't imagine doing anything else."
—*Justin Simonich, animator*

"Probably the worst mistake anyone can make is being too self-confident. People with large egos and big heads make enemies quickly. Whole productions can fall apart because one person has a huge chip on their shoulder. However, too modest of an artist can easily be overlooked. Let your skills speak for you first, then your mouth second."
—*Kyle Neswald, animation artist*

"Learn as much as you can and be passionate about the history of the medium. You need to know what's been done so that you can forge ahead from there and make your own contribution to the art form."
—*Seamus Walsh, stop motion animator*

"If you demonstrate a certain sensitivity, care, and pride in your work with the skills to match, you should do well. It also helps to be personable and have the ability to work with a variety of people and personalities. Avoid burning any bridges. It is a relatively small industry and you will definitely end up in the same building as people you have worked with before, often in positions that could affect your future. Be humble, yet confident. It is a definite balance."
—*Celeste Pustilnick, sheet timer*

"Study everything that inspires you. Look at films. Go to plays. Read books. Look at paintings. Draw everything around you. Keep a sketchbook with you at all times to write down or draw an idea. I feel like I'm learning something new every day when I sit down to work. If you love to draw, you're in the right field because you'll be doing a lot of it. See you in the trenches."
—*Jason McDonald, designer*

> "To me, success is making what you want to make, when you want to make it, and caring an incredible amount about what you do."
> —*Jackson Publick, creator of* The Venture Brothers, *Cartoon Network, Adult Swim*

ANIMATION CAREER STRATEGY SURVIVAL LIST

Make a copy of this and put it on your fridge.

- ✦ Keep building/revising/updating that portfolio/reel as often as you can (every day).

- ✦ When looking for work, the most important thing is to get the meeting.

- ✦ Understand this is a people business. Always make time for networking.

- ✦ If you are working outside of the field to pay the bills, make a list of goals to accomplish each week to get you back into working in the animation industry.

- ✦ Stay inspired by surrounding yourself with your heroes! Get to know your animation heroes in books, films, comics, etc.

- ✦ Push yourself to learn new software/skills to stay marketable.

- ✦ Join an animation society or group.

- ✦ Find inspiration and make important contacts at international animation festivals such as Ottawa and Annecy.

- ✦ Look out for each other and recommend your talented peers when it's appropriate.

- ✦ Set goals and work each day towards creating the career of your choice.

Drawing by Howard Beckerman, showing one path to success. Image courtesy of the artist.

CODA: PRESCHOOL, THERAPY, AND TIME TRAVEL

One of the most valuable career lessons I ever learned was taught to me while I was in my senior year at SVA. Our animation career class instructor, Linda Simensky (then a Nickelodeon development executive), let us choose our own projects for a final assignment. Most students chose to write term papers about their favorite animation heroes. I decided to use the assignment to pitch Simensky (and by default, Nickelodeon) a series starring characters from my thesis film, *Get Off My Back*. Simensky accepted my proposal with a few conditions. First, I would have to pitch in front of the class so everyone could benefit from the experience. Second, I would have to pitch a development executive other than herself. The executive turned out to be Eric Coleman, later to make an enormous splash as a key development executive on *SpongeBob SquarePants*. Coleman was very helpful. Over bagels and cream cheese, Coleman shared the pointers of pitching with me. Most memorably, he showed examples of good and bad pitch books.

Inspired by even the faintest possiblity of success (beyond the class grade), I gathered all my pitch materials together, which consisted of a slick pitch bible, a finished test film, and three-foot-high color cutouts of my characters. The day of the pitch meeting finally arrived and to Coleman's credit, he didn't pull any punches. I believe I was treated as any unknown in the business would have been received. No details of this pitch meeting leap out all these years later except one moment. In his analysis, Coleman felt my pitch idea skewed young. Simensky agreed. I had pitched what I thought was a Nicktoon—in other words, the next *Ren and Stimpy*. Yet, the executives saw my work as gentle, sweet, and for a younger audience.

"This would be more suited for our preschool division," Coleman suggested. What a shocking conclusion, I thought. Maybe even insulting! Preschool content was not something I had gone to school for these four years to do. I was inspired by the best (early) Disney features, animation from the National Film Board of Canada, Chuck Jones, Tex Avery, Bill Plympton, and many others, none of which were preschool. Remember, at this time the purple dinosaur show, *Barney and Friends*, was the hot thing in preschool television. That did little to make me enthusiastic that I had developed a youngish project.

A couple of months later, working on my first job at Michael Sporn Animation, Inc., I found myself assigned to projects for a preschool-age audience. Slowly, I began to see animation as animation, regardless of how old or young the intended audience is. On a project for preschool there may be fewer scene cuts and slower action, but after that, it's all about storytelling. Eventually, Sporn gave me the opportunity to create, write, and design preschool content for a client. I enjoyed that experience more than anything else. Some of the best samples on my reel and in my portfolio were gradually becoming preschool-age material.

Two years later I found myself exploiting this new appreciation for preschool content while working on the biggest preschool hit of our time, Nick Jr.'s *Blue's Clues*. The play-along show with the cute little blue puppy became a pop culture sensation way beyond its undeniable success capturing the imagination of preschoolers. I worked on the show for over seven and a half years, becoming an animation director, helming more than sixty-five episodes of the series. It's so funny to think back to that moment in Simensky's class and imagine there was a time when the term "preschool animation" was a near-insult to me.

You can plan a career, but you'll likely still end up taking turns you hadn't planned on. We don't have a complete map. All I knew is that I wanted to work in animation. In my first jobs, particularly at Michael Sporn Animation, Inc., I put myself in the position to learn. By plugging into the animation community through volunteering at ASIFA-East, I was able to make innumerable invaluable connections that would help steer me towards success at *Blue's Clues* and beyond.

Post–*Blue's Clues* success is starting to come in ways that I don't think I could have imagined just five years ago. For one, writing this book (something I never dreamed of) has allowed me to take stock of my journey and to connect or reconnect with so many others who have inspired my career in animation. Completing the experience, directing on Jim Jinkins' series *Pinky Dinky Doo* at Cartoon Pizza allowed me a fresh start: clearing the air of mistakes I made in a similar role on *Blue's Clues*.

I recently spoke to a class at New York City's Parsons School of Design. At one point, I told the students that a healthy career is like time travel. At the start of a career you work hard and make the best possible career choices along the way. In such a way your younger self sets up all your opportunities ahead, for today and tomorrow.

The author sailing away on Lake Annecy, France.

"I sometimes wish I could go back in time and thank myself," I told the class. They chuckled as if I was kidding, but I really wasn't. Those who put off today for tomorrow may have a lifetime of regrets to look forward to. Why would we choose that path? At a premiere screening for his film *The Incredibles*, Brad Bird told an audience of SVA students and alumni that he is dubious of anyone who peddles the answer to a successful career in animation. Bird went on to correctly point out that no one can simply imitate another one's path and be successful. This author is in full agreement with Mr. Bird. The paths, information, advice, and anecdotes presented here are offered with the hope that they will inspire you to discover your own journey.

We, as animation artists, need to realize three fundamental things: we can create the careers of our choice, it need not be such a bumpy ride, and we don't have to go it alone. Never doubt that our careers (as well as the future of this business) are ours to make, or in our case, to animate.

Appendix
Animation Industry Resource List

ORGANIZATIONS

ASIFA-East

ASIFA is the International Animated Film Society Northeast/New York Chapter. ASIFA (association internationale du Film d'Animation) was formed in 1960 by an international group of animators to coordinate and increase worldwide visibility of animated film. ASIFA-East is the Eastern US chapter of ASIFA, based in New York City. ASIFA-East holds monthly screenings of animated films and publishes a monthly newsletter filled with information of interest to those in the East Coast animation community, as well as fans of the medium. ASIFA-East also conducts a yearly animation festival, a unique showcase for the most groundbreaking independent and commercial animation being produced in the industry today.

ASIFA-East c/o Michael Sporn Animation
35 Bedford Street
New York, NY 10014
www.asifaeast.com

ASIFA-Hollywood

The International Animated Film Society (ASIFA-Hollywood) is a California nonprofit organization established over twenty years ago to promote and encourage the art and craft of animation. Since 1972, ASIFA-Hollywood has hosted an annual awards ceremony to honor individuals who have made significant contributions to the art of animation. Originally designed to honor the lifetime achievements of legendary veterans of the field, the Annie Awards are now awarded in competition for the year's best animation efforts, recognizing outstanding productions in feature films, videos, television programs, commercials, animated interactive productions, as well as individual achievement by artists, writers, and voice talent. Members participate in the nomination process and final voting. The Annie Awards are regarded as animation's highest honor, and the ceremony is one of ASIFA-Hollywood's most prestigious and elegant events.

ASIFA-Hollywood
2114 Burbank Boulevard
Burbank, CA 91506
www.asifa-hollywood.org

ASIFA-San Francisco

ASIFA-San Francisco is the oldest and foremost Bay Area organization for the animation community, with over 300 members ranging from seasoned professionals to students and fans. As a branch of the international organization, membership in ASIFA-SF provides these great benefits: monthly events and screenings that play to overflowing audiences. These include an annual career night with leading animation houses, such as Pixar, ILM, Wild Brain, and PDI; annual open screenings; festival screenings; industry close-ups; and other special events. A monthly newsletter (usually at least 8 pages), chock full of the latest industry buzz, happenings, and reviews, is published with a focus on the Bay Area. You can set up a free link from the ASIFA-SF Web site to your own site (see Web Gallery). This is great for self-promotion and visibility.

ASIFA-SF
PO Box 14516
San Francisco, CA 94114
www.asifa-sf.org

ASIFA-Central

ASIFA-Central is the Midwest Chapter of ASIFA in the US. ASIFA-Central began in Chicago, Illinois, and has involved many of the professional and independent animators in the Chicago area. Today, ASIFA-Midwest has members from Texas to Canada, New York to Colorado, and beyond! ASIFA-Central has co-sponsored many programs and brought in visiting animators including Don Bluth, June Foray, Gordon Sheehan, and Shamus Culhane. For years, the chapter coordinated the judging of animation at the Chicago International Film Festival. The purpose of ASIFA-Central is to promote the art of animation locally and internationally and to promote communication among animators and devotees.

ASIFA-Central
School of Communications
Lake Superior Hall
Grand Valley State University
Allendale, MI 49401
www.swcp.com/animate

ASIFA-Northwest

ASIFA-Northwest is the Pacific Northwest's (Northwest US and western British Columbia, Canada) foremost organization for the animation community, with a collective membership of professional animators, filmmakers, students, teachers, and fans as well as affiliated professions such as voice-over actors, composers, puppeteers, illustrators, and cartoonists. ASIFA-Northwest has a rich history of experimental and independent animation, as well as commercial production in the areas of stop motion, computer graphics visualization, interactive, and video game animation.

The mission of ASIFA-Northwest is to promote the art of animation and foster the development of the animation industry in the Pacific Northwest, including Oregon, Washington, and Western B.C., Canada.

ASIFA-NW
PO Box 4752
Seattle, WA 98194
www.asifa.net/usa-northwest

ASIFA-Canada

ASIFA-Canada members receive two to three issues of the ASIFA-Canada magazine, which profiles Canadian animators and studios, new technology trends, and features up-to-date information on film animation across the country. Membership also includes a $30 discount off passes at the Ottawa International Animation Festival, and free admission to ASIFA-sponsored screenings and events. Student ASIFA-Canada members (with identification cards) receive an additional $10 off the festival's student pass rate. The membership directory includes animation studios, governmental organizations, and a list of all ASIFA-Canada members.

ASIFA-Canada
CP 5226
Ville St. Laurent
Québec, Canada H4L 4Z8
www.awn.com/asifa-canada

Animators, Ink.

Animators, Ink. was founded in February 2001 by SVA students in New York City. Their goals are as follows: keep students informed about the industry; provide recruiters with a venue to scout for new talent, especially on the East Coast; showcase talent for people interested in the craft; create a network between pros and amateurs; and give students the opportunity to communicate with their administration and improve their schools.

www.animatorsink.com

The Toronto Animated Image Society

The Toronto Animated Image Society Animators' Production Cooperative opened their doors in March 2002. Since 1984 TAIS has been a group dedicated to promoting the art of animation. As an extension of TAIS monthly lectures and screenings, the new co-op offers hands-on animation workshops and production facilities catering to traditional cel, 3D, stop-motion, digital 2D, paint on film, under the camera and experimental animation. The TAIS co-op is a not-for-profit organization funded by its members and the Canada Council for the Arts (Media Arts Section), Ontario Arts Council, and the Toronto Arts Council.

The Toronto Animated Image Society
8 King Street East
Suite 301
Toronto, ON M5C 1B5
www.awn.com/tais

The Animation Guild Local 839 (TAG)

The parent organization of TAG is IATSE, the International Alliance of Theatrical Stage Employees, Moving Picture Technicians, Artists and Allied Crafts of the United States, Its Territories and Canada, AFL-CIO, CLC. IATSE represents those involved in animation and CGI as well as representing "below-the-line" film crafts such as camerapersons, sound technicians, editors, live-action storyboard artists, set designers, art directors, scenic artists, etc., in the Southern California area.

The Animation Guild Local 839 4729
Lankershim Boulevard
North Hollywood, CA 91602-1864
www.mpsc839.org

Women In Animation

Women In Animation is a professional, nonprofit organization established in 1994 to foster the dignity, concerns and advancement of women who are involved in any and all aspects of the art and industry of animation. WIA is a networking organization, providing opportunities for you to meet and exchange business cards with interesting and influential people in the animation industry. Through WIA's workshops, meetings, and panels you are bound to gain valuable insight into the industry, opportunities available to you and other educational resources in your area. With most members concentrated in the United States and Canada, their influence and members at large reach into many other countries and is growing all the time.

Women In Animation, Inc.
PO Box 17706
Encino, CA 91416
www.womeninanimation.org

Quickdraw Animation Society

Quickdraw Animation Society is a twenty-one-year-old, artist-run center in Calgary, Alberta, Canada. QAS's mandate is to support and encourage the production of innovative independent animation and to develop the appreciation of all types of animation as a viable artistic medium. The principles engaged in at QAS are: inclusion, cooperation, active participation by youth, and positive support and encouragement among members. Each year QAS offers two scholarships to first-time animators to assist them over the initial hurdles toward making an independent animated film. The competition is open to members and nonmembers. All applications are reviewed by a jury of QAS members. Programming initiatives include their Master Animators Workshop Series, annual Cameraless Extravaganza Week, bi-monthly Free Film nights held in the QAS/EM screening room, as well as special events and exhibitions for the public.

Quickdraw Animation Society
201–351
11 Avenue SW
Calgary, AB T2R 0C7
www.awn.com/qas

ACM SIGGRAPH

ACM SIGGRAPH is dedicated to the generation and dissemination of information on computer graphics and interactive techniques. They are a membership organization that values passion, integrity, excellence, volunteerism, and cross-disciplinary interaction in all of their activities. They are probably best known for the annual SIGGRAPH conference they sponsor, but they also put on a variety of programs year-round and worldwide to benefit the SIGGRAPH community.

www.siggraph.org

National Film Board of Canada

Created in 1939, the Oscar-winning National Film Board of Canada is the world-renowned public producer and distributor of animation and documentary, working with many of Canada's best and brightest new talents. NFBC produces and distributes films and other audio-visual works, which interpret Canada to Canadians and to other countries.

NFBC Head Office
Constitution Square
360 Albert Street
Suite 1560
Ottawa, Ontario K1A 0M9
or
NFBC Operational Headquarters
PO Box 6100
Station Centre-Ville
Montréal, Québec H3C 3H5
www.nfb.ca

Telefilm Canada

Telefilm Canada is a federal cultural agency dedicated primarily to the development and promotion of the Canadian film, television, new media, and music industries.

Telefilm Canada
360 St. Jacques Street
Suite 700
Montréal, Quebec H2Y 4A9
www.telefilm.gc.ca

WEB SITES AND BLOGS TO KNOW ABOUT

Animation World Network

The Animation World Network is the largest animation-related publishing group on the Internet, providing readers from over 145 countries with a wide range of interesting, relevant, and helpful information pertaining to all aspects of animation. Covering areas as diverse as animator profiles, independent film distribution, commercial studio activities, CGI and other animation technologies, as well as in-depth coverage of current events in all fields of animation, AWN gives its readers an easy to navigate, visually and intellectually creative mechanism to electronically access a wealth of information previously unavailable anywhere in the world.

www.awn.com

Cartoon Research

This is Jerry Beck's online depository of all things related to classic Hollywood cartoons. It includes a database of all US-released animated feature films, pages devoted to rare images from Looney Tunes, Fleischer, MGM, and Terrytoons (and other studios), and a FAQ that answers common animation history questions.

www.cartoonresearch.com

Cartoon Brew

Cartoon Brew is an animation blog run by animation historian Jerry Beck (*The Animated Movie Guide*) and animation critic Amid Amidi (AnimationBlast). Beck and Amidi do reviews, news, and commentary on all things animated.

www.cartoonbrew.com

The Big Cartoon DataBase

The Big Cartoon DataBase provides an in-depth, detailed look at your favorite classic cartoons. It is a searchable database of cartoon information, episode guides and crew lists.

www.bcdb.com

Michael Barrier

Barrier is the author of *Hollywood Cartoons: American Animation in Its Golden Age* (Oxford University Press, 2003). His site includes: commentary on current films, books, and comics; essays on a variety of animation and comics-related subjects; interviews with leading creators; brief essays on individual films; and FunnyworldRevisited, a selection of articles and reviews from the magazine publications.

www.michaelbarrier.com

StopMotionAnimation.com

StopMotionAnimation.com began as an effort to inspire and instruct those individuals who wanted to create their own films. Since this site was launched in April 1999, it has become a large community for aspiring animators sharing their ideas, opinions, and questions on the message board.

www.stopmotionanimation.com

TRADE PUBLICATIONS

AnimationBlast

AnimationBlast is a purely independent magazine and has been in print since 1998. Unlike other media sources, they're not subservient to the studios and don't regurgitate their press releases. *AnimationBlast* magazine has been blessed with a wonderful group of writers and artists who have contributed to the first eight issues. They include Jerry Beck, Gabe Swarr, Greg Duffell, David Calvo, Aaron Springer, Will Friedwald, Mark Mayerson, and Shane Glines. AnimationBlast is the brainchild of publisher/editor Amid Amidi. He is currently writing an art book for Chronicle Books, to be released in Spring 2006. Amid recently worked on the new episodes of *Ren & Stimpy*.

Amid Amidi
Animation Blast
PO Box 260491
Encino, CA 91426-0491
www.animationblast.com

Take One

Take One is Canada's English-language magazine devoted to Canadian film and television. *Take One* covers the full spectrum of feature films, television, animation, documentaries, shorts, and independent film and video throughout Canada.

www.takeonemagazine.ca

Playback

Playback is Canada's production, broadcasting, and interactive media journal, a magazine that offers an intimate view of the industry events, trends, and innovations every two weeks.

www.playbackmag.com

FESTIVALS

Animation Block Party

Animation Block is dedicated to exhibiting the world's best independent, professional, and student animation. Their mode of broadcast is always evolving, be it through Internet streaming on their Web site, smaller free screenings for the public, official Animation Block Party festivals, or DVD distribution. Its Web site home page offers three Web selects every month for mass consumption. The program of their NYC Valentine Festival attracted distributors such as Atom Films to pick up festival winners; major studios like Disney called and asked for Valentine show DVDs to review, and large scale animation festivals such as Annecy International Animated Film Festival (France) exhibited some of ABP's world premieres at their 2005 festival.

www.animationblock.com

The ASIFA-East Animation Festival

The jewel of the New York ASIFA-East chapter is its animation festival, for over thirty-seven years. Since many animation festivals are held on alternate years, this might be the longest running animation festival in the world. It appeals to professionals and novices alike—there is no pre-selection committee to eliminate films—and is casual enough for students and veteran animators to mingle, discuss, and toast the subject they love best: animation. In this day and age of home video, digital cable, and the Internet, ASIFA-East brings live bodies together through the festival. Friendships, partnerships, and businesses have been sparked from the ASIFA-East connection.

www.asifaeast.com

The Ottawa International Animation Festival

Founded in 1975, the Ottawa International Animation Festival (OIAF) was first held August 10 through August 15, 1976, creating a gathering place for North American animation professionals and enthusiasts to ponder the craft and business of animation. It also provided their international colleagues with a unique opportunity to gain an appreciation for and access to the North American scene. The OIAF is committed to ensuring the animation profession benefits from exposure to outstanding creativity and originality of emerging work, and young animators gain access to the movers and shakers of their chosen profession.

OIAF
Suite 120
2 Daly Avenue
Ottawa, Ontario K1N 6E2
www.awn.com/ottawa

Withoutabox

Withoutabox is an international online exchange dedicated to expanding access and opportunity for the film community. This self-service system allows filmmakers to enter and manage the world of film festivals, while saving time and money.

www.withoutabox.com/index.php

RECRUITMENT

I Spy Recruiting

I Spy Recruiting provides customized services to help animation and design studios meet their ongoing recruiting needs: animation, design, editing, and production management for the West Coast, East Coast, and everything in between. It is also a place for talent to get maximum exposure for freelance or staff jobs.

I Spy Recruiting
Ila Abramson
45 Main Street #524
Brooklyn, NY 11201
ila@ispyrecruiting.com

GRANTS AND FUNDS

Bell Broadcast and New Media Fund
The Bell Broadcast and New Media Fund provides grants to independent new media and television producers who develop and produce television content complemented and enhanced by outstanding interactive content designed for digital delivery (i.e., Web sites, iTV, mobile content).

The Bell Broadcast and New Media Fund
2 Carlton Street
Suite 1709
Toronto, Ontario M5B 1J3
www.ipf.ca

The Canada Council for the Arts
The Canada Council for the Arts is a national arm's length agency created by an act of parliament in 1957. Its role is "to foster and promote the study and enjoyment of, and the production of works in, the arts."

The Canada Council for the Arts
350 Albert Street
PO Box 1047
Ottawa, Ontario K1P 5V8
www.canadacouncil.ca

Film/Video Arts
Founded in 1968, Film/Video Arts' mission is to make the tools and skills of the media arts available to those who might otherwise not have access to them. Film/Video Arts has become one of the largest nonprofit media arts centers in the New York region during its over thirty-five-year history. Film/Video Arts provides a dynamic environment where emerging and established film, video, and digital media producers, editors, directors, and hobbyists of diverse backgrounds can take courses taught by seasoned film industry

veterans. Film/Video Arts members are eligible to receive fiscal sponsorship for their projects and have access to the tools needed to edit their projects affordably. Over 2,500 individuals and organizations participate in Film/Video Arts programs every year.

Film/Video Arts
25 East 21st Street
3rd Floor
New York, NY 10010
www.fva.squarespace.com

The New York Foundation for the Arts

The New York Foundation for the Arts (NYFA) helps artists turn inspiration into art by giving more money and support to individual artists and arts organizations than any other comparable institution in the US. Their goal is to provide the time and resources for the creative mind and the artistic spirit to think, work, and prosper. By matching donor interest and values with creative people and projects, NYFA gives artists and the organizations that serve them the opportunity to realize their dreams. And, as an advocate for the arts, NYFA plays a pivotal role in engaging and educating the public about the visual, performing, literary, and media arts. Each year, NYFA provides more than $11 million in grants and services and offers fellowships to as many as 170 New York State originating artists.

New York Foundation for the Arts
155 Avenue of the Americas
14th Floor
New York, NY 10013
www.nyfa.org

Telefilm Canada

Telefilm Canada is a federal cultural agency dedicated primarily to the development and promotion of the Canadian film, television, new media and music industries.

Telefilm Canada
360 St. Jacques Street
Suite 700
Montréal, Quebec H2Y 4A9
www.telefilm.gc.ca

SUPPLIES/EQUIPMENT

Cartoon Colour Company

Since 1947, Cartoon Colour Company has manufactured superior artists' paints for the animation industry, as well as for other fields of commercial art. Today, Cartoon Colour Company has expanded its line of quality animation products to include an ARTTOOLS brand of acrylic animation discs, cel punches, and light boxes. They also maintain a complete inventory of specialized art supplies for the animation and commercial artist.

Cartoon Colour Company, Inc.
9024 Lindblade Street
Culver City, CA 90232
www.cartooncolour.com

SCHOOLS

Algonquin College

A three-year program at Algonquin provides students with training in both traditional and digital animation. Following a common first year of studies, students have the option of pursuing either traditional or digital animation. They learn the skills necessary to work effectively as animators in a variety of settings. Graduates acquire the skills necessary to work independently, collaboratively, and in studio settings.

Algonquin College
Woodroffe Campus
1385 Woodroffe Avenue
Ottawa, Ontario K2G 1V8
www.algonquincollege.com

Capilano College

Capilano College is a publicly funded community college, located on the slopes of the coastal mountains in North Vancouver, British Columbia. Affordable tuition, excellent faculty and facilities, and one of the best reputations among Canadian animation schools make the animation programs the first choice of most applicants.

Animation Department
Capilano College
2055 Purcell Way
North Vancouver, British Columbia V7J 3H5
www.gradshow.com

Emily Carr Institute

The Bachelor of Media Arts Animation major at Emily Carr Institute focuses on the development of innovative, well-rounded animation artists working with film, electronic and digital media, as well as traditional studio arts. Students select from courses in drawing, 3D computer animation, experimental animation, commercial animation, and special effects. The program offers a challenging course of study that encompasses drawing, color, storytelling, computing, and also English literature, cultural studies, and written composition. Graduates are equipped to work in animation as it is applied to entertainment, advertising, communication, and independent production of fine art film.

Emily Carr Institute
1399 Johnston Street
Granville Island
Vancouver, BC V6H 3R9
www.eciad.ca

Joe Kubert School of Cartoon and Graphic Art, Inc.

In 1976, Joe and Muriel Kubert founded the Joe Kubert School of Cartoon and Graphic Art. The school is dedicated to aspiring cartoonists who are dedicated to becoming professionals in cartooning, comic book, and the general field of commercial art. The school also offers a major in cinematic animation. Hundreds of the school's graduates have gained acclaim and admiration in high profile positions in comic books, advertising agencies, computer color and separation, animation, advertising, and illustration.

The Joe Kubert School of Cartoon and Graphic Art, Inc.
37 Myrtle Avenue
Dover, NJ 07801
www.kubertsworld.com

California Institute of the Arts

California Institute of the Arts educates professional artists in a unique learning environment founded on the principles of art-making excellence, experimentation, critical reflection, and independent inquiry. Throughout its history, CalArts has sought to advance the practice of art and promote its understanding in a broad social, cultural, and historical context. CalArts offers students the knowledge and expertise of leading professional artists and scholars and a full complement of art-making tools. In return, it asks for the highest artistic and academic achievement. Reflecting its longstanding commitment to new forms and expressions in art, CalArts invites creative risk-taking and urges active collaboration and exchange among artists, artistic disciplines, and cultural traditions.

California Institute of the Arts
24700 McBean Parkway
Valencia, CA 91355
www.calarts.edu

The Art Institute of Philadelphia

Art Institute of Philadelphia students in the Animation Art and Design and the Media Arts and Animation programs all begin with a foundation in drawing, color, design, and computer applications. From this foundation, students develop advanced skills in various aspects of computer graphics and animation. Students learn to use the tools of the animation profession, ranging from computer operating systems to three-dimensional modeling and desktop video production. In addition to software applications, equipment also includes scanners, printers, video, audio, and classroom presentation equipment. These tools enhance students' flexibility and creativity, and enable them to produce an individualized digital portfolio that demonstrates their practical and technical abilities to potential employers. Graduates will be prepared with fully focused, entry-level skills to enter this fast-paced, high-tech field.

The Art Institute of Philadelphia
1622 Chestnut Street
Philadelphia, PA 19103
www.aiph.artinstitutes.edu

Dartmouth College

Dartmouth College combines the best features of an undergraduate liberal arts college with the intellectual vitality of a research university. Founded as an undergraduate institution more than two centuries ago, Dartmouth offers excellent graduate programs within the arts and sciences and in business, engineering, and medicine. The professional schools, among the first established in their respective fields, have had a historic role in defining the school's intellectual values. Dartmouth encourages a love of learning and discovery in every member of its community. It celebrates the diversity of that community, which includes men and women from different backgrounds, abilities, economic circumstances, perspectives, races, religions, national origins, and sexual orientations.

Dartmouth College
Hanover, NH 03755
www.dartmouth.edu

Parsons School of Design

Innovation, exploration, collaboration, and anti-traditionalism drive the BFA in Design and Technology at Parsons. Students use new and emerging technologies and collaborate on real-world projects that take them to the next level. Graduates pursue careers in game design, digital filmmaking, information architecture, interaction design, broadcast design, animation, Web design, and technology-enabled environmental and architectural design, to name just a few. In the freshman curriculum, students receive an intense introduction to the Web, audio and video, interface design, and computer programming skills.

www.parsons.edu

Pratt Institute

The mission of Pratt Institute is to educate artists and creative professionals to be responsible contributors to society. Pratt seeks to instill in all graduates aesthetic judgment, professional knowledge, collaborative skills, and technical expertise. With a firm grounding in the liberal arts and sciences, a Pratt education blends theory with creative application in preparing graduates to become leaders in their professions. Pratt enrolls a diverse group of highly talented and dedicated students, challenging them to achieve their full potential.

Pratt Institute
200 Willoughby Avenue
Brooklyn, NY 11205
www.pratt.edu

Max the Mutt™ Animation School

Max the Mutt™ Animation School is one of Toronto's fastest growing private career colleges offering a three-year diploma program in classical animation basics and a fourth year post-diploma program in advanced animation. Max The Mutt™ has developed a reputation for demanding the Max-imum from its students through small class size with serious individual instruction from some of the industry's top talent. The school admits it is not for everyone. The diploma program's exacting standards, based on Warner Brothers and Disney guidelines, is available to only the most serious students wishing to pursue a professional career in the animation industry.

Max the Mutt™ Animation School
952 Queen Street, West
Toronto, Ontario M6J 1G8
www.maxthemutt.com

The Mel Hoppenheim School of Cinema

The Mel Hoppenheim School of Cinema offers two programs in film animation: a major in film animation and a minor in film animation. The programs are conceived and designed to teach the full process of artful and intelligent frame-by-frame (animated) filmmaking, its theory, and practice. Students are encouraged to develop a personal and creative individual approach to the art of frame-by-frame filmmaking, and to explore various technical and conceptual issues related to it. Rather than emphasizing a single type of animation, the program is designed to enable students to identify, from the widest possible range of techniques, the approach that is most suitable for the expression of their personal, original vision. The goal is to provide, to future filmmakers, a solid foundation for research, discovery, and improvement, and to facilitate the articulation of a style, which affirms each student's unique artistic personality. Students are carefully and individually exposed to the ever-widening possibilities of both digital and traditional technologies.

The Mel Hoppenheim School of Cinema
1455, boul de Maisonneuve oust
FB 319, Montréal, Québec H3G 1M8
cinema.concordia.ca

New York University Tisch School of the Arts

New York University Tisch School of the Arts' animation area serves the needs of all film and TV students for both animation and live-action projects. The curriculum is varied and integrated with both traditional animation and 2D and 3D animation courses at the fundamental, intermediate, and advanced levels, as well as storyboarding, titles, optical and digital effects, life drawing, and history and criticism classes. As well as the dedicated and professional faculty and staff, special guests and visiting artists have included Chuck Jones, Nick Park, Pete Docter, Frank Thomas, Ollie Johnston, Marc Davis, and Faith Hubley. Also, talent recruiters visit yearly from Walt Disney, DreamWorks, Warner Brothers, LucasArts, R/GA, Blue Sky, MTV, and Nickelodeon.

Tisch School of the Arts
721 Broadway
New York, NY 10003
www.filmtv.tisch.nyu.edu

The School of Visual Arts (SVA)

SVA offers undergraduate programs in advertising, animation, cartooning, computer art, film and video, fine arts, graphic design, illustration, interior design, and photography. The undergraduate program is a four-year, full-time Bachelor of Fine Arts degree program with courses offered throughout the day and evening. SVA is considered a primary source of animation talent for both coasts. Graduates have found work at Disney, Pixar, Dreamworks SKG, Blue Sky Studio, and Nickelodeon. You'll learn from more than thirty directors, animation and special effects artists, character designers, and writers.

The School of Visual Arts
209 East 23rd Street
New York, NY 10010
www.schoolofvisualarts.edu

Ringling School of Art and Design

Ringling School of Art and Design is a private, not-for-profit, fully accredited college offering the Bachelor of Fine Arts degree in six disciplines: computer animation, fine arts, graphic and interactive communication, illustration, interior design, and photography and digital imaging. Located on Florida's Gulf Coast, the picturesque thirty-five acre campus now includes sixty-nine buildings, and attracts more than 1,000 students from forty-six states, and thirty-three foreign countries. It is recognized as being among the best and most innovative visual arts colleges in the United States as well as a leader in the use of technology in the arts.

Ringling School of Art and Design
2700 North Tamiami Trail
Sarasota, FL 34234
www.rsad.edu

Rhode Island School of Design (RISD)

RISD (RIZ-dee), founded in 1877 in Providence, RI, is a vibrant community of artists and designers that includes 2,200 students from around the world, approximately 350 faculty and curators, and 400 staff members. Each year more than 200 prominent artists, critics, authors, and philosophers visit the historic College Hill campus.

Rhode Island School of Design
Two College Street
Providence, RI 02903
www.risd.edu

Seneca College's Animation Arts Centre

In less than ten years Seneca College's Animation Arts Centre in Toronto has gained a reputation within the animation industry for attracting top-quality professors and students from across Canada. The three-year diploma program provides a solid foundation of traditional animation before students move on to state-of-the-art computers in the final year. The centre distinguishes itself further with post-graduate certificates that include 3D character animation, special effects, and its award-winning 3D gaming program. Among its many successes, the centre is proud of the Oscar-winning film *Ryan*, which was produced at Seneca and animated by its graduates.

Animation Arts Centre
88 The Pond Road
4th Floor
Seneca at York, Toronto, Ontario M3J 3M6
www.aac.senecac.on.ca

Sheridan College

The animation classical program at Sheridan is known the world over for the creative excellence of its graduates and faculty. The program, with its strong focus on character animation techniques, examines both contemporary and traditional approaches to animation. Animation affords students the opportunity to master their drawing skills and sense of acting and motion, and to apply them to the art of human and animal dramatization and animation storytelling. Sheridan's experienced instructors build upon their professional and teaching insights to provide an education that covers many aspects and eras of animation. Sheridan is the industry leader in enabling students to design and animate with the latest in 3D computer animation and special effects software.

Sheridan Institute for Technology and Advanced Learning
SCAET Building
1430 Trafalgar Road
Oakville, Ontario L6H 2L1
www1.sheridaninstitute.ca

The Art Institute of Toronto

The Art Institute of Toronto's animation art and design nine-month diploma program provides graduates with the art, design, technical, business, and life skills needed to interview for entry-level positions in the fields of animation and related media arts. Multimedia artists and animators are professionals who create special effects, animation, or other visual images using film, video, computer, or other electronic media. Computer animators work in 3D, creating their characters with the subtleties and realistic motion of everyday life. The key is to balance technology with the fundamentals of drawing and animation so that students become animators who can bring characters to life while harnessing the capabilities of the computer.

The Art Institute of Toronto
655 Bay Street
Suite 200
Toronto, Ontario M5G 2K4
www.wherecreativitygoestoschool.ca

The University of the Arts (UArts)

UArts teaches and practices animation as a fine art—a powerful form demanding technical excellence and offering boundless possibilities for exploration and expression. Work within the department spans a broad range, from experimental and mixed media to character animation and under-the-camera animation (painting-on-glass, clay-on-glass, sand animation, cut-out animation) as well as 2D and 3D computer animation. Students are guided by a faculty of accomplished working professionals, as they develop their individual vision and build a strong preparation for professional careers.

The University of the Arts
320 S. Broad Street
Philadelphia, PA 19102
www.uarts.edu

Vancouver Film School

Imagination is the only limit when encountering innovation; artists are faced with a tension between transformation and endurance. At Vancouver Film School this healthy tension allows new forms, new ideas, and new art to emerge. No matter the potency of today's technology, the elements of animation remain constant. Animation is the fine art of telling a story through movement: knowing how to animate life where there is none. Every animated film produced today is actually a hybrid of classical and computer-generated animation methods. The more proficient you are with the foundations of animation, the more skillful will be your use of modern digital technology.

Vancouver Film School
3rd Floor
1380 Burrard Street
Vancouver, BC V6B 2V5
www.vfs.com

ABOUT THE AUTHOR

DAVID B. LEVY is an award-winning independent filmmaker and animation director for Nickelodeon's *Blue's Clues* and the Noggin Channel's *Pinky Dinky Doo*. His animation has been seen on *Saturday Night Live* and HBO, and he is currently the supervising animation director for the Blue's Clues spin-off show, *Blue's Room*. He has lectured and taught at Parsons School of Design and School of Visual Arts and is president of the New York chapter of Association International du Film d'Animation (ASIFA). He lives in New York City.

Index

Books from Allworth Press

Animation: The Whole Story, Revised Edition
by Howard Beckerman (paperback, 6⅞ × 9¾, 437 pages, $24.95)

They'll Never Put that on the Air: Breaking Taboos in TV Comedy
by Allan Neuwirth (paperback, 6 × 9, 256 pages, $19.95)

Makin' Toons: Inside the Most Popular Animated TV Shows and Movies
by Allan Neuwirth (paperback, 6 × 9, 288 pages, 82 b&w illus, $21.95)

The Educa
edited by M ges, $19.95)

Making Sl
by Jim Pip , $24.95)

Mastering).00)
by Peter Ra

Documen
by Liz Stut

Shoot Me:
to Rousin
by Roy Fru
56 b&w ill

The Healt
by Monona

Directing
by Christop $19.95)

The Filmn
by Vincent F 19.95)

Making In
by Liz Stub
42 b&w illi

Please write to end a check
or money order clude $5
for shipping an dollars plus
$1 for each add sales tax.

To see our com at
www.allwo

DATE DUE

OCT 2 8 2013		
NOV 2 2 2013		
GAYLORD		PRINTED IN U.S.A.

DISCARD